TEXTBOOK VIOLENCE

Textbook Violence

Edited by James R. Lewis, Bengt-Ove Andreassen
and Suzanne Anett Thobro

SHEFFIELD UK   BRISTOL CT

Published by Equinox Publishing Ltd.

UK: Office 415, The Workstation, 15 Paternoster Row, Sheffield, South Yorkshire, S1 2BX
USA: ISD, 70 Enterprise Drive, Bristol, CT 06010

www.equinoxpub.com

First published 2017

© James R. Lewis, Bengt-Ove Andreassen, Suzanne Anett Thobro and contributors 2017

All rights reserved. No part of this publication may be reproduced or transmitted in any form or by any means, electronic or mechanical, including photocopying, recording or any information storage or retrieval system, without prior permission in writing from the publishers.

British Library Cataloguing-in-Publication Data
A catalogue record for this book is available from the British Library.

Library of Congress Cataloging-in-Publication Data
Names: Lewis, James R., editor. | Andreassen, Bengt-Ove, editor. | Thobro, Suzanne Anett, editor.

Title: Textbook violence / edited by James R. Lewis, Bengt-Ove Andreassen and Suzanne Anett Thobro.
Description: Sheffield, UK ; Bristol, CT : Equinox Publishing, Ltd, [2017] |

Includes bibliographical references and index.
Identifiers: LCCN 2016020803 (print) | LCCN 2016035968 (ebook) | ISBN 9781781792582 (hb) | ISBN 9781781792599 (pb) | ISBN 9781781795132 (e-PDF)

Subjects: LCSH: Religion in textbooks. | Violence--Religious aspects. | Conflict management--Religious aspects.

Classification: LCC LB3045.84 .T49 2017 (print) | LCC LB3045.84 (ebook) | DDC 379.2/8--dc23

LC record available at https://lccn.loc.gov/2016020803

ISBN: 978 1 78179 258 2   (hardback)
ISBN: 978 1 78179 259 9   (paperback)
ISBN: 978 1 78179 513 2   (e-PDF)

Typeset by CA Typesetting Ltd, www.publisherservices.co.uk
Printed and bound in the UK by Lightning Source UK Ltd., Milton Keynes and Lightning Source Inc., La Vergne, TN

CONTENTS

Introduction   1
Bengt-Ove Andreassen and James R. Lewis

1. Reading Beyond the Lines:
   What Students Learn from their History Textbooks   7
   Michael H. Romanowski

2. This is not a Religion!: "The Treachery of the Images"
   of Aum, Yasukuni and Al-Qaeda in Japanese Textbooks   27
   Satoko Fujiwara

3. Ignore the War: Concentrate on Peace: Textbook Analysis of
   Strategies in Post-conflict Societies: A Praxeological Approach   53
   Zrinka Štimac

4. Colonial Conflicts: Absence, Inclusion and Indigenization
   in Textbook Presentations of Indigenous Peoples   71
   Torjer A. Olsen

5. Talking about Conflicts in Pursuit of the Common Good,
   or How to Handle Sensitive Topics while Learning about
   Religions: The Approach of the Ethics and Religious Culture
   Text-Books in Québec   87
   Sivane Hirsch

6. Representations of Anti-semitism and the Holocaust in RE
   Textbooks for Norwegian Upper Secondary School   98
   Suzanne Anett Thobro

7. Aniconism and Images in Norwegian RE Textbooks:
   Representations and Historical Change   126
   Sissel Undheim

8. Undermining Authority: The Representation of Buddhism and Discourse on Modernity in Religious Education Textbooks 151
Kai Arne Nyborg

9. Significant or Insignificant Absence? Religion and Violence in RE Textbooks for Norwegian Teacher Education 176
Bengt-Ove Andreassen

10. Toward an Appreciation of Non-normativity: A Quasi-autobiography 196
Aaron W. Hughes

11. Self-contradictions and Projected Otherness: Images of Sikh Militancy in the Writings of Orientalist Scholars and Contemporary Textbook Authors 210
James R. Lewis

Index 220

INTRODUCTION

Bengt-Ove Andreassen and James R. Lewis

From the Crusades to the nerve gas attack on the Tokyo subway, and from the wars of the Reformation to the attacks on the World Trade Center, religion and violence have been intimately related throughout human history. In the words of Leo D. Lefebure (2000: 14):

> The brutal facts of the history of religions impose the stark realization of the intertwining of religion and violence: violence, clothed in religious garb, has repeatedly cast a spell over religion and culture, luring countless 'decent' people—from unlettered peasants to learned priests, preachers and professors—into its destructive dance.

Religion and violence have been intimately related throughout most if not all of human history. However, because our cultural conception of "religion" makes a rough equation between "being religious" and "being good, moral, and decent," the violent aspects of religion tend to be seen as either aberrant and isolated incidents in our own tradition, or the *sine qua non* of someone else's belief. We avoid the dark side of faith because it challenges our very notions of what religion is "supposed" to be. In many ways, however, violence lies at the very heart of religion. Religion and violence has thus challenged scholars in the academic study of religion. How should the relation between religion and violence be understood? Is it the scholar's job to "make sense" of religiously motivated violence? Analyzing the interrelation between religion and violence is indeed a challenging task.

In the last ten to 20 years, university courses on religion and violence have become commonplace. After 9/11, 2001, there was a rapid growth in the number of publications focused on the topic of religious violence (cf. Avalos 2005; Cavanaugh 2009; Eller 2010; Juergensmeyer 2008, Kimball 2002, Rennie and Tite 2008 to mention only a few). In the years after the wave of books on religious violence post-9/11, the first reference books on the topic were published. The first was *The Blackwell Companion to Religion and Violence*, edited by Andrew R. Murphy (2011), followed two years later by *The Oxford Handbook of Religion and Violence*, edited by Mark Juergensmeyer, Margo Kitts and Michael Jerryson (2013). These two are the only comprehensive handbooks that exist thus far (in 2016) but a Cambridge University Press companion on religion and terrorism is on the way.

In a collection of essays edited by Brian Pennington (2012) under the title *Teaching Religion and Violence*, examples of how to approach religion and conflict and violence in the classroom are presented. This volume does not offer a coherent presentation of religion and violence in all religious traditions. The different chapters rather indicate points for further interrogation for students by way of select examples from some traditions. Together with the handbooks from Blackwell and Oxford, the discourse on religion and violence is now dealing with epistemological questions regarding what religious violence is and how it can be studied.

UNDERSTANDING VIOLENCE IN "RELIGION AND VIOLENCE"

The question concerning how the term "religious violence" should be understood, is indeed a difficult one. Such questions are addressed by John D. Carlson (2011) and William T. Cavanaugh (2009: 15–54, 2011) in *The Blackwell Companion to Religion and Violence*, and demonstrate the complexity of this matter. In his book *The Myth of Religious Violence* (2009), Cavanaugh offers an extensive review of important works on religious violence. Cavanaugh finds that a common feature in these works is an absence of adequate conceptualizations of religion and violence, and thus religious violence. The meanings of religion, violence and conflict vary, and are generally unclear in most contributions, according to Cavanaugh. This calls for an extensive—bordering on exhaustive—task of clarification, but nevertheless an important one. The handbooks from Blackwell and Oxford try to offer this, as well as books published after Cavanaugh's challenge to this field of scholarship (cf. Eller 2010).

In the introduction to *The Oxford Handbook of Religion and Violence* (2013), the editors emphasize that there are a variety of ways in which religion and violence might be understood, and formulate the question: "From whose perspective and at what point is an act to be deemed violent?" Understandings or definitions of violence might thus be very different. To formulate a more coherent understanding of religion and violence such as Cavanaugh calls for is therefore a difficult task.

Being aware of these epistemological reflections on "religion and violence," this volume rather shows how diverse this might be. The different contributions deal with violence in a broad sense of the term. The primary reason for this diversity is that the textbooks analyzed in this volume are designed for different levels of the education system.

TEXTBOOK VIOLENCE

In the study of religions at universities, courses and literature that address conflict and violence are now well-established. However, it still seems that issues of conflict and violence are treated explicitly in specialized courses and more implicitly, if at all, in introductory courses on different religions.

Textbooks designed for introduction courses in the academic study of religion at universities seems often to avoid religion and violence instead of dealing with it overtly. In these books, the main focus is usually rather to provide an introduction to how a religious tradition appeared; its founder, texts, rituals, internal disputes and divisions, geographical spread, diaspora and so on. In such a classic approach to a religious tradition, there is often no place for religion and violence. Probably because it is regarded as a disruptive force, presenting a religious tradition from an insider's perspective does not typically include treatments of conflict or violence. To find scholarly literature that deals with religious violence one has to find books and articles that explicitly deal with these matters.

RELIGION AND VIOLENCE IN RELIGION EDUCATION IN SCHOOL

In Religion Education (RE) in public schools, the topic of religion and violence seems to be an ever bigger challenge than at universities. A clear tendency in most countries is that textbooks for primary, secondary and upper secondary school completely avoid the subject of religious violence. The current situation appears to be the same as English scholar Liam Gearon (2006) described ten years ago, namely that most textbooks instead point to religions as an ethical alternative and as an inspiration for being good. In RE it is still a question of whether religious violence should be part of the curriculum at all because it might be challenging for pupils to deal with. Or, whether it is a topic that might be introduced to pupils in secondary and upper secondary school because it is—whether one likes it or not—a challenging question about religion today.

Based on the analysis of RE textbooks in this volume, textbooks in RE from different parts of the world more than ever seem to present religion as something good and as a source for ethical reflection. Satoko Fujiwara's chapter in this volume is especially interesting in relation to this theme. It is interesting to read how Japanese authorities actively censor textbooks, and at the same time argue that groups that perform violent acts (and/acts of terror) are not religions.

THE CONTRIBUTIONS IN THIS VOLUME

Eight of the 11 contributions in this volume deal with religion and violence in textbooks for RE in school. **Michael H. Romanowski** begins with a theoretical discussion of textbooks and how they are important artefacts of culture. He then turns to several examples of studies that have examined various textbooks from several nations and how authors address issues such as religion, 9/11 and America's war on terror and the Arab-Israeli conflict. Finally, several practical suggestions are offered for teachers and students, providing them with opportunities to challenge textbook doctrine and read textbooks in a more critical manner.

That the textbook is an important artefact is evident in Satoko Fujiwara's chapter. Fujiwara begins her chapter with her own experience as a high school textbook writer and how she came to argue with the Japanese Ministry of Education over how to teach about the relationship between religion and violence. The Ministry's view was that if a group commits violence, they should not be regarded as religious. The Ministry insisted that religion is, by definition, free of any violence. Since all school textbooks in Japan must be authorized by the Ministry, Fujiwara had to accept the Ministry's opinion because, otherwise, her textbook would not have been published. Fujiwara argues that the Ministry's attitude will increase rather than decrease the prejudice among young Japanese people against religions, Islam in particular, because the Ministry's view flatly contradicts the information these young people receive from the Internet, which many of them trust more than their teachers.

In her contribution, **Zrinka Štimac** discusses how textbooks for RE—Islamic, Catholic and Serbian-Orthodox—miss the opportunity to deal with war atrocities, violence and ongoing conflicts in the society after the most recent war in Bosnia and Herzegovina. Instead—to a different extent and in a different quality—they concentrate on their own history and identity, which is connected with war-related discourse. Štimac argues that they do not, or only seldom, deal with the communist past and the violence committed during that period of time. She further argues that the neglected debate on conflict and violence is not an indication of intellectual and pedagogical inability to deal with the war. Instead, it is firstly a strategy to deal with historical ambivalences and social problems that cannot be solved. Secondly, she argues, it is a strategy of Churches and Religious Communities to deal with their own inner tensions; and thirdly, it seems to be a normative "must," that religious organizations after the war are responsible for "peace and freedom" discourse.

Historical ambivalence is also a part of **Torjer A. Olsen's** analysis of Norwegian textbooks in RE and history, and the presentation of colonization and conflicts related to the Sami, the Indigenous peoples of northern Finno-Scandinavia. He analyzes presentations of the Christianization process in the 18th century and the so-called Kautokeino Rebellion of 1852. Olsen argues that in both cases, the relationship between majority, state and church on one side, and an ethnic and religious minority on the other side, is an issue. The Christianization process was part of an explicit colonization in which the state set out to convert the Sami into both Norwegians and Christians. The Kautokeino Rebellion has an almost mythical status. Here, a group of Sami Christians brutally attacked representatives of the local authorities. Two were killed in an act of violence. In Sami history, this incident is, however, something more than a story about violence. These two incidents are important parts of Sami and Norwegian history. As such, the way textbooks treat these incidents can be seen as an articulation of the relationship between the majority and the minority when it comes to both religion and ethnicity. The major focus of the article is on textbooks currently used in today's public schools. Additionally, Olsen examines presentations of the same incidents in older textbooks.

Sivane Hirsch writes about textbooks designed for the "Ethics and Religious Culture" (ERC) program in Quebec. The subject tries to achieve two primary objectives: the recognition of others and the pursuit of the common good, while placing an emphasis on "the search for common values, the promotion of projects that foster community life and respect for democratic principles and ideals specific to Quebec society." Hirsch examines the treatment of religious conflicts in the ERC textbooks. In addition to providing a general portrait of this treatment, Hirsch also discusses its strengths and weaknesses through an analysis that considers recommended approaches for teaching sensible topics appearing in established literature. Thus, she demonstrates not only the difficulties of discussing this subject in a secular society like Quebec, but also the importance of doing so.

Suzanne A. Thobro discusses continuity and change in RE textbooks' representations of anti-Semitism and the Holocaust, covering the period 1970–2014. Thobro argues that both the textual and the iconographic representations presuppose substantial prerequisite knowledge, and in textbooks one can find three intertwined strategies for distancing readers from the problem of anti-Semitism.

Iconographic representations of religion and violence is also a focus in **Sissel Undheim's** contribution. Undheim uses the impact of the cartoon controversy of 2005 as a point of reference when she analyzes and discusses the palpable changes in the use of iconographic material in RE textbooks for primary school. By studying changes in visual representation of Islam and Judaism in two "generations" of textbooks, she discusses different interpretations of Islamic aniconism expressed in textbooks from four different publishers.

Kai Arne Nyborg analyzes and compares Australian and Norwegian RE textbooks for upper-secondary school. From the perspective of postcolonial criticism (Said) and cultural theory (Bourdieu), he discusses whether the textbook's presentation of Buddhism can be understood as symbolic violence when using Christianity as a point of reference. And as a consequence, whether explaining Buddhism with terms drawn from the presentation of Christianity, based on unqualified concepts and comparison, potentially could result in a discriminative religious education.

The chapter by **Bengt-Ove Andreassen** is based on textbooks for teacher education at universities and university colleges. The chapter analyzes textbooks in RE designed for Norwegian teacher education. An analysis of 23 books shows that topics concerning religion and violence, conflict and extremism are rarely mentioned. As a consequence, future RE teachers are only minimally introduced to issues that relate religion to violence, conflict or extremism. Using theoretical concepts from Norman Fairclough, Andreassen discusses whether this can be described as a significant or insignificant absence.

In an autobiographical account of how he came to write his own textbook—*Muslim Identities: An Introduction to Islam* (New York: Columbia University Press, 2014)—**Aaron W. Hughes** examines the unwillingness of most textbooks on Islam to deal with issues of violence, terrorism, or similar issues. Hughes provides an author's perspective on the dominant trend in the development on textbooks on

Islam in his discussion of textbooks and the absence of violence, terrorism and similar issues.

In his chapter, **James R. Lewis** looks first at how the assumptions and interests of scholar-officials in the British Raj shaped their representations of Sikhs and Sikhism. Secondarily, he discussed how these often inaccurate images of the Sikh religion were picked up and redeployed by the authors of world religions textbooks that were written in the latter half of the 20th century. More specifically, Lewis provides an overview of the roots of the images of the Sikh militancy found in Western scholarship—militant images derived from the Enlightenment-informed Orientalist discourse about the imputed pacifism/militancy of the Sikh gurus.

REFERENCES

Avalos, Hector. 2005. *Fighting Words: The Origins of Religious Violence*. New York: Prometheus Books.
Carlson, John D. 2011. "Religion and Violence: Coming to Terms with Terms." In *The Blackwell Companion to Religion and Violence*, ed. Andrew R. Murphy, 7–22. Oxford: Blackwell.
Cavanaugh, William T. 2009. *The Myth of Religious Violence: Secular Ideology and the Roots of Modern Conflict*. Oxford: Oxford University Press.
Eller, Jack D. 2010. *Cruel Creeds, Virtuous Violence: Religious Violence across Culture and History*. New York: Prometheus Books.
Gearon, Liam. 2006. "Human Rights and Religious Education: Some Postcolonial Perspectives." In *International Handbook of the Religious, Moral and Spiritual Dimensions in Education. Part One*, eds. M. de Souza et al., 375–85. Dordrecht: Springer.
Juergensmeyer, Mark. 2008. *Global Rebellion. Religious Challenges to the Secular State, from Christian Militias to al Qaeda*. Berkley, CA: University of California Press.
Juergensmeyer, Mark, Margo Kitts and Michael Jerryson, eds. 2013. *The Oxford Handbook of Religion and Violence*. Oxford: Oxford University Press.
Kimball, Charles. 2002. *When Religion Becomes Evil*. San Francisco, CA: Harper Publishing.
Lefebure, Leo D. 2000. *Revelation, the Religions, and Violence*. Maryknoll, NY: Orbis Books.
Murphy, Andrew R., ed. 2011. *The Blackwell Companion to Religion and Violence*. Oxford: Blackwell.
Pennington, Brian K., ed. 2012. *Teaching Religion and Violence*. New York: Oxford University Press.
Rennie, Bryan, and Philip L. Tite, eds. 2008. *Religion, Terror and Violence: Religious Studies Perspectives*. New York and London: Routledge.

1. READING BEYOND THE LINES: WHAT STUDENTS LEARN FROM THEIR HISTORY TEXTBOOKS

Michael H. Romanowski

INTRODUCTION

School textbooks are a dominant educational tool used in classrooms throughout the world. One could easily argue there is no other educational tool that shapes national culture more powerfully than textbooks. "Textbooks are not only among the first books most people encounter; in many places they are, along with religious texts, almost the only books they encounter" (*The Economist* 2012). In fact, textbooks are granted authority similar to religious texts where knowledge is sanctioned as infallible truth beyond criticism. Students are taught to memorize and master rather than to question or criticize textbook content.

However, textbooks do not deserve this reputation as simple impartial educational tools that teach students facts and skills. Rather the selected knowledge written on textbook pages is, "never neutral or objective but is ordered and structured in particular ways" (McLaren 1998: 169). For example I argue elsewhere:

> history textbooks incorporate attitudes and ways of looking at the world. In making judgments about what should be included and what should be excluded and how particular episodes in history should be summarized, textbooks authors assign positive or negative interpretations to particular events, thereby asserting a set of values. The fact that these values are often not declared explicitly, but remain implicit does not make them less powerful (Romanowski 1996: 170).

It is vital to consider that knowledge that is selected for inclusion into textbooks is not random but rather "it is selected and organized around sets of principles and values that come from somewhere, that represent particular views of normality and deviance, of good and bad, and of what good people act like" (Apple 2004: 61). Even textbooks that adopt a "fact stating" format still send powerful messages to students because all textbooks are written from a particular perspective or worldview. The end result is "what goes into school textbooks—and, even more, what is left out—spurs concern and controversy all over the world" (*The Economist* 2012) because textbooks embody, promote and legitimize particular values, ideologies, interests, assumptions, and beliefs.

Critical theorists have long argued that textbooks not only provide a generation of citizens a sanctioned version of their historical past, but the version presented is a highly politicized, ideological device that shapes students' views and understandings of the world (Cherryholmes, Heilman and Segall 2005; Apple and Christian-Smith 1991; Anyon 1979). The issue is history textbooks contain selected "narratives and stories that nations choose to tell about themselves, their people and their relationship with other nations" (Foster 2011: 5). These stories create what a society has recognized as legitimate knowledge by signifying particular constructions of reality that members of society want transmitted to their children (Apple and Christian-Smith 1991). More importantly, the school textbook has an important social function, "to represent to each generation a sanctioned version of human knowledge and culture" (de Castell, Luke and Luke 1989: vii). Given the significant role textbooks play in the educational systems of some countries, this chapter provides a discussion that offers teachers and students insight into the narratives and messages transmitted to readers and suggestions that develop skills to challenge textbook narratives by reading textbooks with a critical eye.

To accomplish these goals, several themes are discussed utilizing examples in textbooks from around the globe. The themes are as follows:

1. Textbook Language
2. Omissions, Controversy and Conflict
3. Narratives Transmitted to Students
4. Moral and Ethical Concerns

In what follows, I offer a brief yet significant discussion addressing the power and authority of textbooks that render the knowledge and narratives above criticism. Next, I provide discussion for the above themes offering several examples from various content analyses I conducted that examined high school history textbooks from several nations focusing on how authors address issues such as the American Japanese Internment during World War II, religion, 9/11 and America's war on terror and the Arab-Israeli conflict. Each theme is presented separately to provide a more focused examination although the four themes overlap at various points. Finally, practical suggestions are offered for teachers and students that provide opportunities to learn to challenge textbook doctrine and begin to critically read textbooks. These include important questions that must be considered when engaging textbook knowledge and several facets of understanding that if used in the classroom, can aid students in gaining comprehensive understandings of textbooks and uncovering embedded narratives allowing for critique and questioning.

THE AUTHORITY OF TEXTBOOKS

When comparing Japanese and US textbook usage and students, Richard H. Minear, a Japanese historian stated, "As far as the effects on students go, the difference is not great... our students believe absolutely what they read in textbooks." Fitzgerald (1979: 7) argues when it comes to the understanding of history, "to students, American history textbooks are the truth of things. They are American history." The major educational concern is that most students trust and do not question historical accounts in textbooks (Hsiao 2014). This illustrates the power that textbooks have to place knowledge beyond criticism.

Textual authority can be defined as the power granted to the written word that sanctions the knowledge and messages communicated as truth. This authority enables the printed word to be accepted as infallible presenting truth that is beyond questioning. Regarding textbooks, one aspect of the authority of the textbook is embedded in the idea that in most cultures, books have power because they serve as an authority on issues of dispute (Olson 1989). By simply being in print, authority is attributed to statements that originate elsewhere separating the author from the reader. This separation of author and reader plays a significant role in legitimizing textbook authority and also gaining the trust of readers. This separation makes the words impersonal objective and above criticism. When the knowledge found in textbooks does not originate from a person with limited experience but rather in the textbooks that are consulted by parents and teachers, the knowledge is assumed to have great authority and truth.

However, although it is impossible for history textbooks to be written with historical objectivity (Shin and Sneider 2013), the impersonal style of textbooks allows textbook content, interpretations and the framework to appear to readers as objective, and lacking any particular viewpoint, which in turn contributes to its alleged neutrality and objective authority (Luke, De Castell and Luke 1989). Most readers assume the authors are well qualified to write the textbook and this expertise is simply accepted thinking that what appears in the textbook must be the truth. Because students trust their textbooks, they are "willing to devote serious and prolonged study to books, rather than simply reading them" (Olson 1989: 239).

In some sense, the textbook and its usage develop the similarity of a religious ritual, both possess a truth-value originating from a transcendental source. Olson argues:

> Textbooks, like religious ritual, have both some validity and a transcendental source. Textbooks, like religious ritual, are devices for putting ideas and beliefs above criticism...knowledge so stored carries great authority because it appears to originate in a transcendental source, at least in a source other than the present speaker or a member of his or her peer group (Olson 1989: 241).

Like religious sources, textbooks are seldom challenged or questioned. Having been legitimized by school authorities, textbooks are granted a special power to provide the official version of a society's valid knowledge (Olson 1989). Students learn their role is to master textbook knowledge treating textbooks like documents, seldom are they challenged or interpreted but rather they are simply cited (De Castell 1990). Thus, there is little doubt that textbooks have the authority to present sanctioned knowledge to students who seem to simply accept the author's interpretations. With the above in mind, the following discussion addresses several themes and presents examples of how bias textbooks are and how the author's presentation of historical events can shape how students understand history and the world around them.

TEXTBOOK LANGUAGE

Williams (1985) notes that there are keywords that have multiple meanings and uses such as "democracy," "culture," and "citizenship." These meaning are often termed a floating signifier "a signifier that is overflowed with meaning because it is articulated differently within different discourses" (Torfing 1999: 301). These terms do not necessarily have an essential meaning but rather are used by different groups with different agendas. More importantly, the words found in history textbooks are loaded with important historical associations and the meanings are often utilized by conflicting groups to create an impression that promotes and supports their own narratives. Actually, these words often move around on a continuum of meanings. The point here is that the careful selection of words plays a key role the creation of an impression that plays a role in the construction of particular narratives and when coupled with textual authority, are legitimized and placed beyond criticism.

This is important to understand and consider when examining or reading history textbooks because textbook language creates impressions of particular historical events and these impressions not only play a role in the construction narratives but as Fitzgerald argued over 30 years ago:

> what sticks to the memory from those textbooks is not any particular series of facts but an atmosphere, an impression, a tone. And this impression may be all the more influential just because one cannot remember the facts and the arguments that created it (Fitzgerald 1979: 18).

The following example illustrates this concern. Although somewhat dated, I would argue that this example provides an excellent example to illustrate how textbook language creates impressions and shapes thinking. These examples were found in two American Secondary History textbooks used in the mid 1990s and their portrayal of the internment of Japanese Americans during World War II.

As we know during World War II, the American government forced the relocation and incarceration of Japanese Americans living in the United States shortly after Japan's attack on Pearl Harbor. I argue elsewhere (Romanowski 1995; 1996) when addressing the internment of Japanese Americans, Bragdon, McCutchen, and Ritchie (1992) write the Japanese Detainees had as little as 48 hours to make arrangements for their homes, businesses, and farms before being relocated to internment camps located throughout the US Many were forced to sell their property at a loss or abandon it with such short notice. This provided American citizens opportunities to purchase Japanese Detainees' property or businesses. The authors select the term "bargain hunters" to describe individuals who profited from the internment, in terms of property, money, and material items. "Bargain hunters descended on them, taking advantage of their plight." In American culture, the expression bargain hunters constitute a positive image that downplays the responsibility of individuals who sold and gained economically from the internment. The term justifies economic gain at any means instead of addressing the ethical issues regarding the exploitation of the victims. The term creates an overall impression that conceals significant ethical issues related to "taking advantage of their plight" which remains unquestioned. In this sense, students learn that injustices are deemed appropriate in the name of economic advancement or "getting a bargain."

In contrast, the textbook *American Voices* (Berkin et al. 1992: 669) selects the term "human vultures," to describe these "bargain hunters" constructing a strikingly different impression. The selection and use of this term constructs a completely different narrative by framing the event not as receiving a bargain but rather focuses on individuals preying upon victims of injustice in order to receive benefits. The term "human vultures" raises issues of fairness and justice regarding the selling and profiting from confiscated Japanese American citizens' property. Thus, this example clearly illustrates how textbooks can create impressions that shape how students understand American history. As these examples demonstrate, the selected language used within history textbooks develops narratives that are by far objective and neutral.

The term Zionism provides another useful example that illustrates the impact of language. Several textbooks used in Iraq, Jordan and the US illustrate how the definition of Zionism shapes students' thinking.

Zionism is a racist, aggressive and colonial movement aimed at gathering the Jews of all nationalities around the world in Palestine through the migration and displacement of the Arab people. Zionism also aims to impede Arab's unity and to erase their cultural identity for the purpose of achieving a Jewish state stretching from the Euphrates to the Nile (Mothfer and Mohamad 2009).

Zionism is a racist political movement founded by the Jews of Russia in the mid-eighteenth century, aimed to raise Jewish Diaspora and establishing a homeland in Palestine...The Zionist thought is characterized as: Racial,

Settlement and Diversionary thought...Zionism emerged when the Jews rewrote the Torah and built an imaginary history and rights in establishing a homeland in land of Palestine...Jews were invited to the reunion and return to the Promised Land and colonize Palestine and establish the State Israel (Al Abedlaat et al. 2009: 125).

These excerpts create an impression supporting a narrative that rejects Israel's national identity and describes Israel as the "occupied lands" (Mothfer and Mohamad 2009: 69). The narrative includes language such as racist, aggressive and a colonial movement that displaces Arab people and prevents Arab unity. The Jews are accused of rewriting the Torah, the five books of the Hebrew Bible, commonly known to non-Jews as the Old Testament.

However, American textbooks provide quite a different impression describing Zionism as seeking a Jewish homeland. Only one American textbook uses Zionism and the authors define the term as follows: "The UN plan was a victory for Zionism the movement seeking a Jewish homeland in Palestine" (Boyer and Stuckey 2005: 564). One can easily see the two radically different definitions and use of the term Zionist and how interests and politics play a role in presenting historical events.

These are just a few of the numerous examples that explain the importance of language and word selection as authors present knowledge, desired by the particular nation that constructs impressions and narratives that shape students' understandings and views on particular issues. For example, terms such as religious fundamentalist, Jewish extremist, Palestinian extremist, patriotism, native, immigrant, invasion, settlement, colonization and nationalism have emotive meaning that students must decipher. Even when textbook authors fail to provide a definition or discussion to unpack an important term, students must trust their own understandings that are often linked to media portrayals and stereotypes that shape their understandings of the particular term and/or event. In other words, without contemplating written words or without providing some opportunity to engage in dialogue about meanings, it is less likely that students will be able to understand how language might spark their emotions, bias and understandings of particular people or events and in turn affect their perspective and possibly behavior.

OMISSIONS, CONTROVERSY AND CONFLICT

Certainly the knowledge that finds its way onto textbook pages is important as described above. However when examining textbooks, it is critical to understand not merely the facts, narratives, impressions and the language used to legitimize the knowledge in textbooks, but also the knowledge that is disqualified or omitted from the story. Eisner argues that the knowledge schools do not teach is as important as what they do teach. He points out that "ignorance is not simply a neutral void; it has important effects on the kinds of options one is able to consider, the alternatives that one can examine, and the perspectives from which one can view a situation or problem" (Eisner 1994: 97).

It is neither possible for textbooks to include all information nor unusual for authors to omit knowledge. However, it is often the case that textbooks exclude controversy, conflict and omit anything that might reflect badly upon national character (Loewen 1995). For example, school textbooks in both Israel and Palestine largely eliminate one another's existence in maps (Miller 2013) and most Chinese students complete their high school studies believing that China has only engaged in wars in self-defence, never aggressively or in conquest, in spite of the People's Liberation Army's invasion of Tibet in 1950 and the war with Vietnam in 1979 (French 2004). The key here is that omitted knowledge has important effects on students because it limits the alternatives and perspectives from which they can view particular problems, events, or situations. Possible reasons for omissions might be a political agenda, prejudices, deliberate distortion, the cultural climate, activists' groups or less likely, simply an oversight. These omissions are significant because the knowledge and the historical interpretations presented affect how students view their country and understand the "other."

An excellent example of these omissions can be found in both US and Arab textbooks regarding an aspect of the Arab-Israeli conflict, Palestinian Refugees. Palestinian Refugees are individuals whose normal residence was Palestine between June 1946 and May 1948, who lost both their homes and means of livelihood as a result of the 1948 Arab-Israeli conflict (United Nations Relief and Works Agency n.d). Beyond simple mentioning, not a single textbook provides a substantial discussion regarding the Palestinian refugees that many would consider to be a fundamental concern in the Arab-Israeli conflict (Romanowski and Alkhateeb 2011). Al Tarwneh et al. (2009a); Al Tarwneh et al. (2009b) write "Thousands of Palestinians were forced to leave their lands on the West Bank and Gaza Strip." No further explanation is provided. The knowledge omitted is the process of settlement activity. Settlement camps are located in various areas such as Jordan, Lebanon, the Syrian Arab Republic, the West Bank and Gaza Strip. The camps are located on land leased by the host government–meaning that the refugees do not own the land but have the limited right to use the land. The United Nations Relief and Works Agency (UNRWA) points out that the socio-economic conditions in the camps are generally poor with a high population density, cramped living conditions and inadequate basic infrastructure such as roads and sewers. Today, 4.7 million Palestinian refugees are eligible for UNRWA services. The hardships of the Palestinian refugees and personal struggles are omitted. There are no Israeli homes that have been demolished by Palestinians, whereas 24,145 Palestinian homes have been demolished by Israel since 1967 (Israeli Committee Against Home Demolitions 2009). The question one must ask is if students had this knowledge, would they look at this historical event differently? In response, the information clearly hampers students from developing complex understandings of Arab-Israeli conflict and this knowledge clearly serves particular interests.

Examining America's War on Terror, often US textbooks omit significant information that shapes students' understanding of the War on Terror. The majority of the textbooks exclude any discussion of the hardships and casualties of the invasion, authors do not address the impact of war on the civilian population and there is no discussion of the millions of Afghans starving to death and dying of disease or of civilian casualties. I point out elsewhere "the lack of information regarding civilian casualties provides students with a sterile and unrealistic view of the invasion of Afghanistan. More important, without proper attention to the human element, the disastrous consequences of war and the invasion of Afghanistan in particular go unreported and unquestioned" (Romanowski 2009b: 293).

Another important example deals with patriotism. This example illustrates the avoiding of conflict or controversy in some US textbooks' portrayal of the effects of 9/11 on America. Regarding 9/11, it is quite common to read about and view photos depicting such as photos of American icons such as the Statue of Liberty with the smoke from the 9/11 attacks in the background; Congress singing "God Bless America" on the Capitol steps; fireman raising the American flag with a backdrop of the Twin Tower debris; American flags in yards, on front doors and draped across fences and bridges. These textbooks clearly illustrated the uniting of the nation after the 9/11 attacks. They showed photos of Americans donating money and holding candlelight vigils and prayer services. Headings and language in the text used terms such as "America Unites," "A Nation Pulls Together," "A Nation United," and "American Comes Together: From Shock to a New Unity." One textbook even stated that there was support for Arab-Americans. Certainly there is truth in these statements and photos however there is a limited view of patriotism presented.

Textbooks unquestionably presented patriotism as an outstanding virtue targeted against the perpetrators who attacked the US and as a benefit to the nation. Americans are presented as united and committed to the challenge facing the country. However, the dark side of patriotism such as the possibility that America's post 9/11 patriotism combined with fear of terrorism could influence individuals and organizations to act in ways that might never be accepted during peacetime is never addressed. For example, misplaced anger demonstrated toward Arab Americans, Muslims and South Asians failed to make the pages of these textbooks. There is no mention of the incidents of harassment and hate crimes that were reported against Middle Easterners and other "Middle Eastern-Looking" people. There were no examples of reports of bomb threats to a Muslim school in Detroit or the 300 protestors who stormed a Chicago area mosque. There was no discussion of other behaviours with ethical dimensions, such as the singling out of Arab Americans in airports. One of the most valuable lessons that students should learn from 9/11 is how patriotism can be a force to unite a nation and how it can also be a tool of oppression when laced with fear but this is difficult when textbooks avoid conflict and controversy through the omission of this vital information.

Another US history controversy avoided in many textbooks is the invasion and occupation of Iraq. Textbooks set the context for war by informing readers that Saddam Hussein possessed weapons of mass destruction (WMDs), was a dictator linked to terrorism and that the invasion was the next logical step in the war on terror. However, textbooks omit an important element of the Bush Administration's justification for war. That is, the Administration claimed Hussein had recently sought significant quantities of uranium in Africa, and that US intelligence sources had reported that Hussein had also attempted to purchase high-strength aluminium tubes suitable for nuclear weapons production. These claims were eventually proved false, which raised questions about the Administration's motives and honesty (Romanowski 2009a). Declassified material now indicates that there was considerable doubt in the intelligence community about the uranium allegations before Bush's speech (National Security Archive 2008; Miller and Gerstenzang 2003). This significant information could change students' views about the Iraq invasion. However, this expanded perspective might provoke conflict and controversy—which authors generally try to avoid, no matter how important the knowledge might be in developing a complex understanding of the Iraq invasion (Romanowski 2009a).

When it comes to controversy, Adwan et al. (2002) point out that students often learn only one side of the story and usually it is their own perspective portrayed as the correct one. Textbooks justify one side and offer a negative portrayal of the other, in a sense "one side's hero is the other side's monster" (Adwan et al. 2002: i). For example, China along with other countries criticized Japan for using textbooks that whitewash the country's history glossing over Japanese war crimes while Palestinian textbooks present an "imbalance, bias, and inaccuracy" and failed accurately to depict today's political reality (*The Economist* 2013). History textbooks either omit important information or simply mention events without providing opportunities for students to fully consider controversy. More important, textbooks report controversies as if they were already resolved (Romanowski 2009a). Students must realize that ethics, morals and democratic values cannot be set aside in the name of patriotism or to further national interests and security.

Considering conflict and the invasion of Afghanistan, US history textbooks present facts that are generally accurate. However, several textbooks fall victim to the criticism that textbook authors present conflict as already solved or as about to be solved. The following excerpt from an American history textbook illustrates this criticism.

> a bombing campaign, known as 'Operation Enduring Freedom,' began on October 7th, and was followed by attacks by ground troops. Within two months, the United States defeated the Taliban, ending their five-year rule. They failed, however, to find bin Laden. Bush claimed that the defeat of the Taliban was the first victory in the war on terrorism (Ayers et al. 2007: 744).

Although some textbooks state that it is an on-going struggle, the majority of textbooks claim that the United States and rebel Afghan forces defeated the Taliban and shattered al-Qaeda's operations in Afghanistan in just two months and "within weeks, anti-Taliban forces captured the capital of Kabul and by early December the Taliban was defeated" (Ayers et al. 2007: 744). The impression conveyed to readers is that the invasion was a quick, and easy military endeavor, but, as we know, the fighting in Afghanistan continues and the War in Afghanistan is now considered the longest in US history.

The absence of conflict is again evident when considering Iraq and WMDs. Although United Nations inspectors found no WMDs, textbooks leave this information unexamined. For example, one textbook states "United States forces found no evidence that Iraq possessed weapons of mass destruction, and a serious link between Saddam Hussein and al-Qaeda was not discovered" (Appleby et al. 2007: 916). Although a true statement, the authors fail to question either the government's actions or foreign policy, and legitimize Bush's misleading claim as a "miscalculation" without presenting an explanation of how the president made such a blunder.

When textbooks do question the lack of evidence of WMDs, they present the conflict as resolved. For example, one textbook states, "Bush named a blue-ribbon panel to investigate United States intelligence regarding the claims of Iraq possessing WMDs" (Boyer and Stuckey 2005: 842). The authors omit any dialogue about the findings of the self-appointed panel, concerns about the panel members' objectivity, and any findings from the panel. More important is the use of the term "blue-ribbon panel," indicating that members of the panel were experts and could be trusted. The members are never listed, and readers are left to assume that Bush acknowledged the misinformation and addressed the problem, although no outcome is discussed. According to textbooks, the case is closed. For several textbooks, the answer to the lack of WMDs is that Bush overcame these criticisms to be re-elected. Since the American people re-elected Bush, suggesting that the WMD issue is irrelevant and implying the issue was resolved. Olson points out that textbooks help "to preserve the social order by minimizing dispute" (1989: 241). Historical events are void of conflict and presented as fixed, complete, and beyond criticism in order to accomplish this goal.

NARRATIVES TRANSMITTED TO STUDENTS

I earlier addressed how the language of textbooks constructs various narratives that students have the opportunity to learn. The discussion centred on the selected words used by textbook authors and how these develop impressions and narratives that students have the opportunity to learn. We now turn to the particular narrative that is embedded within the textbook pages. Embedded within these narratives are messages that students have the opportunity to learn. For example, Hamerman (2011) reports findings from a review conducted by The Institute for Monitoring Peace and Cultural Tolerance in School Education of 118 textbooks currently used in Palestinian schools. Findings indicated that these textbooks blame Israel for all environmental problems, there is a total denial of the existence of Israel and any Israeli presence is usually extremely negative. In geography textbooks, Israel usually does not appear in maps of the Middle East, instead "Palestine is shown to encompass Israel, the West Bank and the Gaza Strip. Jaffa is also shown on maps of Palestine, but Tel Aviv and other predominantly Jewish cities, such as Ramat Gan, Kibbutzim and Moshavim, are not displayed. The study also found that "Palestinian textbooks include many references to martyrdom, death, jihad and refugees returning to cities and towns in Israel—and frequently demonize Israelis and Jews." It is quite obvious that these textbooks legitimize a Palestinian narrative evident in the language presented and the knowledge omitted.

Another example dealing with the Arab-Israeli conflict illustrates how US and Arab nations present and legitimize different narratives for students to learn. Arab textbooks suggest several reasons why Israel is a threat to the Arab world. This includes Israel's expansionist policy that forces Arab countries to remain on standby in case of Israeli aggression. This impacts Arab countries' budgets by forcing Arabs to funnel finances into a military budget instead of investing in other development projects. Second, Israel plays a role in the obstruction of Arab unity and prevents communication between Arab States in Asia and Africa. Finally, Israeli nuclear threat is considered the most serious danger for the Arab nations.

Contrary, US textbooks position Israel more as a victim. Several textbooks clearly state that the US supports Israel and provide explanations of US support because of Palestinian attacks and the Arab world's rejection of Israel as a national entity. American textbooks seem to present the US not so much as an ally of Israel but rather as a country seeking peace in the region. Most of the coverage in these textbooks is spent on the US attempts at various summits in the development of peace agreements between the Arab nations and Israel (Romanowski and Alkhateeb 2011).

Finally, an interesting example from an American textbook that addresses religion by creating a narrative about Christians in the following textbook excerpt; "He [President Jimmy Carter] symbolized the reawakening of an American religious spirit, especially among conservative Protestants. Despite radical movements and unprecedented scientific breakthroughs, the tide of popular religion had continued to rise" (Garraty 1994: 1107). By implication, the authors put forth the idea that Christians (conservative Protestants) are profoundly anti-modern and that their faith and beliefs are incompatible with science and radical movements. The textbook makes an authoritative knowledge claim where the meaning is fixed and presented as fact. Based on this statement, students are introduced to a narrative in which people who hold to a conservative Protestant faith (or any religion for that matter) are individuals who fail to understand or even intellectually consider the role science and technology play in the development of knowledge and understanding (Romanowski 2003). One can see how omitted knowledge helps build this particular narrative. The author never names these radical movements and unprecedented scientific breakthroughs that conservative Protestants have dismissed. The textbook never addresses why these radical movements and unprecedented scientific breakthroughs are incompatible with Christianity. In this case, the reader is given "the false impression that religion is something that used to matter a long time ago but no longer makes much difference in the lives of modern people" (Nord and Haynes 1998: 90). More important, the narrative created by this excerpt could possibly develop new stereotypes in readers or reinforce commonly held stereotypes such as Christians or individuals of any faith are anti-intellectuals who oppose science and modernity and cling to an irrational faith.

AVOIDANCE OF ETHICAL ISSUES

In the same vein as avoiding conflict, history textbooks also avoid the raising of and any discussion regarding ethical and moral issues because these areas often stir controversy or create conflict. Because history textbooks are written using an instrumental narrative that presents information in a law-like manner with fixed meanings, they often expel the inescapable moral and ethical components of historical events. The authors make too little effort to raise ethical issues such as inequality or injustice because of conflict or controversy as discussed above. Thus, they rely on presenting facts. For example, one of the darkest moments for the US in the war in Iraq was the discovery of the abuse of detainees at Abu Ghraib. One textbook addresses the event as follows:

> The failure of inspectors to find any weapons of mass destruction in Iraq further weakened his [Bush's] support, as did the scandal at the Iraq prison of Abu Ghraib where some Iraqi prisoners of war were abused by their American guards and interrogators. These events provided an opportunity for the Democrats to mount a serious challenge in the 2004 presidential election (Appleby et al. 2007: 820).

This description is limited to facts and placed within a framework of politics avoiding any discussion regarding morality and ethics. Instead of ethical aspects of prisoner treatment, the textbook limits the discussion to the political realm by suggesting the democrats could use the scandal to their advantage. This excerpt is so poor that they do not even provide information about the scandal. Linking back to previous categories earlier discussed, what important knowledge is missing and how does this avoid ethical concerns? What about the details of the abuse? Beginning in 2004, accounts of abuse, torture, sodomy, and homicide of prisoners came to the public's attention. The abuse was found to include such things as urinating on detainees, jumping on a detainee's wounded leg and preventing proper healing, pounding detainees' wounded limbs with a metal baton, pouring phosphoric acid on detainees, sodomizing detainees with a baton, and tying ropes to detainees' legs and dragging them varying distances. These serious charges are never revealed to readers and instead emphasis is placed on American politics. By simply presenting the "facts," one could see how readers would not be led to raise questions about ethical behavior. There are some who would argue the specific details should be omitted, but, nevertheless, this behavior could be presented in a tactful and meaningful manner that sheds light on the seriousness of the abuse raising issues that centre on morality and ethics. The key is that this textbook portrayal excludes any discussion of the moral and ethical implications of prisoner treatment such as the appropriate treatment of prisoners of war and the Geneva Conventions.

This same approach is used by textbook authors when addressing the Gaza Strip where 1.5 million Palestinians suffer daily hardships such as malnutrition of children, a lack of water supplies and drainage, food, fuel and medicine deliveries are made difficult or stopped altogether and children die for lack of healthcare (Snorre and Wilhelmson 2008) is important knowledge for students to grasp the complexities of the Arab-Israeli conflict. Yet textbooks remain silent on this issue. Knowing this information clearly adds an important element to understanding the Arab-Israeli conflict and provides opportunities for students to understand multiple perspectives and to understand the human features of history. More importantly, this omitted information prevents students from viewing the historical event from this particular perspective but textbooks are successful in avoiding controversy.

Many of the examples provided are void of moral or ethical concerns. Consider the examples above. Are there ethical issues that need to be raised in the lack of WMD's and Bush's justification for the invasion? What type of ethical questions should be raised regarding the consequences of invading Iraq? What about the numerous soldiers and civilians killed and wounded in the war that is never discussed? Just consider the internment of Japanese-Americans, the use of torture at Abu Ghraib or the numerous ethical issues embedded in the Arab-Israeli conflict. All of these are loaded with ethical concerns that are mostly omitted by textbooks.

READING TEXTBOOKS CRITICALLY

Even with the development of advanced technology, there is little doubt textbooks, in some form will remain a mainstay in education. Having said that, the purpose of this chapter is not to examine particular historical events or the quality of particular textbooks, but rather to provide examples that illustrate how knowledge presented in history textbooks legitimize particular narratives and impressions and how textbooks convey desired messages to students.

Although textbooks have textual authority, teachers can either participate in granting authority to textbooks or play a role in delegitimizing textbook narratives. Teachers, due to their institutionally defined authority, still control the textbook. When the door to the classroom closes, teachers have power over textbooks because they must mediate the content to students and decide the value of any textbook and the knowledge within. It is important that teachers not only focus on teaching historical content but also deliberately teach particular thinking skills that prove useful for students when reading their textbooks and also beyond the classroom walls. With that in mind, let me offer several suggestions for teachers and students that might aid in developing a critical eye when engaging textbooks.

First, teachers cannot simply assume all students have understandings of important terms used in textbooks. Based on previous examples, teachers should take time to discuss the complex meanings and multiple perspectives embedded in authors' word choices. When textbooks or teachers fail to unpack terms, students are left to rely on their own understandings, media portrayals and most likely stereotypes that shape their understandings of the particular term and/or event. One strategy that could be used is to have students brainstorm the various meanings so students not only learn the complexity of a term but also the skills needed to dissect the meanings. Teachers would do their students well if they challenged stereotypes that often accompany various terms and also demonstrate how particular interests can shape the meaning of particular terms.

Second, teachers need to teach students that the textbook version of a particular event is limited and only one of many narratives. Clearly textbooks cannot include every piece of information or all perspectives so students need the skills and ability to raise questions regarding the impressions and narratives produced in history textbooks. This can be accomplished by engaging in a narrative-based approach to history instruction. This approach to history activates critical thinking and provides the opportunity for students to take the "other's" view of history. However, students must be taught that narratives are also interpretations of history and they should be encouraged to question all narratives. Lee (1998) argues that students should be exposed to different versions of historical events but they must also be taught to account for the difference.

Loewen (1995) suggests that teachers could challenge textbook doctrine and deal with textbooks in a more critical manner by utilizing five questions. These questions are the initial stage of uncovering others' narratives. Loewen's questions are as follows: Why was a particular event written about? Whose viewpoint is presented, omitted and whose interests are served? Is the account believable? Is the account backed up by other sources? and How is one supposed to feel about what has been presented? These questions provide opportunities for students to begin to grasp the meaning of a "frame of reference," oppositional narratives and how these play a role in selecting, and organizing the information that makes up their history textbooks. Arida (2006) points out that when teachers or textbooks provide opposing narratives and viewpoints, the student benefits by gaining an understanding that conflicts are multidimensional and dynamic rather than one-dimensional and static. More importantly, students will learn how to recognize their own personal biases and the ideologies that directly influence their perceptions and understandings of historical events.

Third, Wiggins and McTighe (2005) provide six facets of understanding. Teachers can use this framework to provide opportunities for students to gain comprehensive understandings of textbook knowledge and to uncover and critically examine textbook narratives. More importantly, questions are provided that should be asked and answered to aid in the development of complex understandings. Table 1 is adapted from G. Wiggins and J. McTighe (2005) and develops these categories.

Table 1: Six Facets of Understanding

Explanation	Students possess the knowledge to be able to develop complicated explanations. They should be able to ask and respond to questions such as: Why is that so? What explains such events? What accounts for such actions? To what is this connected? What is an illustrative example? How does this work? What is implied? Understanding is not just basic knowledge of facts but rather the ability to make inferences about why and how providing evidence, connections and illustrations with logic. Explaining requires one to support, justify, generalize, predict verify and substantiate. In addition, students should be able to identify and explain the moral and ethical dilemmas that might surface in particular events. A very important aspect of explanation is developing in students the ability to ask questions.
Interpret	To give meaning by providing interpretations, narratives and translations. They should be able to *ask* and *respond* to questions such as: What does it mean? Why does it matter? What does it illustrate in the human experience? How does it relate to me? What makes sense? This requires the student to be able make the subject of study personal or accessible through images, anecdotes, analogies, and models.
Application	Students are able to transfer knowledge to new situations and diverse contexts. They should be able to *ask* and *respond* to questions such as: How and where can we use this knowledge, skill or process? How should my thinking and action be modified to meet the demands of this particular situation? This requires teachers to provide real-world problems for students to engage and solve. They should also understand that morals play a role in defining personal character and ethics involve the application of those morals in a social system. Students should be able to apply their own code of morals to various contexts.

Perspective	Students must have the ability to be able to identify and understand differing points of view through critical eyes that allow them to develop a more complete story of an event. They must be able to produce critical and insightful points of view and be able to *ask* and *respond* to questions such as: From whose point of view? What is the point of view of the authors of the textbook concerning what is true, verified and important? What are the other viewpoints? To what extent do textbooks distort and simplify ideas to satisfy audiences? What is assumed or tacit that needs to be made explicit and considered? What is justified or warranted? Is there adequate evidence? Is it reasonable? What are the strengths and weaknesses of the idea? Is it plausible? What are the limits? Students must be able to expose questionable and unexamined assumptions, conclusions and implications in textbooks.
Empathy	The ability to understand another person's feelings and worldview. Students need to find value in others' narratives and experiences and come to sensitively understand the different lives and experiences of others. Empathy is a form of insight because it allows students to find meaning in an others' experiences and requires respect for people who live different lives and are different from us.
Self-Knowledge	Students are able to critically reflect and uncover their personal narratives, prejudices and habits of the mind that both shape and impede their understandings. They should be able to *ask* and *respond* to questions such as: How does whom I am shape my views? What are the limits of my understanding? What are my blind spots? What am I prone to misunderstand because of prejudice, habit or style? They are also able to identify their limitations and how knowing just one perspective hampers understanding. Self-knowledge demands that students and teachers question their own ways of seeing the world and understand and accept the limits of our thinking. More importantly, students should be able to identify their own code of morals and how these should be applied to the particular situation.

Teachers must be creative in developing lessons and activities that provide opportunities for students to develop the six facets of understanding. If given these learning opportunities, students will begin to grasp how their individual biases and limited views shape how they view the history and how this limits their understandings.

Furthermore, photos are excellent ways to encourage critical thought. Students can be given textbook photos that can be used to isolate important pieces of information. Teachers can instruct students to write several paragraphs based on the information and list questions about the photo. For example, students could view a photo of a United States tank rolling into Baghdad (Cayton et al. 2007) with children running alongside. Students would select information and write their paragraphs, and the teacher would engage them with questions such as: Why did you choose this particular information? What is missing from the photo? What do the children add to the photo? How do you feel when you see the photo? What message is sent to readers by the inclusion of this photo? Pictures and photos can be used in numerous ways to develop thinking skills, uncover messages and raise ethical issues.

Finally teachers can access various readings and/or books that can provide a more balanced perspective on various historical events and conflicts. Teachers should provide opportunities for students to write their reflections about not only their own perspective and understandings of the historical events and conflict but learning oppositional viewpoints allows them to develop an understanding that a textbook's interpretation of an event is only one of the many possible perspectives.

In closing, schools are of the utmost importance because they socialize future citizens shaping their understanding of their country and the global community. I suggest that instead of telling students *what to think*, teachers must encourage students *to think* and teach them to develop thinking skills that are needed to analyze textbook knowledge. The argument can be made that "if we understand what has caused what in the past, we may be able to predict what will happen next and even adopt national policies informed by our knowledge" (Loewen 1995: 281).

ABOUT THE AUTHOR

Michael H. Romanowski is Professor of Education and Coordinator of Graduate Programs in the Department of Educational Sciences at Qatar University. He earned his PhD from Miami University. A former high school teacher in the American Public School System, Professor Romanowski brings to the classroom diverse educational experiences including academic positions in the United States, China and currently Qatar. He has published his research and scholarship in various academic books and international journals and has managed external and internal research grants examining various important educational issues, recently addressing the national education reform in Qatar. He continues to research and write on various educational and culture issues.

REFERENCES

Adwan, Sami, Dan Bar-On, Adnan Musallam and Eyal Naveh. 2002. *Learning Each Other's Historical Narrative: Palestinians and Israelis*. Beit Jallah, PNA: Peace Research Institute in the Middle East.

Al Abedlaat Mohammed, Fadi Badawi, Jamal Badran, Salem Ismail, Hassan Ahmad and Ibrahim Azabi. 2009. *The History of the Arabs and the Modern World*. Amman, Jordan: The Ministry of Education.

Al Tarwneh, A., Al Kareem Ahmad A., Al Abedlaat M., Ismail S., and Al Tarawneh M. (2009a). The Modern and Contemporary History of Arabs, Part 1 Grade 10. Amman, Jordan: The Ministry of Education.

Al Tarwneh, A., Al Abedlaat M., Ismail S., and Al Tarawneh M. (2009b). The Modern and Contemporary History of Arabs, Part 2 Grade 10. Amman, Jordan: The Ministry of Education.

Anyon, Jean. 1979. "Ideology and United States History Textbooks." *Harvard Educational Review* 49(3): 361–86.

Apple, Michael. 1993. *Official Knowledge: Democratic Education in a Conservative Age*. London: Routledge.

Apple, Michael. 2004. Ideology and Curriculum, 3rd Ed. New York and London: RoutlegeFalmer.

Apple, Michael, and Linda Christian-Smith. 1991. *The Politics of the Textbook*. London: Routledge.

Appleby, Joyce, Alan Brinkley, Albert Broussard, John McPherson and Douglas Ritchie. 2007. *The American Republic*. New York: McGraw-Hill/Glencoe.

Arida, Holly. 2006. "Teaching the Middle East: The Perspectives Method." *Teaching History: A Journal of Methods* 31(2): 74–85.

Ayers, E., J. de la Teja, R. Schulzinger, & D White. 2007. *American Anthem*. Austin, TX: Harcourt/Holt.

Berkin, Carol, Alan Brinkley, Clayborne Carson, Robert W. Cherny, Robert A. Divine, Eric Foner, Jeffery B. Morris, Arthur Wheeler and Leonard Wood. 1992. *American Voices*. Glenview, IL: Scott Foresman and Company.

Boyer, Paul, and Sterling Stuckey. 2005. *The American Nation*. Austin, TX: Holt, Rinehart and Winston.

Bragdon, Henry W., Samuel P. McCutchen and Donald A. Ritchie. 1992. *History of a Free Nation*. Westerville, OH: Glencoe/Macmillian/McGraw-Hill.

Cayton, Andrew R. L., Elisabeth Perry, Linda Reed and Alan Winkler. 2007. *America: Pathways to the Present*. Boston, MA: Pearson/Prentice Hall.

Cherryholmes, Cleo H., Elizabeth E. Heilman and Avner Segal. 2005. *Social Studies—The Next Generation: Re-searching in the Postmodern (Counterpoints Studies in the Postmodern Theory of Education)*. New York: Peter Lang.

De Castell, Suzanne. 1990. "Playing by the Book: The Problem of Textbook Knowledge." *The Journal of Educational Thought* 24(3A): 110–13.

De Castell, Suzanne, Allan Luke and Carmen Luke. 1989. *Language, Authority and Criticism: Readings on the School Textbook*. London: Falmer Press.

The Economist. 2012. "Textbooks Round the World: It Ain't Necessarily So." *The Economist*, October 13. Available at: http://www.economist.com/node/21564554. Last accessed 14 April 2015.

Eisner, Elliot W. 1994. *The Educational Imagination: On the Design and Evaluation of School Programs*. 3rd edn. New York: Macmillan.

FitzGerald, Frances. 1979. *America Revised*. New York: Random House.

Foster, Stuart. 2011. "Dominant Traditions in International Textbook Research and Revision." *Curriculum Inquiry* 2(1): 5–20.

French, Howard W. 2004. "China's Textbooks Twist and Omit History." *The New York Times*, December 6. Available at: http://www.nytimes.com/2004/12/06/international/asia/06textbook.html?_r=0. Last accessed 3 March 2015.

Garraty, John A. 1994. *The Story of America*. Orlando, FL: Holt, Rinehart and Winston.

Hamerman, Joshua. 2011. "Israel Absent or Only Negative Presence in PA Textbooks." *The Jeru-

salem Post, May 13. Available at: http://www.jpost.com/Diplomacy-and-Politics/Israel-absent-or-only-negative-presence-in-PA-textbooks. Last accessed 3 March 2015.

Hsiao, Yi-Mei. 2014. "Taiwanese Students Understanding of Differences in History Textbook Accounts." In *Understanding History: International Review of History Education Vol 4*, eds Ross Ashby, Peter Gordon and Peter Lee, 49–61. London: Routledge.

Israeli Committee Against Home Demolitions (ICAHD). 2009. *Statistics on House Demolitions (1967-2009)*. Available at: http://www.badil.org/es/monitoreo-continuo-de-los-desplazamientos/item/1365-forced-eviction. Last accessed 28 March 2015.

Lee, Peter. 1998. "Making Sense of Historical Accounts." *Canadian Social Studies* 32(2): 52–54.

Loewen, James. 1995. *Lies My Teacher Told Me: Everything Your American History Textbook Got Wrong*. New York: The New Press.

Luke, Carmen, Suzanne De Castell and Allan Luke. 1989. "Beyond Criticism: The Authority of the School Textbooks." In *Language Authority and Criticism: Readings on the School Textbook*, eds Suzanne De Castell, Allan. Luke and Carmen Luke, 245–60. Philadelphia, PA: The Falmer Press.

McLaren, Peter. 1998. *Life in Schools: An Introduction to Critical Pedagogy in the Foundations of Education*, 3rd edn. White Plains, NY: Longman.

Miller, Elhanan. 2013. "Israeli and Palestinian Textbooks Erase the Other Side, Report Finds." *The Times of Israel*, February 4, 2013. Available at: http://www.timesofisrael.com/israeli-and-palestinian-textbooks-erase-each-other-report-finds/. Last accessed 28 March 2015.

Miller, Greg, and James Gerstenzang. 2003. "Classified Iraq Data Released." *Los Angeles Times*, July 19 Available at: http://articles.latimes.com/2003/jul/19/world/fg-intel19. Last accessed 8 March 2015.

Minear, R. H. (n.d.). *Support Statements of Nominators and Supporters*," Nomination of Prof. Ienaga Saburo for Nobel Peace Prize. Available at: http://vcn.bc.ca/alpha/ienaga/support.htm. Last accessed 18 March 2015.

Mothfer M and Mohamad, K. I. 2009. The Modern and Contemporary History of Arab Countries. The Ministry of Education, Baghdad, Iraq. 2009.

National Security Archive. The National Security Archive, 2008, 2015. Available at: http://www.gwu.edu/~nsarchiv/NSAEBB/NSAEBB254/index.htm. Last accessed 8 March 2015.

Nord, Warren A., and Charles C. Haynes. 1998. *Taking Religion Seriously Across the Curriculum*. Alexandria, VA: ASCD.

Olson, David. R. 1989. "On the Language and Authority of Textbooks." In *Language Authority and Criticism: Readings on the School Textbook*, eds. Suzanne De Castell, Allan Luke and Carmen Luke, 233–45. Philadelphia, PA: The Falmer Press.

Romanowski, Michael H. 1995. "Impressions of the Democratic Ideals of Justice and Equality in US History Textbooks: The Treatment of Japanese Americans During world War II." *Journal of Social Studies Research* 19(1): 31–49.

Romanowski, Michael H. 1996. "Problems of Bias in History Textbooks." *Social Education* 60(3): 170–73.

Romanowski, Michael H. 2003. "Religion in Contemporary US History Textbooks." *The Social Studies* 94(1): 29–34.

Romanowski, Michael H. 2009a. "What You Don't Know Can Hurt You: Textbook Omissions and 911." *The Clearinghouse* 82(6): 290–96.

Romanowski, Michael H. 2009b. "Excluding Ethical Issues from U.S. History Textbooks: 911 and the War On Terror." *American Secondary Education* 37(2): 26–48.

Romanowski Michael H., and Hadeel Alkhateeb. 2011. "Truth Against Truth: American and Arab History School Textbooks Portrayal of the Arab-Israeli Conflict." *Near and Middle Eastern Journal of Research in Education* 1: 1–14, doi: 10.5339/nmejre.2011.1

Shin, Gi-Wook, and Daniel C. Sneider. 2013. *History Textbooks and the Wars in Asia: Divided Memories.* London: Routledge.

Snorre, Lindquist, and Lasse Wilhelmson. 2008. "Revoking Israel's UN Membership. The *Palestine Chronicle*, December 3. Available at: http://www.palestinechronicle.com/old/view_article_details.php?id=14445. Last accessed 8 March 2015.

Torfing, Jacob. 1999. *New Theories of Discourse: Laclau, Mouffe and Zizek.* Oxford: Blackwell.

United Nations Relief and Works Agency. n.d. Palestine Refugees. Available at: http://www.unrwa.org/palestine-refugees. Last accessed 8 February 2015.

Wiggins, Grant, and Jay McTighe. 2005. *Understanding by Design.* Alexandria, VA: Association for Supervision and Curriculum Development.

Williams, Raymond. 1985. *Keywords.* New York: Oxford University Press.

2. THIS IS NOT A RELIGION! "THE TREACHERY OF THE IMAGES" OF AUM, YASUKUNI AND AL-QAEDA IN JAPANESE TEXTBOOKS[1]

Satoko Fujiwara

INTRODUCTION

As a specialist in the study of religion, I have been writing upper secondary school social studies textbooks since 2008. All Japanese school textbooks up to the upper secondary school level go through a state authorization process every four years. In 2011 my co-authored textbook was examined by the Ministry of Education[2] for the first time. Suggested by the Ministry's textbook investigators, my publisher removed two entire pages from a section on religion and world peace; one on the terrorist attacks in America on September 11, 2001 (also known as 9/11), the other on the contemporary Islamic revival. The investigators held the view that, if a group commits violence, the members of that group should not be regarded as religious. They insisted that religion is, by definition, free of any violence and, therefore, it is inappropriate to include anything about the terrorist attacks when discussing religion in a textbook. I had little choice but to accept their opinion and follow the publisher's decision because, if I did not, the textbook would not have been published and my publisher would have incurred a great financial loss. As a result, the published version of the textbook includes only one paragraph on the terrorist attacks and no religion is mentioned in relation to those attacks.

The Ministry has apparently chosen a safe path for teaching the issue of religion and violence by defining the issue out of existence. Ironically, the Ministry's attitude would increase rather than decrease the prejudice among Japanese young people against religions. This is especially the case for Islam as the Ministry's view flatly contradicts the information that young people who use the textbook receive from mass media, which many of them trust more than what their teachers say.

Generally speaking, when dealing with controversial issues in the setting of democratic education, it is usually recommended to give the opinions of both sides. In this particular case of teaching about religion, the use of essentialist labels of "good/authentic religion" and "bad/pseudo-religion" is to be avoided. It is also a common practice among scholars of religions to show the internal logics of those religions. In cases where violence is involved, scholars also tend to explain the historical and social contexts that have likely driven people to what is called "terrorism" or "mass suicide," for example. Such contextualization is necessary in order to avoid demonizing violent actors in a way that, nonetheless, does not affirm their actions.[3] The Ministry did not agree on any of these points.

This chapter starts with a detailed explanation of the descriptions in my co-authored textbook that the Ministry regarded as unpublishable. I will then expand my arguments by examining how Aum Shinrikyō (the Buddhist New Religious Group responsible for the 1995 Tokyo sarin gas attack), Islamic extremists, and State Shinto (particularly the Yasukuni Shrine) are treated in secondary school textbooks.

Before delving into my analysis, however, allow me to provide a basic background of religious education in Japan. Following the US model, the current (postwar) Japanese Constitution is shaped by the idea of the separation of church and state. As such, religious education as a separate subject is not a part of public school curricula. It is widely agreed, however, that education about religions, which is considered to be neutral,[4] can be given in any school, and private religious schools are permitted to have confessional RE classes. Visible references to religions in textbooks appear in secondary education, which covers ages 13-18 (ages 13-15 for lower secondary schools and 16-18 for upper secondary schools). I will focus on social studies textbooks, which include religious topics in accordance with the official "Course of Study (Curriculum Guidelines, *gakushū shidō yōryō*)," provided by the Ministry of Education. Social studies subjects for secondary education consist of three main categories: Geography, History and Civics. The textbook I have co-authored is for "Ethics," which is one of several Civic Studies subjects designed for upper secondary school students, and is the subject that most extensively deals with religious issues.

1. THE MINISTRY'S DEFINITION OF RELIGION DISCLOSED DURING THE AUTHORIZATION PROCESS

When I was asked to join the group of authors for an Ethics textbook by a textbook publishing company,[5] I personally conducted a bit of field research at public (state-funded) secondary schools in Tokyo to see how textbooks are actually used in classrooms. The publisher told me there was no need for such research because they had already given a questionnaire to school teachers who had used their textbooks and been willing to provide some feedbacks. Nevertheless, I thought it was important for a textbook writer novice such as myself to visit classrooms since most textbook writers are university professors who rarely visit local schools and do not have any first-hand knowledge of the students who will be reading their textbooks.

I visited middle- and lower-middle-ranked schools, which have a variety of students. These schools have both college-bound and career-bound students. Some students come from families who are members of new religious groups and others have come to Japan from abroad. Among the Ethics teachers I interviewed, two left me with a strong impression regarding the actual practice of teaching about religions. One of them was teaching at a school in a downtown area where new religious groups such as Soka Gakkai had been active for decades. He said that he felt safer teaching only about religions in the past. He felt it could be risky to discuss contemporary religions and living people of faith because he would have to refer to the new religious groups to which some of the students in the class belong. He said that if he highlighted the importance of living together with, say, Muslim and Hindu immigrants in Tokyo, students from new religious groups, who sometimes feel they are discriminated against by their neighbors due to their faith, might wonder why their teacher only problematizes Islamophobia or xenophobia. The other teacher, looking straight into my eyes, insisted that textbooks should stop avoiding difficult issues and explain why there are religions that legitimize violence such as terrorism. He needed reliable teaching materials that would help him deal with world news on religions.

Interviewing with such teachers was encouraging and convinced me of the importance of the role of scholars of religion in textbook production. A large number of Ethics textbook authors are university professors from departments of philosophy and ethics who do not specialize in the study of religions, especially contemporary religions or "lived" religious traditions. In the course of narrating the history of Western/Eastern philosophy, these scholars only introduced the teachings of Jesus, Buddha, and several Christian, Buddhist and Chinese religious thinkers in the same manner they presented the philosophical thoughts of Socrates, Descartes, Kant and so on.[6] None of them had dared to tackle the theme of religion and violence in the actual world. That was an area in which scholars of religions could make a difference.

In fact, the Ministry of Education had recognized the importance of teaching contemporary global issues, including conflicts and dialogues, in a way that students can relate to and think over. The Ministry revised the "Course of Study" for upper middle school programs in 2009 and added a new chapter titled "Culture and Religion." The chapter, along with chapters on "Life," "Environment," "Family," "Community," "Information Society," and "International Peace and the Welfare of the Humankind," was included in a larger part on "Contemporary Challenges and Ethics." As for the chapter "Culture and Religion," the "Course of Study" (precisely, its detailed version published in the same year) asked educators to:

> let students understand various cultures and religions from a wide perspective, and respect them by realizing that all of them, though varied in appearances, have been formed from a common wish of human beings. Let students recognize the importance of understanding and living together

with people of different cultures, customs and values. Although cultures and religions are human intellectual heritages from the past, due to the development of transportation and information networks, *different cultures and religions have crossed national borders and come into contact with each other, which sometimes results in serious conflicts. In this chapter it is also important to let students relate themselves to the challenges of human welfare and international peace from the viewpoint of equality and justice and to let them contemplate the harmonious coexistence of different religions.* In addition, let them have a sense of identity as Japanese while helping them realize that contemporary international societies exist in close mutual relationships and that there are chances to contact visitors, various cultures and religions from overseas in their daily lives. This is necessary so that they can think over such situations as their everyday challenges (Ministry of Education, Culture, Sports, Science and Technology 2009: 36, emphasis added).

The editors from my textbook publisher had decided to invite me to their team for Ethics precisely because none of the other members could write this new chapter. Both the Ministry and teachers demanded new writings on conflicts and peace related to religion, and I was ready to provide such material.

I wrote a three-page chapter with two sections titled "Why There Are Religions that Legitimize Terrorism" and "Religious Revival Movements," respectively. After some revisions requested by the editor-in-chief and the publisher, the chapter was submitted to the textbook examination board of the Ministry of Education. As mentioned above, I had to rewrite two entire pages, leaving no traces of the two sections.

Before reproducing the pages here, let me give some examples of more common revisions the Ministry asks for because it is uncommon for textbook publishers to replace an entire chapter. The following examples from one Ethics textbook authorized earlier in the 2000s were provided by my publisher, and can also be viewed in a reference room of a public Textbook Library in Tokyo.

Parts requiring revision	Reason (as recorded in official documents)
1. "shudra (slave)"	incomprehensive expression about the caste system
2. a footnote for the caste system	incomprehensive expression about the caste system
3. "Gautama Siddhartha"	inaccurate name
4. "Nichiren's teaching shared something in common with Dogen's in that he emphasized the importance of chanting a *daimoku* prayer."	This expression can be misread that Dogen thought of chanting a *daimoku* prayer as highly as Nichiren did.

These suggestions must puzzle not only the readers of this chapter but also Japanese people who are unfamiliar with the system. In order to avoid excessive governmental control, there is a strict rule that textbook investigators can specify problematic parts but cannot suggest corrections or replacements for those parts. Upon notifying publishers of the results of their inspection, the investigators and Ministry officials meet the textbook editors face-to-face and tell them in more detail what is wrong with parts for which they have suggested revision. Even then they refrain from explaining too much, giving publishers only hints, and make them surmise the "right answers" in the investigators' minds.[7]

As for the first point suggested for revision above, my publisher guessed that "slave" was an overly direct expression and changed it to "service provider." For the second point, they asked the author of the footnote to use more nuanced expressions. The third point is a matter of transliteration in Japanese (Pali and Sanskrit expressions were mixed. It is a simple mistake, but it was strange to point it out for a textbook composed in the 2000s because the previous version of the textbook with the same expression had been circulating for a long time). The fourth point is more a matter of sentence structure than of historical facts. In addition to these four points, the investigators also pointed out a few misprints. The publisher made all the corrections and resubmitted the textbook, which was then passed and authorized.

While Japanese History textbooks, known as the loci of controversies over the descriptions of World War II, always draw public attention during the authorization process, Ethics textbooks have not been involved in such turmoil. As there are only around 10 textbooks in use for Ethics, the lack of public attention makes them easier for investigators to control if they so wish. Nonetheless, the above examples suggest that they have been meddled with in terms of small or "scholastic" matters rather than supporting particular ideological agendas.

Now, to turn to my chapter on "Culture and Religion," I used the first page to write about globalization and multiculturalism, using such key words as "living together," "Edward Said," "Orientalism," "stereotypes," "ethnocentrism," "nationalism," and "identity." I titled the second page "'The Clash of Civilizations' Arguments and Terrorism" and wrote:

> Some pessimistically or skeptically say that peace does not arrive so easily. S. Huntington argued in *The Clash of Civilizations and the Remaking of World Order* (1996) that, after the Cold War between capitalism and communism, global conflicts would occur most violently between different civilizations. Predicting that, above all, conflicts between the Western civilization and the Islamic/Sinic civilizations would intensify, Huntington ignited controversies.

The September 11 terrorist attacks in the USA in 2001, which gave a grave shock to the world, reminded people of Huntington's arguments. The US government started the 'War on Terror,' that is, War in Afghanistan and in Iraq. However, terrorist attacks kept on occurring in Iraq, Israel, England, Indonesia and other places.

It is considered that these terrorist attacks have political and economic backgrounds: most notably, the rage of Islamic societies in Africa and Asia against the economic and political dominance of the USA and other Western nations. Social critics argue that the attacks are meant to be protests against increased global inequality that has arisen as a result of globalization which unfairly profited Western, multinational companies. They also argue that terrorism is a protest against USA-supported Israel's suppression of Palestinians—a group of people largely consisting of underprivileged Muslims. However, these attacks not only called for serious reflection over global inequality but also strengthened the stereotype that 'Islam is violent and terrifying.' Muslims in Western societies have been having a hard time. In order to cope with the problem, American and European educators have been promoting intercultural education that advocates tolerance and understanding for other people's religions.

(With a photo of the World Trade Center buildings)

Feature: Why There Are Religions that Legitimize Terrorism
It is argued that international Islamic terrorist groups are involved in recent major terrorist incidents, regarding them as 'just wars.' If that is true, religion, which is supposed to save people, seems to legitimize terrorism. Why is this the case?

There are two opposing views on this question. Some say that terrorists are a tiny group of radicals who distort Islam. True Islam never allows terrorism. Others say that, since the underprivileged in Islamic counties have already been victimized and damaged by Western nations, they deem their attacks to be legitimate self-defense. For them it is logical to think that their God approved the actions.

To take a closer look, this debate discloses that, while many people believe that the question is a matter of religion, it actually is not. The underlying, fundamental question is another tough issue, namely, whether it is possible to distinguish between permissible and impermissible uses of armed force.

My intention was not to replace "Islam is dangerous" with "Islam is peaceful" (since both are equally essentialist remarks) but rather to replace the initial question with another question which can better involve Japanese young readers, many of whom do not regard themselves as being religious.

The third page, titled "The Necessity of Understanding Religions," explains why learning about religions in the world matters today for Japanese students.

According to world surveys, respondents in Japan show a lower rate of religious affiliation than people in other countries. Up until the mid-20th century, scholars predicted that religions in the world would decline in the process of modernization ("secularization"). However, since around the mid-1970s, traditional religions have been reviving in the various corners of the world ("religious resurgence"). For example, the 1979 Islamic revolution in Iran was largely brought about by Islamic revival movements, which aimed to reconstruct the social order by basing it on Islam. As interactions between different people increase in the process of globalization, it has become more important than ever in Japan to become familiar with the diverse ways of thinking and living among various religions.

Religious Affiliation by Country (From World Values Survey, 2005)

	Religious affiliation Yes	*No (including NA)*
Japan	36.5%	63.5%
South Korea	71.2%	28.8%
USA	70.4%	29.6%
France	49.7%	50.3%
Italy	87.9%	12.1%
Iraq	99.8%	0.2%

Feature: Religious Revival Movements
Why is it that some people return to traditional religious faiths in modern society, where science and technology have developed? Under the set of modern values, people appreciate, above all, liberty. Yet, if everybody does whatever he/she likes, following their desires and pursuing profits, society will fall apart. Those people who thought that only old-time faiths, which repress human desires, would be able to save society came to rehabilitate religion. In particular, Islamic revival movements can be viewed as attempts to keep the identity of Islam among people who have realized that their society was in critical condition, having been influenced by liberal Western cultures and losing traditional morals such as modesty.

However, frictions can arise between people who always try to follow their faith and secular society, which separates politics and public life from religion. For example, in France Muslim students are forbidden to wear a headscarf for a religious reason at public schools. It is debated whether

this policy is appropriate to build a harmonious society among people of different cultural backgrounds.
(With a photo of a young Muslima in France marching for the freedom of wearing a headscarf).

On the scheduled day the editors of my textbook publisher went to the Ministry of Education to have an interview with investigators. As soon as they returned, they told me that I had to rewrite the entire chapter. As explained above, the investigators only conveyed their suggestions orally and indirectly, and it was the editors who wrote them down. Therefore, there is a possibility that they misheard or misinterpreted what the investigators said, although such a possibility is small. It is at least safe to say that the editors heard and interpreted what the investigators said as follows.

As for the topic of "religion and terrorism":
In the chapter we see phrases such as 'whether religion legitimizes terrorism' and 'terrorist attacks as legitimate self-defense.' The Ministry of Education have an understanding that 'terrorism and religion are two entirely different things,' 'terrorism cannot be permitted by any means' and 'there is no religion that legitimizes terrorism. If it does, then it is not a religion.'
There are many other examples of cultural conflicts that are moderate and appropriate for the chapter. The author could write about such cases instead of terrorism.

As for the page titled 'The Necessity of Understanding Religions':
As an example of religious revival movements, the author mentions the Iranian Revolution, but it is abrupt because general trends in the world are not explained, such as cults and conservative religious groups in the USA.
The feature 'Religious Revival Movements' starts with arguing, 'Liberty is appreciated in modern democratic society' and 'society falls apart if people do whatever they want,' but then, again, abruptly moves on to the case of France.
The author, while addressing the case of France, relates religious revival movements with the principle of the separation of religion and the state. This part can cause misunderstanding because the author does not explain the historical background of the French separation of religion and politics.

As is clear from the above quotation from my pre-authorized textbook, I presented the view of "terrorist attacks as legitimate self-defense" only as one of two opposing opinions. Neither of the two opinions was endorsed by the textbook. However, my publisher's editors told me that, from the interview, they had got a strong impression that the Ministry of Education was quite worried about textbooks discussing religion and terrorism together by any means. No matter how many different opinions or interpretations were added, putting the words "religion" and "terrorism" on the same page was totally unacceptable. The editors also said, as for the page on "The Necessity of Understanding Religions," they believed that the Ministry simply did not want Islam to stand out in the context of conflicts between religious people and the secular states. They concluded that, in short, the Ministry required us to minimize descriptions of Islam, especially Islamic radicals or activists. They insisted that the Ministry did not want us to refer to 9/11 at all.

Since the publisher was willing to revise the textbook as the Ministry of Education suggested (because they did not have any strong opinion of their own), I did not dare to trouble them by refusing the revision, though I was deeply disappointed and expressed my wish to leave the authorial team after the term. The publisher did not want to make it a public issue—they had already been stressed out enough by disputes over History textbooks—and there was no media coverage on this incident.

I replaced the pages "'The Clash of Civilizations' Arguments and Terrorism" and "The Necessity of Understanding Religions" with new pages titled "The Contemporary World and Religion" and "Frictions over Religion and Living Together." I first outlined historical changes in religion and the world in the 20th century, referring to the secularization thesis (though without using the technical term), countercultural movements and young people's interest in Eastern religiosity, and religious revivals among Christian conservatives and Muslims. On the next page I briefly mentioned the Muhammad cartoon controversy in Denmark in 2005, and emphasized communities' efforts to live together with Muslims in Japan. I included a picture of a halal food booth with a smiling Muslim cook at a university's cafeteria in Kyoto. For the rest of the page I wrote about how Christmas is celebrated in Western multi-cultural societies, especially the American debate over the signs of "Merry Christmas" and "Happy Holidays."

I thus consented to delete all the provocative articles. Nevertheless, I insisted that 9/11 and other terrorist incidents in the 2000s should be included somewhere in the textbook. The publisher finally agreed with me. They inserted five lines on "the backgrounds of recent major terrorism and conflicts" at the end of the next chapter on "International Peace and the Welfare of the Humankind," which is also the very last page of the entire textbook. Yet, they allowed me to do so upon one condition: Do not use the word "religion" or "Islam" in the five lines. I could not write who the suspects of 9/11 were or even hint that terrorist attacks had anything to do with religion.

It is true that Muslims living in Japan have been troubled by Japanese people who associate Islam with violence; the same problem that Muslim immigrants have been facing in Western countries. They would rather prefer Japanese textbooks not link terrorism and Islam in any manner. They would likely support my publisher's decision. An Egyptian associate professor who teaches at a university near Tokyo, for example, says that, every time the media reports on violent attacks by Al-Qaeda related groups or the so-called Islamic State, people around him ask the same question, "Why do they kill people for a religious reason? I cannot understand." He has been saying over and over again, "Islam appreciates life. Muslims have absolutely nothing to do with the small group of radicals" (Asahi Newspaper, May 4, 2015).

Nonetheless, if an official textbook authorized by the Japanese government distinguishes between true Islam and false Islam, or between good religions and bad religions, it implies that the government is violating the constitutional rule of the separation between church and the state because the state is authorizing a certain form of religion based on a particular, substantive definition of religion. That is as much problematic as Islamophobia. Neither the textbook investigators nor my publisher was aware of the problem.

2. HOW OTHER TEXTBOOKS TREAT RELIGION AND TERRORISM

Auditing interviews between textbook publishers and investigators is forbidden. Therefore, examining authorized and published textbooks is the only way to find out the possibility—even though only a possibility—that the Ministry of Education has uniformly required all textbook publishers not to mention religion or Islam when discussing terrorism such as the attacks of 9/11. I have examined five major Ethics textbooks.[8] Since all textbooks follow the "Course of Study," their chapter structures are similar to each other. In the case of Ethics textbooks, the issues of religions in the contemporary world appear in the last two chapters: "Culture and Religion" and "International Peace and the Welfare of the Humankind," although in some of them the chapter titles are changed slightly.

2.1. Ethics Textbooks on Terrorism

The first finding is that, while two out of the five textbooks use the word "terrorism" and the other three textbooks use the phrase "ethnic and religious conflicts (conflicts between religions)," all do so in a very general and abstract way, without referring to any specific incident such as 9/11 or any particular religion. To quote from each:

> (In the chapter "International Peace and the Welfare of the Humankind")
> Today, we, who live in an "affluent" society, are often frightened by the threat of terrorism. Many of the terrorist attacks in the modern world are caused by conflicts between different ethnic groups or religious sects. They also occur as a sudden attack by "poor" and "isolated" people against "affluent societies" or as an attack by those who are scared by the intrusion of "poor" people into "affluent societies." It has become clearer that human beings cannot build peace in the future if they only pursue "affluence." (Tokyo E 2014: 200–201. Throughout this chapter, citations from textbooks are shown by their publishers' names. Japanese textbooks are identified by publishers, not by authors).

(In the chapter "International Peace and the Welfare of the Humankind")
Since Immanuel Kant wrote an essay "Perpetual Peace" in the 18th century, human beings have experienced two world wars. They are still groping for world peace, fighting against ethnic conflicts and terrorism. (Yamakawa E 2013: 198–199)

The latter textbook, on the same page, has a photo of the fire-engulfed World Trade Center buildings after two airplanes flown by terrorists crashed into them. It is the only textbook among the five with a picture of the events of 9/11. However, the particular incident is not explicitly related to any part of the main text. It merely has a short caption in the smallest fonts, which reads "Terrorism in New York: On Sept. 11 2001, airplanes hijacked by Islamic radicals smashed into the World Trade Center buildings" (Yamakawa E 2013: 199). There is no account of why the attack took place. It only says, as a general rule, "The causes of conflicts are prejudice and discrimination born out of exclusivistic group mentalities, poverty or the inequality in the distribution of wealth, and the lack of the solid idea of human rights" (Yamakawa E 2013: 199).

Another textbook, which is the top-seller of the five, has titled the chapter as "The Age of Globalization and Ethics" instead of "Culture and Religion." It argues that:

In the age of globalization, different cultures and religions come into contact with each other more often than ever before (multi-cultural, multi-religious situation). This contact is often accompanied by the problem of cultural and religious tension and friction due to the lack of understanding between different cultures and religions. Such tension sometimes becomes a factor of serious conflicts by intensifying the contentions between different ethnicities and religions. In order to live in a society of the future, we need to admit the existence of different cultures and religions from a wide perspective and to try to understand them (Shimizu E 2013: 207).

Whilst it does not draw any concrete examples in this chapter, this textbook includes specific descriptions in facing pages that I find quite problematic in an earlier chapter on the history of world religions. On the left page, which is about Christianity, it is written in bold letters that Christianity teaches "Human Dignity Based on Love." On the right page, which is about Islam, it highlights the word "jihad." It says, "Muhammad organized an Islamic order, conquered Mecca and made it an Islamic holy land. Since then the zeal to spread Islam has also come to take the shape of *jihad*, which has a purpose of propagating God's words" (Shimizu E 2013: 47). The stereotypical association of Christianity with love and that of Islam with conquer and propagation are intensified by putting them side by side. The textbook investigators passed and authorized this juxtaposition and the particular wording of its content.

The fourth textbook also argues about religious conflicts only on a general level. Its chapter titled "Religion, Culture and Ethical Challenges" starts by discussing different religious customs. It focuses on dietary prohibitions along with a picture with several Muslim students at a halal food restaurant at a college. It then moves on to argue:

Religious Conflicts and a Road to Reconciliation
Looking back at world history, there have been many bloody wars between different religions or sects with contested understandings of doctrines. Not only purely religious reasons but also social and economic oppositions or cultural tensions have caused such religious conflicts. Even now, such wars continue in various parts of the world, and are one of the serious problems of modern society.

Japan has been advocating the spirit of harmony since the ancient times. Traditionally, Buddhism, Shinto and Confucianism coexisted in Japan, where Christianity has also been accepted since the modern era. Using our traditional wisdom, we can tell people in the world about reconciliation and coexistence among different religions. In order to do so, we first have to know religions in the world (Daiichi E 2013:197).

These paragraphs can easily be argued against by reminding the authors of (so-called) State Shinto, which was heavily implicated in the violence associated with Japanese ultra-nationalism, or the persecution of Christianity in Japan. Similar to the way the textbook elides discussion of violence when talking about Japanese religion, in an earlier chapter it describes contemporary Islamism as "a way of thinking which emphasizes a sense of Muslim identity and encourages followers to realize a political and social system centered upon the Islamic faith" (Daiichi E 2013: 49). When any religion is specified, the textbook avoids discussing wars and armed conflicts.

The fifth textbook also treats religious conflicts in a general tone.

(In the chapter titled "Understanding Various Cultures and Religions")
In today's world many states are multicultural, multilingual and multinational. Under these circumstances, where different cultures and religions compete with each other, it becomes difficult to integrate society. This, in turn, increases the danger of conflicts due to mutual misunderstandings. As conflicts in various areas of the world show, peace gets endangered above all when religious differences are accompanied by the interests of both groups. This is so especially because religion gives human beings a reason to live and orients their way of living. Religion becomes the core of a particular view of life or a set of ethical values. On the other hand, the same circumstances of multicultural states that breed potential misunderstandings can also give birth to a new culture. This can happen because of contact with different cultures, including religions. It can be a

precious chance to create a more diverse and richer society. The history of Japanese culture eloquently evidences this possibility.

In order to live in peace, we in the 21st century have to solve religious disputes and ethnic conflicts and also to endeavor to find a way of living together with different cultures (Sūken E 2013: 211).

However, on the corner of the same page it shows a small picture of a particular example of religious conflict: a clipped newspaper article on the French law which bans burkas. Just like the textbook with the picture of 9/11, this textbook does not explain the picture at all in the main text. It is unclear how the picture is related to the above arguments. It only has a short caption: "a newspaper article reporting on a ban on wearing burkas in France. A burka is a Muslim woman's dress which covers her entire body including her face" (Sūken E 2013: 211). It does not even say when the law was passed. There is a possibility that the author first explained the French case to some extent in the main text, but then the textbook investigators demanded that he not do so, and as a result only the picture was left in the published version of the textbook.

2.2. Politics and Economy/Contemporary World Textbooks on Terrorism

I have also looked into textbooks for the other civic studies subjects to see whether concrete terrorist incidents, the 9/11 terrorist attacks in particular, appear along with religion. More specifically, I have looked at textbooks for the subjects of "Politics and Economy" and the "Contemporary World" (a comprehensive subject with an emphasis on the present). The investigators who look at textbooks for Politics and Economy are different from those who look at Ethics textbooks. Investigators for Contemporary World textbooks are mostly a combination of people who look over textbooks for Ethics and Politics and Economy, respectively.

All of the eight current Politics and Economy textbooks I examined refer to the 9/11 terrorist attacks, yet all but one simply describe the sequence of events without explaining its background or possible causes. Furthermore, five of them specify the attackers as "Islamic radicals" (and one of them uses the expression "Islamic terrorist organization" along with the name of Osama bin Laden). One of the other three textbooks calls the attackers "an international terrorist group named Al-Qaeda." The remaining two textbooks mention neither Islam nor Al-Qaeda. To quote from the one with the expression of "Islamic terrorist organization,":

The terrorist attacks in the USA that took place on September 11, 2001 were unparalleled, indiscriminate terrorist incidents that killed over 3,000 people. The Bush Administration declared that it was an act of Al-Qaeda, an international Islamic terrorist organization, with Usama Bin-Ladin as its leader. ... The Bush administration then initiated the War against Terrorism ... (Jikkyo P 2014: 96).

The only textbook with some explanation of the political conditions of the event relegates it to a footnote to a paragraph on the 9/11 attacks. It reads:

> The perpetrators of the incident collaborated with each other over national boarders for the purpose of re-ordering the Islamic world. They regarded American foreign policies such as support for Israel, sanctions on Iraq, and forces stationed in Saudi Arabia as 'destructive to the Islamic faith.' They insisted that the USA and Israel were forcing such 'injustices' by power. For them, the terrorist attacks against the USA and Israel were 'holy wars,' bearing the meaning of 'the weapons of the socially disadvantaged.' They took suicide bombings for 'martyrdom' and believed that God blessed the bombers (Shimizu P 2014: 106).

The textbook does not say whether the terrorists' logic of justification is right or wrong, or what "true Islam" should be. The Politics and Economy textbook investigators allowed it to be printed for some unknown reason. At a guess this may be due to the general descriptive overtone of Politics and Economy textbooks, which are written and inspected by political scientists and economists, whereas Ethics textbooks are largely written and screened by graduates from philosophy and ethics departments, which are more hermeneutic in nature. That is, people from philosophy and ethics departments are supposed to provide more than a descriptive account of the world and to analyze texts in different ways than political scientists and economists. These factors perhaps combine, to create a situation in which investigators examine Ethics textbooks with more caution. Another possible reason that this comment was allowed may be that it is modestly put into a footnote, while the explanation in my textbook was highlighted as a featured article.

I have also noticed that the former editions of Politics and Economy textbooks published around five years before the current textbooks (in other words, textbooks that followed the previous "Course of Study") devoted more space to the 9/11 attacks. Many of them also used the expression "Islamic fundamentalists/ism" to describe the attackers and the context of those terrorist acts. It appears that the textbooks now treat the attack as just another event of the past rather than as something special while at the same time becoming more cautious of wording used to describe the attackers. On the other hand, previous editions of Ethics textbooks are completely devoid of recent terrorist attacks, Islamic revivals and religious conflicts because the previous version of "Course of Study" did not require educators to deal with issues of religions in the present world.[9]

The Contemporary World textbooks are, in general, virtually an abbreviated version of both Politics and Economy and Ethics textbooks. That is to say, they mention the 9/11 attacks in passing in a similar yet simpler manner than Politics and Economy textbooks do. Some of them have failed to update wordings and information: one of them identifies the attackers as the members of an "Islamic *fundamentalist* organization, Al-Qaeda" (Shimizu C 2013: 156), and another says that the "validity and effectiveness of the US military actions in Afghanistan and Iraq are *now* questioned" (Shimizu C2 2013: 149).

2.3. Contemporary World Textbooks on "Cults"
A more noteworthy point of the "Contemporary World" textbooks is that two out of the 11 that I researched address the problem of "cults," a topic that textbooks for other subjects do not deal with. Educational interests in the topic reflect the 1995 terrorist attack in Tokyo by Aum Shinrikyō, a Japanese New Religious group, many core members of which were highly educated young people. One of them uses the word "cult" and gives a short description under the heading of "Faith and Religion" as follows:

> Some religious groups with radicalized faiths may confront society or separate themselves from society. Religious orders of fanatics are called 'cults.' They form a mystic and exclusivistic group by brainwashing and, characteristically, completely obey their leader who claims to have a special talent or power (Shimizu C2 2013: 68).

The above quote is attached as an additional explanation on a page about "Religion and Contemporary Society," which reads:

> Since human beings are limited and imperfect, suffering, sorrow and uneasiness remain irrespective of the developments of science and technology. Religion faces such fundamental contradictions and absurdity of life and provides a meaning or goal of life, as well as inner peace.
> On the other hand, since religion is accompanied by faith in superhuman beings and is related to worldviews, beliefs and norms, conflicts may occur between different religions and sects. Political and economic interests can intensify these conflicts. In the contemporary world, where different thoughts and values exist, it is necessary for different religious groups to be willing to recognize each other and live together.
> It is said that Japanese people are non-religious and have moved away from religious matters in the modern era. However, it can also be argued that in contemporary society, where values have been relativized and no single value is firm enough to base oneself on, Japanese people have an increased interest in their inner lives and spiritual matters. Human beings are *homo religiosus* and religion is a key to understand people and society (Shimizu C2 2013: 68).

The other textbook does not use the word "cult" but implies that young people should be careful not to be recruited to deviant religious groups.

Young People and Religion
During adolescence, people seek their identities. In other words, they set off on a journey to find out their true self. Such a sincere search may drive some people to look inside themselves and take interest in the human mind and psychology. It may direct other people to something transcendent or mystical. In this sense, young people are likely to be attracted by religious things. However, while seeking for quick answers and convictions, they might lapse into self-righteous ideas or thoughtlessly take socially unacceptable actions. There are also young people who become fascinated with groundless superstitions and fortune-telling or the occult.

It is not easy to reach a truly convincing answer for the big questions of life. It is important to think deeply, learn from those who came before us about their lives and thoughts, and also to listen to the teachings of various religions (Shimizu C 2013: 39).

Among textbooks published four or five years earlier, I found another textbook that mentions the problem of cults as follows.

It is often said that terrorist attacks and wars in today's international societies are caused by religious conflicts. However, it is more often is the case that ethnic or religious conflicts are born or at least intensified in the bigger frameworks of global politics and economy. In addition, people with anti-social ideas sometimes mobilize a group and commit crimes while claiming that the group is a religion (these groups are called cults). We have to learn from history and judge with prudence whether religion is really causing conflicts, and whether conflicts would cease if there were no religion (Tokyo C 2007: 28).

The textbooks that were published shortly after the Aum Affair in 1995 may well treat cults as a problem, but, as far as I have investigated, only one textbook does so explicitly. Yet even that textbook addresses the issue of cults *without* using the particular example of Aum or the word "cult."

Religion guides people who are at a loss or provides support for people who are vulnerable. However, by burying its head in the sand, religion sometimes turns to 'self-righteousness' or 'superstition.' People should be aware that if they deny science, reason and rational judgments, they will lose themselves. Exclusivist beliefs and religious practices can lead to antisocial, deviant actions. In order to live a better life, people should try to understand the world and human beings deeply by asking "why" (Hitotsubashi C 1998: 155).

It is understandable that the word "cult" does not appear because in Japanese it came into the media and popular usage only after the Aum Affair. It was too new in 1998 to be included in any textbooks. However, it would have been possible to refer to Aum.

In contrast, Japanese History textbooks explicitly mention Aum Shinrikyō, but *not as a religious issue*. Just like Politics and Economy textbooks, History textbooks are largely descriptive and refer to Aum only in describing the sequence of recent events. For example:

> In 1995, shocking affairs that caused Japanese people to lose their trust in the 'safety' of their society occurred one after another. Specifically, the Hanshin-Awaji Great Earthquake, Aum Shinrikyō's Tokyo subway gas terrorist attack, and some bank failures all occurred in that year. Anxiety spread among Japanese people (Yamakawa H 2010: 386).

The History textbooks reveal that the Ministry of Education is not trying to avoid the publication of the name "Aum" all together. One possible reason for the absence of Aum in Ethics and Contemporary World textbooks is that, at the time of publication, legal trials for members of Aum were ongoing. The total picture of the affair was still unclear, and textbook writers refrained from identifying its causes and discussing it as a religious and ethical issue. At present, the Aum trials have mostly finished and its leader has been found guilty and sentenced to death. Nonetheless, textbooks continue to not discuss the Aum Affair in any detail.[10]

2.4. Definitions of Religion in Textbooks

While textbooks do not treat the Aum Affair in any detail, "lessons" from the affair are implied in the definition of religion given by some of them. That is to say, some current textbooks define religions as unrelated to violence and as life-cherishing, implying that a group like Aum is not a religion. To take an example from an Ethics textbook:

> It can be said that religion was born when our ancestors started to feel gratitude and awe toward the source of life and feel fear or sorrow for death, the loss of life ... Religions in the world teach different things, but they have one thing in common in their beliefs: *a feeling of awe and gratitude toward the source of life*. Therefore, religion is a universal culture of human beings (Yamakawa E 2013: 198, emphasis added).

Another example from a Contemporary World textbook:

> Conflicts and terrorism have arisen from oppositions between different religions and sects in the contemporary world. On the other hand, there are also many people of faith who take action for peace. *Religion intrinsically aims* to stabilize people's mind and *to bring peace* (Kyōiku C 2013: 41, emphasis added).

These definitions are in striking contrast with a definition of religion as an otherworldly salvific system. To quote an example of the latter from a different Ethics textbook:

> Religion sheds light upon people's life in this world from a transcendent view of true justice and ultimate truth. It teaches how the world is formed, what is good and bad, what the meaning of life is and how to live rightly. It thereby awakens those of us who are lost and attached to this-worldly interests. It attempts to save our souls (Daiichi E 2013: 45).

Though the definition of religion varies between textbooks and some do not give any definition at all, looking over textbooks published during these 40 years, it is safe to say that the definition which focuses solely on cherishing life is quite new in the textbooks for these subjects.[11] I could not find a single textbook published before the early 2000s which says that every religion, by nature, values this-worldly life (in the sense of being alive rather than the activities of everyday life)[12] and peace. One Ethics textbook published in 1995 (that is, authorized right before the Aum Affair) presents a remarkably opposite view of religion. On the first page of its chapter on religion, it presents an introductory story titled "Young People and Religion" and a picture of a monumental relief of the Twenty-Six Martyrs of Japan, a group of Christians who were executed by crucifixion in the 16th century, when the shogunate government was persecuting Christians in Japan. The story focuses on a 12 year-old martyr, Saint Luis Ibaraki, who refused to abandon his faith and gave up his life, and asks readers "What is Christianity such that it made the 12 year-old boy so strong?" (Shimizu E 1995: 44) The author must have believed that the page would be an eye-catching introduction for young readers who likely did not think religion mattered at all. Nevertheless, both the picture and the story were deleted from the revised version of the textbook published after the Aum Affair. Another textbook published in 1994 has a paragraph on religion and peace, but it argues that religions ought to create peace, not that religions essentially love peace.

> There are various religions in the world, but sometimes differences between religions unfortunately give rise to contentions and conflicts ... These various religions should aim for the achievement of peace and happiness of humankind by means of their respective methods (Yamakawa E 1994: 94).

It is remarkable that the same publisher (Shimizu) that wrote about the courageous young martyr under the heading of "Young People and Religion" in 1995 warns readers of deviant religious groups in 2015 under exactly the same heading. It is also of note that the same publisher (Yamakawa) that made the normative claim in 1994 that religions *should* aim for peace and stop fighting with each other simply argues in 2015 that all religions have gratitude toward the source of life by nature.

3. DO TEXTBOOKS WRITE ABOUT THE YASUKUNI SHRINE?

Across all subjects, the most internationally controversial is the portrayal of Japanese military aggression against neighboring countries during World War II in History textbooks. The controversy has heated up since the Ministry of Education approved a textbook in 2001 which critics claim glorifies Japanese history and downplays its colonialist and ultra-nationalist past. At the time of writing this chapter (spring, 2015), the primary controversial issues concern military "comfort women (sex slaves)" and the Nanking Massacre. For Geography textbooks, sovereignty over particular islands around national boarders has also become a highly contested issue.

In relation to those issues, both the Japanese and the international media have often given prominent coverage to Japanese prime ministers' and other politicians' visits to the Yasukuni Shrine, a controversial Shinto shrine that honors World War II criminals. To take a recent example from *The Guardian*, allow me to quote from an article titled "Japanese MPs make provocative visit to Tokyo's Yasukuni war shrine,"

> Japanese parliamentarians on Wednesday paid homage at the Yasukuni war shrine, risking fresh anger from Asian neighbours that fell victim to the country's aggression last century.
>
> A cross-section of MPs, 106 in all, paid their respects at the shrine in central Tokyo as part of the spring festival. However, no cabinet ministers were seen among them.
>
> The shrine honours those who fought and died for Japan, but also includes a number of senior military and political figures convicted of the most serious war crimes.
>
> 'I feel very grateful anew that we have maintained peace for 70 years,' said Hidehisa Otsuji, a member of the conservative ruling Liberal Democratic Party (LDP), who lead [sic] the group. 'The souls (of the dead) must also be pleased with this.'
>
> China and South Korea see the shrine as a symbol of what they say is Japan's unwillingness to repent for its military misdeeds. The US tries to discourage visits, which it views as unnecessarily provocative.
>
> Japan's prime minister, Shinzo Abe, drew sharp rebukes from China and South Korea on Tuesday after sending a symbolic offering to the shrine. He has not visited since December 2013.
>
> He has also said he may not repeat a formal apology for his country's second world war transgressions in a forthcoming statement on the 70th anniversary of the end of the war.
>
> (*The Guardian*, April 22, 2015)

It might seem strange that, despite the popular controversy surrounding the Yasukuni Shrine, its presence or lack thereof in textbooks has not attracted critical attention. How is it described in textbooks?

It is noteworthy that Yasukuni, without doubt one of the most oft-mentioned Japanese shrines in this century, rarely appears in textbooks. None of the Ethics textbooks mention it, even though it has a chapter on international peace as a contemporary ethical issue. Many Politics and Economy textbooks refer to it in a section on the separation of religion and state (in Japanese, *seikyō bunri*, which literally means the separation between politics and religion). Yet, all of them do so in their explanations of two lawsuits regarding the constitutionality of the public performances of Shinto ceremonies unrelated to Yasukuni, but even that is in noticeably smaller fonts. For example:

The Public offerings for shrines in Ehime Prefecture Case; The Shrine groundbreaking ceremony at Tsu-city Case (Ehime Tamagushi Ryō Soshō and Tsu Jichinsai Soshō)

The first case is about controversies over the constitutionality of the public offerings to the Yasukuni Shrine and the Gokoku Shrine[13] in the form of 'tamagushi ryō (literally, fees for offerings in the form of a tree branch).' The Supreme Court ruled the *tamagushi* offerings using public funds were unconstitutional in 1997. Although the Supreme Court had ruled the second case constitutional in 1977, namely, the use of public funds to give a Shinto-style groundbreaking ceremony in Tsu-city, in the *tamagushi* case, it was considered that the local government favored particular religious groups. As for Prime Ministers' visits to the Yasukuni Shrine, which have harshly been criticized by Asian countries, Prime Minister Koizumi's public visit was ruled unconstitutional by the High Court (2005), but the Supreme Court did not judge whether it was constitutional or unconstitutional (2006). (Jikkyo P 2009: 39)

The textbook does mention that Yasukuni is a politically controversial shrine, but what is at stake in the above passage is a general principle of the separation between the state and religion rather than the relationships between the shrine and war or ultra-nationalism. That is to say, the ruling of these cases, which is the only controversy regarding the shrine included in the textbooks, is that the same judgment should be applied to all Shinto shrines, or further, to all religious institutions—at least logically.[14]

At a glance, it appears that the textbooks are minimizing references to the Yasukuni Shrine as well as hiding its most controversial aspect, which symbolizes the ideology of State Shinto. Upon closer inspection, however, it is clear that the textbooks do not evade the problem of the State Shinto ideology altogether. The Politics and Economy textbooks attach the abovementioned two court cases to the main text, which emphasizes the importance of freedom of religion precisely because it was severely limited under the State Shinto system until the end of World War II. The textbooks critically argue that Japanese people back then were compelled to follow State Shinto. Moreover, many lower secondary History

2. THIS IS NOT A RELIGION! 47

textbooks, which are the focus of most on-going international textbook controversies, insert a picture of the Chosen Jingū (Korean Shrine) in Seoul and explain that the Japanese colonial government forced State Shinto on Korean people and made visits to local Shinto shrines created by the Japanese obligatory. They do not mention Yasukuni, but do criticize the religious imperialism of pre-war and wartime Japan.

Accordingly, there is no doubt that these textbooks with few or no references to Yasukuni are not whitewashing the past (though some may argue that they should problematize it more). Rather, the name of Yasukuni can readily become *the* hot button which immediately turns a textbook into an ideological battlefield between right- and left-wingers. It is most likely that the textbook publishers are trying to save their textbooks from being attacked by both parties. No matter how they write about it, Yasukuni can easily make them the targets of polemics. Even the Politics and Economy textbooks which mention Yasukuni do not put the word in their indexes.

This point becomes clearer by comparing these textbooks with the controversial textbooks produced by right-wing intellectuals. Since the first authorization of a right-wing textbook in 2001, three publishers[15] have created such textbooks both for History and Civic Studies that critics regard as dangerously "revisionist." Although they have only issued textbooks for lower secondary schools, which contain far fewer pages than upper secondary school textbooks examined so far in this chapter, the difference from other, standard textbooks is quite clear.

The History textbooks of these three publishers do *not* mention Yasukuni. Instead of arguing that Yasukuni is an important shrine for Japanese people, they have chosen not to discuss the issue. This is likely because they have decided not to discuss the liaison between Shinto and the state before World War II. Not only can the word "State Shinto" not be found anywhere (because right-wingers consider "State Shinto" to be an invention of the left), but there is also no mention that Shinto was granted special status by the Meiji Government (because the right-wingers inherit the pre-war rhetoric of "Shinto as non-religion"[16] and argue that the freedom of religion was protected in pre-war Japan). Needless to say, there is no reference to the Chosen Jingū.

As for Civics Studies textbooks published by those three publishers, one of them does put the Yasukuni Shrine in its index. It appears under the topic of freedom of religion and the separation of religion and state. It shows a picture of Prime Minister Koizumi visiting Yasukuni and says in the caption, "There are discussions over the relationships between Prime Minister's and MP's visits to the Yasukuni Shrine and the constitutional principle of the separation between religion and state." It also says in the text adjacent to the picture:

> In order to protect the freedom of religion, the constitution adopts the principle of the separation between religion and state. ... However, in reality it is difficult to divide clearly between religion and politics, as seen in the example of the US Presidential inaugural ceremony in which the Bible

is used for making an oath. The principle is interpreted[17] as meaning that it is necessary to inhibit relationships seen as excessive by ordinary people; for example, the installation of religious education or the accordance of privileges to particular religions by national or local governments (Ikuhosha CS 2011: 59).

The textbook refrains from mentioning that Prime Minister's visit to the shine is criticized for being illegal and indirectly tries to justify those visits. Furthermore, this textbook describes "Japanese traditional religion" as follows.

> Religion also holds an important position in culture. Many Japanese people visit shrines when babies are born in order to pray for their healthy growth and to request funeral services as religious rites. In this manner, they perform the unique rites of passage which are deeply related to Shinto and Buddhism. In addition, they are tolerant to religions and are pluralistic, as seen in people who make New Year's Day visits to shrines and temples several days after celebrating Christmas.
>
> In this manner, the Japanese traditional view of religion seems to place value not on belief in one God and everyday faith-keeping but rather on the awareness of one's own role and responsibility in the society to which he/she belongs—an awareness maintained by performing periodical religious rites (Ikuhosha CS 2011: 8).

The textbook thus promotes the value of placing individuals' responsibilities for society over individuals' freedom by presenting a positive image of what they take for traditional Japanese religion.

Two other textbooks do not mention Yasukuni at all while they also have a paragraph on the freedom of religion. However, it is remarkable that the phrase "the separation of religion and state" is missing in the paragraph. Instead of treating the Yasukuni issue, they simply try not to surface the "separation between religion and the state" issue, especially the point that the freedom of religion is institutionally guaranteed by the principle. In so doing, they tacitly support the view that the Prime Minister's public visit to the shrine is not a problem.

To add, one of the two textbooks juxtaposes a picture of a resident's campaign against Aum to the paragraph on religious freedom. The picture has the caption, "Residents protesting against the settlement of a religious group which has plunged society to chaos. It is difficult to reconcile the freedom of residence and change of residence with people who complain that they feel uneasy [due to the group]" (Fusōsha CS 2005: 82). In the picture, the name of Aum is recognizable but it is not used in the caption. Moreover, it is notable that the textbook author does not present it as an issue of the freedom of religion. ("The freedom of residence" means that a citizen has the liberty to reside in any part of the country they wish to reside in).

CONCLUSION

To recapitulate the above findings, when Japanese textbooks treat the issue of religion and violence, they either discuss the issue very generally, without referring to any concrete case or identifying specific religions or religious groups, or they limit the range of violence discussed to conflicts caused by misunderstandings between religions. In so doing, they exclude the consideration of the broader causes of terrorism and its relation to religion. Some Ethics textbooks contain pictures in which a particular case or a religion is identifiable, but such pictures are left out of context. When textbooks explicitly mention the name of a certain group (Aum or Al-Qaeda) or religion, they are only describing the sequences of events in recent history. In other words, they are not discussing religious matters *per se*. The legacy of the Aum Affair appears in the use of the word "cult," but more significantly, in the definition of religion. Some textbooks have started to define religion as life-cherishing by nature (entailing that religion is intrinsically unrelated to any kind of violence): a definition that matches the Ministry of Education's view of religion disclosed in the interview with my publisher during the authorization process. On the other hand, when textbooks dare to refer to the Yasukuni Shrine, they replace the particular issues surrounding the shrine with discussion of the general issue of the separation of religion and state. In contrast, right-wing textbooks argue that the separation of religion and state is not an issue, implying that what their opponents call State Shinto is not a religion. Despite the adoration of the Yasukuni Shrine among right-wingers, their textbooks do not mention it when describing pre-war history, most likely in order obscure the existence of any state religion-like system at that time. In these ways, Japanese textbooks deal with the issue of religious violence by either hiding religion or showing religion with the caveat that it is not truly religion. They play this religion-peekaboo quite coherently, although there is neither a law nor a guidebook instructing them to do so.

From a study-of-religion perspective, the change in the textbooks' definition of religion is particularly worth noting. It is likely that the "religion as life-cherishing" definition will appear more regularly in future textbooks, given the recent media coverage of the so-called Islamic State and of Aleph, a successor of Aum Shinrikyō that continues to attract young people. There is also a tendency to tell readers that it is a (unique and honorable) Japanese tradition to create harmony among different religions. In addition, the right-wing identification of the function of religion as inducing awareness of one's own role and responsibility in society may be merged with the communitarian view of religion as community-serving, which has lately become popular in discourses on public religion or socially-engaged religion. It might be difficult for textbook readers to tell the ideological difference between the two views of religion. In short, there is the possibility that textbooks' view of religion will increasingly become religiously liberal or secularist (with an emphasis on the this-worldly and tolerant aspect of religion) and politically conservative (with an inclination to homogenize and harmonize religions, eliminating anti-social or anti-Japan elements).

ABOUT THE AUTHOR

Satoko Fujiwara is Professor, Department of Religious Studies, Faculty of Letters, at the University of Tokyo. Her related Publications include "Problems of Teaching about Religion in Japan: Another Textbook Controversy against Peace?," in R. Jackson and S. Fujiwara (eds.), *Peace Education and Religious Plurality: International Perspectives* (Routledge, 2008), and *Religions in Textbooks: Religious Education that Is Not Supposed to Exist in Japan* (in Japanese, Iwanami, 2011), "Establishing Religion through Textbooks: Religions in Japan's 'Ethics' Program," in B.-O. Andreassen and J. R. Lewis (eds.), *Textbook Gods* (Equinox, 2014). Email: fujiwara@l.u-tokyo.ac.jp

REFERENCES

Fujiwara, Satoko. 2014. "Establishing Religion through Textbooks: Religions in Japan's 'Ethics' Program." In *Textbook Gods: Genre, Text and Teaching Religious Studies*, eds. Bengt-Ove Andreassen and James R. Lewis. Sheffield: Equinox Publishing.
Hussain, Amir. 2012. "Confronting MisoIslamia: Teaching Religion and Violence in Courses on Islam," in *Teaching Religion and Violence*, ed. B. K. Pennington. Oxford and New York: Oxford University Press.
Nitta, Hitoshi. 2000. "Shinto as a Non-religion: the Origins and Development of an Idea." In *Shinto in History: Ways of the Kami*, eds. J. Breen and M. Teeuwen. Abingdon and New York: Routledge.
Ministry of Education, Culture, Sports, Science and Technology. 2009. *Kotogakko gakushū shidō yōryō kaisetsu komin-hen*.
Pennington, Brian K. ed. 2012. *Teaching Religion and Violence*. Oxford and New York: Oxford University Press.

Asahi Newspaper, May 4, 2015. "Isuramu Kyoto te Nani? (What Is a Muslim?)."
The Guardian, April 22, 2015. "Japanese MPs Make Provocative Visit to Tokyo's Yasukuni War Shrine," http://www.theguardian.com/world/2015/apr/22/japanese-mps-make-provocative-visit-to-tokyos-yasukuni-war-shrine

Textbooks
NOTE: The referencing below is ordered by publishers' names. It is designed to highlight continuities and discontinuities between Japanese textbooks published by the same publisher over several decades.

Key to Textbook References:
C = *Contemporary World*
CS = *Civic Studies*
E = *Ethics*
H = *History*
P = *Politics and Economy*

Daiichi, E. 2013 = Ochi, M. et al. 2013. *Rinri*. Tokyo: Daiichi Gakushūsha.
Fusōsha, CS. 2005 = Yagi, S. et al. 2005. *Atarashii Kōmin Kyōkasho*. Tokyo: Fusōsha.
Hitotsubashi, C. 1998 = Nitani, S. et al. 1998. *Kōkō Gendai Shakai*. Tokyo: Hitotsubashi.
Ikuhōsha, CS. 2011 = Kawakami, K. et al. 2011. *Atarashii Minna no Kōmin*. Tokyo: Ikuhōsha.
Jikkyo, P. 2009 = Miyamoto, K. et al. 2009. *Seiji Keizai*. Tokyo: Jikkyo.
Jikkyo, P. 2014 = Miyamoto, K. et al. 2014. *Seiji Keizai*. Tokyo: Jikkyo.
Kyōiku, C. 2013 = Kawai, H. et al. 2013. *Saishin Gendai Shakai*. Tokyo: Kyōiku.
Shimizu, C. 2013 = Fujita, H. et al. 2013. *Gendai Shakai*. Tokyo: Shimizu.
Shimizu, C2. 2013 = Ikeda, S. et al. 2013. *Shin Gendai Shakai*. Tokyo: Shimizu.
Shimizu, E. 1995 = Komaki, O. et al. 1995. *Gendai Rinri*. Tokyo: Shimizu.
Shimizu, E. 2013 = Kanno, K. et al. 2013. *Shin Rinri*. Tokyo: Shimizu.
Shimizu, P. 2014 = Nakamura, K. et al. 2014. *Gendai Seiji Keizai*. Tokyo: Shimizu.
Sūken, E. 2013 = Katayama, Y. et al. 2013. *Rinri*. Tokyo: Sūken.
Tokyo, C. 2007 = Sasaki, T. et al. 2007. *Gendai Shakai*. Tokyo: Tokyo Shoseki
Tokyo, E. 2014 = Takeuchi, S. et al. 2014. *Rinri*. Tokyo: Tokyo Shoseki.
Yamakawa, E. 1994 = Hamai, O. et al. 1994. *Gendai no Rinri*. Tokyo: Yamakawa.
Yamakawa, E. 2013 = Hamai, O. et al. 2013. *Gendai no Rinri*. Tokyo: Yamakawa.
Yamakawa, H. 2010 = Ishii, S. et al. 2010. *Shōsetsu Nihonshi*. Tokyo: Yamakawa.

College Textbooks
Sakurai, Y., and H. Miki. 2007. *Yokuwakaru Shūkyo Shakaigaku*. Kyoto: Minerva.
Takahashi, N., H. Tsukada and R. Okamoto. 2012. *Shūkyo to Shakai no Furontia*. Tokyo: Keisōshobō.

Endnotes
1. I thank Michael Berman for editing the draft and making helpful suggestions.
2. Precisely, the Ministry of Education, Culture, Sports, Science and Technology.
3. See, for example, the American Academy of Religions' Series book, *Teaching Religion and Violence* (Pennington 2012). In the chapter "Confronting MisoIslamia," its author argues, "It is also understandable that a young Palestinian man who has no hope for a reasonable future in the Occupied Territories would volunteer to blow himself up if his family would receive financial support from a sponsoring organization;" while at the same time making it clear that "I condemn all terrorism and violence" (Hussain 2012: 135, 136).
4. It is often argued that such liberal-democratic education has a secularist bias. However, the case of Japan is paradoxical: it is secularist in principle but confessional in practice. See Fujiwara (2014).
5. Most school textbooks are published by publishers that specialize in the genre. There are currently around ten major textbook publishers.
6. Ethics textbooks are divided into three sections:
    1. History of philosophy, both western and eastern (Japanese in particular), from ancient Greek philosophy to contemporary philosophy.
    2. History of religions, with a focus on the life and the teaching of Jesus, Muhammad, Buddha and other major religious leaders in the world and in Japan.
    3. Contemporary issues of ethics, such as bioethics, environmental ethics, information ethics, conflicts and dialogue.

7. Textbook investigators have a Master's degree and a field of specialization, but do not belong to a university.

8. Together with the textbook I have co-authored, the textbooks comprise over 90% of the Ethics textbooks used by college-bound students.

9. To be precise, there was one exception. The former version of the textbook issued by my publisher devoted a third of a page to the 9/11 attacks with a picture of the World Trade Center buildings (although there was no description of Islamic revivals or other related religious issues). Further, it also explained the political and economic backgrounds of the terrorism as I did, rather than simply condemning the attacks. It also inserted a photo of a group of young Muslimas in headscarves who were mourning over the loss of the victims of the 2005 terrorist attack in London. The textbook investigators passed the textbook in their previous authorization — likely because they had not yet decided what to do with religion and violence issues or because the relationship between religion and violence was unclear in the explanation.

10. Some college textbooks provide a marked contrast. A group of scholars of religions published a college textbook in 2007 which not only has a chapter on cult (with no quotation marks, which customarily show that "cult" is a problematic label and not an academic term) but also clearly identifies four religious groups as cults (the chapter is divided into seven sections, four of which have a religious group's name as its heading) (Sakurai and Miki 2007). This textbook reflects a new trend among some Japanese scholars of religions who argue that they should distinguish between good and bad religions, especially when teaching students. They believe that failure to do so partly caused the Aum Affair. A younger group of scholars published another college textbook with a similar idea in 2012 (Takahashi, Tsukada and Okamoto 2012).

11. I have also been investigating RE textbooks used in England (around 80 textbooks published since 2000), which take a multi-religious, non-confessional approach. In contrast to Japanese Ethics textbooks, they rarely define religion *per se*. Such a lack of definition may be due to the long empiricist tradition of England, but it also seems to function well in the multicultural society because the textbooks can avoid essentializing religion, which inevitably results in implying that some religions are more essential than others. One textbook published in 2011 has a chapter titled "What is religion?" but there it presents Ninian Smart's "seven dimensions of religion," which only give readers seven ways to analyze religion, instead of a substantial definition, which uniformly determines an essence. On the other hand, since the majority of Japanese Ethics textbooks are written by authors specializing in philosophy more of the continental than of the Anglo-American tradition (German philosophy has been exerting the greatest influence upon Japanese philosophers, especially those who have an interest in religion), they share a deductive tendency to give an abstract definition for every major concept at issue.

12. In Japanese, "*inochi*" or "*seimei*" is applied to the first meaning for life, while "*seikatsu*" or "*jinsei*" is applied to its second meaning. The two meanings are thus very easily and clearly distinguishable.

13. The Gokoku Shrines are smaller, local versions of the Yasukuni Shrine.

14. Strictly speaking, it is not the textbooks but the court that has tried to put a veil over the particularity of the Yasukuni Shrine.

15. One of them is a branch of another.

16. See Nitta (2000).

17. This interpretation is shared only among conservatives.

3. IGNORE THE WAR, CONCENTRATE ON PEACE – TEXTBOOK ANALYSIS OF STRATEGIES IN POST-CONFLICT SOCIETIES – A PRAXEOLOGICAL APPROACH

Zrinka Štimac

INTRODUCTION

What can religious education and textbooks achieve in a post-conflict situation? While there can be no straightforward answer to this question, the literature on education in armed conflict and in processes of post-conflict reconciliation, points towards a general tendency. Ideas in this respect are based on the following approaches: Sobhi Tawil and Alexandra Harley have developed a phase model of intervention for the United Nations High Commissioner for Refugees (UNHCR), according to which Bosnia and Herzegovina (henceforth BiH) finds itself in a post-conflict status in which the primary focus is placed on the reconstruction and establishment of social and civil life (Sobhi and Harley 2004: 11). A state-of-the-art examination of the present situation of education in emergencies and reconstruction and a guideline for planning education in reconstruction environments was given by Margaret Sinclair (Sinclair 2002). The problems surrounding education in pluralist societies are the focus of Lynne Davies' work, which is based on the assumption that the school can merely reflect the situation within a state. She also ascertains that education under conditions of difficulty and distress usually follows top-down models (Štimac 2016). These, however, are revealed to be entirely unsuitable for the task of appropriately addressing the needs of children and young people (Davies 2004). Kenneth Bush and Diana Saltarelli "show how educational systems can be manipulated to drive a wedge between people, rather than drawing them closer together. In short, education reflects the society around it. The attitudes that flourish beyond the school walls will, inevitably, filter into the classroom" (Bush and Saltarelli 2000). They assume that no inter-ethnic conflict that is based on patterns of identity can be solved by education alone, but only together with all involved state-based and non-state entities (Bush and Saltarelli 2000: 8). They come to the conclusion, however, that a mere "good education" is not good enough for post-conflict countries: "In many conflicts around the world, education is part of the problem, not the solution" (Bush and Saltarelli 2000: 32).

The following analysis might reveal to which extent this statement is applicable to the situation in BiH. For this purpose firstly the 'religious field' of BiH will be outlined in order to identify and locate the individuals and institutions whose responsibilities include the content matter and production of religious education textbooks. The study inquires as to whether there might be a correlation between the textbook contents used by this community and the latter's position within the 'religious field' of BiH. Secondly, it analyses the textbooks based on the praxeological *HabitusAnalysis* (Schäfer 2015a) approach, with which both textbook contents and the strategies employed by diverse entities within a post-conflict situation can be reconstructed. Finally the study analyses the religious education textbooks of one of the institutions: the Islamic Religious Community. The perception and strategies are reconstructed and related to socially relevant statements on violence and peace. This outlines the religious habitus that is supposed to be developed in the future.

LOCATING THE ISLAMIC RELIGIOUS COMMUNITY WITHIN THE RELIGIOUS FIELD OF BOSNIA AND HERZEGOVINA

The following addresses the model of the "religious field" developed by Leif Seibert in the course of the project The Ethos of Religious Peacebuilders (Der Ethos religiöser Friedensstifter) at the University of Bielefeld, based on theoretical approaches by Weber, Yinger and Bourdieu, and applied to the situation in BiH (Seibert 2010: 89–117). A wealth of diverse religious institutions are active in BiH, participating in both religious and also political or education policy-related debates and decision processes. Unlike the Weber perspective, here it is not a matter of a stable religious field in which there is one inclusivist institution such as the Church or a specific religious community while many smaller exclusivist bodies advocate revolutionary standards (Seibert 2010: 94). For this reason, and also because Seibert prefers to work with a model that "conceives of multiple interwoven relations between the social positionings of individual and collective actors, autonomy and heteronomy, power balance and 'rules of engagement' as a system," he selects the approach developed by Bourdieu (Seibert 2010: 100). According to the latter, the battle within the religious field is a struggle for religious capital, which is understood as a variation on social capital that is closely related to the development of networks (institutions) and trust ("charisma" in Weber's term). The battling parties are religious specialists (priests, prophets); their clientele, however, is excluded. The faith of the laity can thus only be indirectly transported within the field as invested faith. The laity delegates religious activity to religious experts by declaring the latter representatives of their faith qua denomination (Seibert 2010: 101). In the development of his field model,

Seibert does not use Weber's terms such as "institution" or "charisma"; rather, he works with the analytical factors of complexity and credibility, based on the assumption that they sufficiently explain the majority of differences in status between religious representatives. Complexity (Organisiertheit) refers to "the power of religious actors in their function as disseminators of social dynamics." Alongside the number of experts and active members, these also include the laity and passive members (Seibert 2010: 106). Credibility or religious authenticity is understood in terms of Bourdieu's concept of fidelity and refers to a quality of individuals and institutions whose actions appear to be free of—or only marginally shaped by—interests foreign to their field. Nevertheless this credibility is to be understand as ascribed credibility; "a credible actor benefits from the effects of being (inter)subjectively perceived as a—and thus objectively effective—figure of numinous authority. This credibility can be measured in terms of religious and social competence" (Seibert 2013: 155), in this case via statistics gleaned from the project mentioned above. The religious landscape in BiH then appears thus:

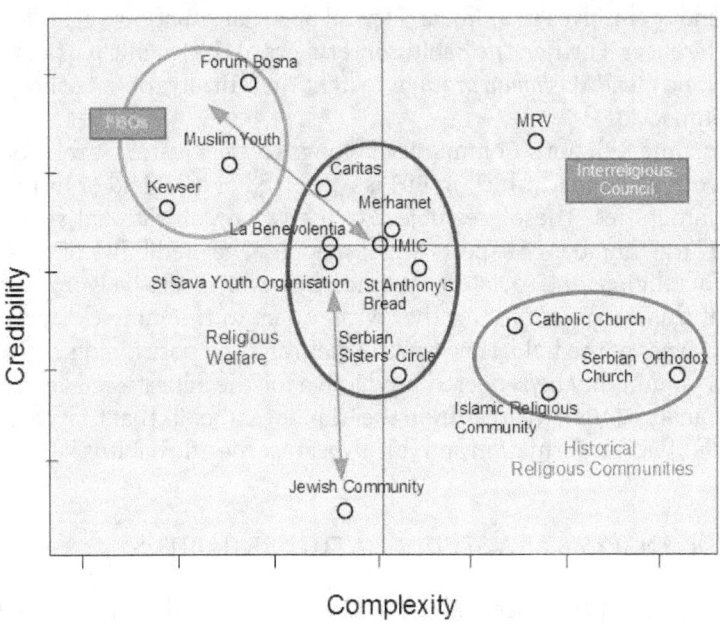

Figure 1: Religious Field of BiH (Seibert 2010: 113)

The high level of religious authenticity then goes hand in hand with the largest possible identification with the *nomos* of the religious field (Bourdieu and Wacquant: 1996). In other words, the strongest actor latently defines the semantics and what is to be understood within society as "religion"– and thus in turn the *nomos* of the field (Bourdieu and Wacquant 1996: 110). This is defined by the Interreligious Council (visible in Figure 1 as MRV, *Medjureligijsko vijeće*), which is a collaboration between individual historic churches and religious communities, and therefore includes the Islamic Community. The Inter-religious Council focuses primarily on dialogue between the different religions and other issues of interest to *all* historical churches and religious communities. Figure 1 further shows several clusters of actors: historical religious communities (Islamic Religious Community, the Catholic Church and the Serbian Orthodox Church), Church/Muslim/Jewish welfare (Merhamet, St. Anthony's Bread, Caritas, Benevolentia, Jewish Community, IMIC-Together, Youth Organisation St. Sava and Serbian Sisters' Circle) and faith-based organizations (Forum Bosna, Kewser and Muslim Youth). While a discussion of the relationships between these clusters would exceed the scope of this essay, it is important to emphasize that there are synergies and conflicts between them, not necessarily along religious lines but in terms of social stratification (Seibert 2013). It is assumed that those subject to these groupings possess similar dispositions and thus operate in *habitus* formations. The HabitusAnalysis of some of these parties points towards a wealth of symmetry in terms of both content and organizational aspects exhibited when institutions or individuals find themselves in a similar societal or social situation, regardless of religious differences. Further, the habitus interviews of the Islamic participants such as *Kewser* and *Mladi Muslimani* brought to light their firmly rooted concept of education (Štimac 2011).

The Islamic Religious Community belongs to the cluster of religious stakeholders within the field which in BiH is conceived of as a field of historical religious communities. These are subject to a strict organizational structure and involve a large number of experts and laypeople. The credibility of these groups in terms of religious and social competence, however, is relatively low, which suggests that this community—together with others in the same cluster—deviates from the *nomos* of the field. How can this field and the positioning of the Islamic Religious Community be rendered productive for the educational landscape and textbook analysis? Can we infer from the Islamic textbooks that they (a) belong to a particular habitus formation and (b) advocate a specific habitus?

TEXTBOOK ANALYSIS AS A STUDY OF A FUTURE HABITUS?

How are war, conflict, peace and related issues portrayed in religious education books of the Islamic Community, and what strategies are employed with which to address these topics? This question is addressed here via a combination of two qualitative procedures which capture the fundamental structure of the text and reconstruct the most important relationships.

Firstly, the relevant passages and topoi are filtered using the method of text analysis as a specialist area of content analysis. The central task here is the reconstruction of meaning beyond the individual texts which provide only an excerpt of a process of communication. The conditions under which carriers of meaning evolve and are used provide the interpretative framework and must equally be taken into consideration. An inductive procedure was chosen for the study, with the result that single observations can indicate initial tentative connections that are then reinforced by further systematic observations.

The second step of the analysis addresses the relational aspects.[1] To this end, the method of HabitusAnalysis as employed by empirical sociology and developed by Heinrich Wilhelm Schäfer at the University of Bielefeld (Schäfer 2003: 161), was selected as the point of departure and applied from a hermeneutic perspective. The focus here is placed on the logic of the statements and the relationships between the concepts referred to, alongside the terms used and their negations. According to Schäfer, these (logical) relationships indicate transformations of experience with a societal impact which will be described in more detail below. Particularly interesting about this procedure—and indeed important from the viewpoint of textbook research—is the combination of two perspectives. On the one hand there is society, which is governed—according to Bourdieu—by a "logic of practice" in the sense of "that's how it is done" (Bourdieu 1987: 107). On the other hand, according to Schäfer, either individuals or collective parties operate on the basis of their own "practical logic" in the sense of "that's how I/we do it"– inspiring a sense of identity and with a direct impact upon society (Schäfer 2005: 259-82). These two perspectives are connected by the actual habitus or by the collective habitus intended by the textbook and envizaged for the future.

For Bourdieu, the term "habitus" refers to an accumulation of cognitive, emotional and somatic dispositions by which situations are interpreted and judged, ethical and aesthetic norms are developed, and which ultimately result in actions. These dispositions are on the one hand triggered by everyday situations, societal and private events, and social interaction. On the other hand, they have direct repercussions on the situations and contexts of the relevant persons on account of perception, judgment and actions (Bourdieu 1987: 107). The habitus is incorporated by a specific kind of socialization and is conceived of as an "internalisation of a certain type of social and economic conditions" (Bourdieu 1996: 136). How can we work with an idea that can be described as a consequence of past perceptions and actions and as relatively stagnant, within the field of education and textbook analysis? While the term has been subject to some critique within education science, it is, however, repeatedly referred to because it unites the individual and society, thus revealing the complex relationships between perception, meaning and action, and the latter's social conditions (Höhne 2013: 261–84). Here, the term "habitus" can be understood—amongst other aspects—as a mode of appropriation that can help us to understand the practice of socialization on the one hand, and processes of individualization on the other.[2] In this respect, the textbook analysis can be seen as a contribution to the emergence of a habitus because, while the intended habitus may be clearly articulated, it is not yet fully developed. A subsequent investigation could shed light on whether or not the attempt to influence the habitus via education was successful.

HABITUSANALYSIS AS AN ANALYTICAL BASIS

How can we methodologically analyse a connection between the social and the individual? Schäfer provides an answer to this question with his HabitusAnalysis, based on Greimas' semiotic square, and developed into his own praxeological square. The latter is to be understood as a transformations model which allows the reconstruction of the development of identity and strategy of an entity or of a text/document (Schäfer 2015b: 285). Schäfer explains:

> It [the square] brings perception, judgement and actions [...] in relation to one another. The result is *schemata* in the strict Kantian sense: a combination of concept (*Begriff*) and experience (*Erfahrung*). [...] In the first *schema*, the perception of experience is combined with the perspective of change and thus with judgement, from which the new position on social injustices emergences. This new position is transformed into a plan of action by its contextualisation within the sources of social injustice.

The praxeological square renders the following visible: The subject or the text adopts a position by completely affirming, completely negating, partially negating or partially affirming a thing. The model therefore comprises the basic levels of experience of practice and the interpretation of the latter, as well as its positive and negative impacts (see Figure 2, Schäfer 2009).

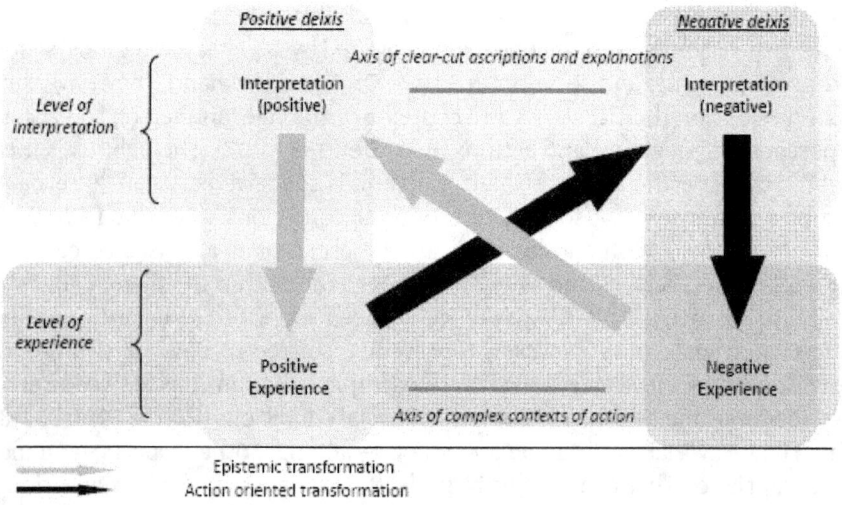

Figure 2: Epistemic and Action Oriented Transformation

The analysis of experience transformation (epistemic transformation) takes as its point of departure the open question of the most pressing problems for the various entities (in the model the position "negative experience") and the most obvious approaches to solving them (Schäfer 2003). The negative experiences are linked to the highest religious hopes and most important religious ideas of redemption and motives (position "positive interpretation"). It is from these positive elements that the various entities derive their self-conception, which in turn leads to the self-description ("positive experience"). Finally, the identity of the group is reconstructed via these three steps. On the other hand, the strategy of the collective actor can be reconstructed, beginning with the positive experience, e.g. within a specific group. On the basis of their beliefs, practice and institution ("positive experience"), a group or a movement discusses the particular social injustice at hand and identifies its specific causes and reasons ("negative interpretation"). Once the reasons behind certain social injustices have been identified, strategies can be developed with which the negative experiences may be counteracted. In other words, the action-orientated transformation can be reconstructed. Within these different positions of the square we find three logical relations: implication, contrariety and contradiction, which are most helpful for the textbook analyses as we will see below.

ISLAMIC RELIGIOUS BOOKS AND THE HABITUS TO BE DEVELOPED

The religious education textbooks of the Islamic Community in BiH will be examined in the following based on the HabitusAnalysis model. In concrete terms, this study will first investigate the positive and negative experiences. Which textbook contents relating to war and peace are used to inspire the future habitus of Bosnian Muslims in their modern state? Which strategies for attaining this habitus do the textbooks propose?

The first step of the analysis ascertains that war and violence are not explicitly addressed. There are, however, some implicit portrayals concealed behind contents on the Bosnian state, on neighbouring states and/or on societal and interpersonal competencies and qualities that Muslims of the future are supposed to have developed. There are many aspects of the content matter, however, which can be interpreted as "positive experience." These equally harbour implicit suggestions of war, to be addressed at a later stage. As on balance the positive experiences are clearly in the majority, and these are constantly subject to an explicit portrayal, these will be analyzed first. The focus is on various religious statements with a direct impact on society, such as statements on everyday life, on the lifeworld and the global environment (including nature), on the state of BiH, on the national cultural heritage and on national and religious festivals.

The analysis takes as its sample the textbooks for Islamic religious education currently authorized for primary/lower secondary schools in BiH (age 7-14).[3] Primary schooling in BiH covers eight years, similar to primary school and the first level of secondary school. There is only one textbook for each stage of schooling, as only the publishing house of the Islamic Community can design and publish the books. The version used today in standardized Bosnian included many terms, particularly of a religious nature, which in previous standard languages in this country (e.g. in former Serbo-Croatian or Croato-Serbian) were considered loanwords or Turkicisms. Now, however, these terms are given in both Bosnian and Turkish.

POSITIVE EXPERIENCES AND THEIR ONE CAUSE

a. The Islamic World and the Islamic Local Environment
In the first two years of primary school, the beginning of religious education is given an emphatic positive experience—an Islamic name (Religion textbook for year one, p. 5, in the following: R1, 5) (Begović 2005) and with the Islamic greeting in the local language: "es selamu alejkum" (R1, 7). Other people are greeting with "good morning" or "good afternoon" (R1, 9). The book emphasizes that the Islamic greeting enhances the love between Muslims (R1, 19). In year one, all contents focus on the introduction to the Islamic religious teachings. Otherwise, the lessons address personal faith, mosque construction, memorizing of various surahs, how to write the surahs in Arabic, and depictions of various religious festivals.

In year two, the lesson entitled "My New School Friends" does not provide names for the friends but leaves blank spaces where the pupils can enter the names of their own friends (R2, 15) (Tinjak 2006). It becomes apparent from the rest of the book, however, that these friends are without exception all Muslims. The text with the heading "We help each other" illustrates various everyday situations such as help with learning, with carrying a heavy rucksack, visiting those who are sick, and reconciling persons in conflict. The comment, "He who helps his Islamic brother when he is in need will be helped in his own need by Allah" (R2, 23). This is followed by a lesson on *džemat* (Turkish: Cemaat); in this case a religious group of Muslims who go to school and to the Mosque together and resemble religious and moral unity (R1, 41ff). This concept reappears in the material for year four; here, however, in a more narrow sense—of communal prayer, whether at the Mosque or at home (R4, 126f) (Nistović 2007). Later, in year eight, various forms of communal Islamic life are summarized—family, local religious community and Ummah—and understood as expressions of social life (R8, 101) (Grabus et al. 2011). No other forms of social life are mentioned.

If we are to believe the book for year two of primary school, all neighbours are also Muslims. The lesson, "Taking Care of our Neighbours" addresses good behaviour and portrays it as a positive experience. We should not only behave well towards our neighbours, the book tells us, but we should also celebrate festivals with them (R2, 125). It is not until the fifth year, in the lesson entitled "Diversity in my Neighbourhood," that for the first time neighbours are mentioned who have a different religion to Islam. An Islamic boy who has met some Christians and Jews reports on the festivals of these neighbours, such as Christmas, Easter, the Sabbath, Passover and Hanukah (R5, 115ff) (Prljača and Halilović 2008). The accuracy of this information is not relevant for this study, which focuses on positive and negative experiences as related to society. The attitude taken by the textbook towards these religions, however, is indeed relevant. The pupils are required to write a letter to a Christian or Jewish friend, filling in the blank spaces in the textbook. The text reads:

> I am a Muslim and I [love] my customs. I feel [comfortable] with them. In my country there are [Christians] as well as [Jews]. All of them have their own religious [customs]. I am sure that they all feel [comfortable] with their own customs. This is why we respect the customs of [others]. Then we all feel [good]. This is why my country is BiH [religiously diverse?] (R5, 118).

The crucial factor in this exercise becomes clear when we examine its objective. The result—as a supplementary explanation informs us—is supposed to direct pupils to the sixth line of the surah *Al-Kafirun* (The Disbelievers): "You have your religion and I have mine." What may sound like an advocation of respect for other religions ends in a complete segregation of religions. The surah reads as follows:

> ¹Say [Prophet], Disbelievers: ²I do not worship what you worship, ³you do not worship what I worship, ⁴I will never worship what you worship, ⁵you will never worship what I worship: ⁶you have your religion and I have mine (Haleem 2004: 441).

This surah is again significant in year six, when it is presented in full (R6, 89) (Grabus and Bašić 2009). There are two aspects that are essentially suggested by this lesson: firstly, that moral values can only be attained via the religion of Islam and, secondly, that other religious persons are the "disbelievers," to whom one should nevertheless maintain a correct relationship. The historical background and the context of the Surah are not discussed.

The textbook for year six also suggests for the first time that Muslims should help each other in the sense of the Ummah. Here the explicit norms of the community of Medina are listed as understood by the authors. No precise sources are given. All Muslims should form a union; they should help one another, free of sin and injustice. They should create a society with "the best and fairest laws," which guarantees "the right to practice religion and the right to the property of non-Muslims," which does not tolerate criminals; they should "build a state in which every person has the right to move freely" and where "both Muslims and non-Muslims protect the country they share" (R6, 78). These are highly ambitious religious goals to be achieved in a secular country—as BiH is supposed to be. The emotional level of learning is appealed to with a poem in order to convey the message that the union of Muslims also means mutual support, and that the rich should assist the poor (R6, 79).

This paradigm of surrounding persons being exclusively Muslim is continued in year seven (R7, 22f). (Sulejemanović and Husić 2010) Guidelines for moral behaviour are presented only within a religious context. A particular example of this is to be found in the lesson entitled "Wishing for others what we wish for ourselves" (R7, 52f). A native Muslim war refugee who has lost everything in the war chances upon a large sum of money. As a good Muslim, he is not tempted to keep the money for himself, but rather goes in search of the rightful owner and returns his money to him. A while later, the refugee and his family coincidentally—in the sense of the hand of fate—are given a house and the gift of fulfilling the *Hajj* at the expense of the Islamic Community of BiH (R7, 53). There are statements such as that difference in race, nation, skin colour and religion are God's gift to mankind (R7, 24), which can clearly be included in the positive experiences. These are, however, only mentioned in passing and out of context, and are not connected to any guidelines for positive behaviour. One exception can be found in the context of "non-Muslims" as a minority in the lesson entitled "Relationships between People" (R7, 49): "Mohammad says: Should anyone treat the persons of a different faith unjustly [...], I will complain about that person on Judgement day." In the same year, the book further proclaims that *the one Islam* teaches that all persons are equal before God, but that they differ on account of their deeds and are one large family (R7, 97). Here too, however, we must assume that this sentence primarily refers to Muslims.

b. Our Homeland: Islamic and Ottoman
The issue of BiH as a Muslim state is addressed as early as in the second year of primary school (R2, 16f), and categorized as a positive experience. To this end, the book illustrates the flag and coat of arms of BiH and names the cities and towns of Sarajevo, Trebinje, Jajce, Mostar, Blagaj and Visegrad. There is strategy behind this selection, as Blagaj is not a town of great significance for BiH but rather a small village with a dervish house, known as a place of Islamic pilgrimage. The towns are depicted via symbolic drawings. All drawings with only one exception portray the cultural heritage only from the Ottoman period.[4] Even if BiH is indeed strongly influenced by the Ottoman heritage, the cultural history of the country is considerably older and richer than suggested by these drawings. This narrowing of religious and cultural heritage to cover only the Ottoman aspects can in this context only be interpreted as an emphasis on the Muslim religion and the Muslim perspective and understanding of BiH. There is no sign in these drawings of the alleged religious pluralism of BiH.

The idea of the Muslim state is addressed once again in the textbook for year three of primary school, and once again described using positive adjectives. Alongside the flag and the coat of arms, the book also presents a map of BiH. This time the cities of Sarajevo, Tuzla, Zenica, Mostar, Banja Luka and Bihac are mentioned; the cultural heritage remains in this lesson too, however, focused on the Ottoman period. This becomes apparent in the list of Ottoman architectural features, such as the *sebilj* (drinking fountain; Turk. *Sebil*), the *šadrvan* (fountain for ritual ablutions; Turk. *Şadrvan*), the *hamam* (steam bath; Turk. *hamam*), and the *bezistan* (covered market; Turk. *Bedesten*) (R3, 152) (Pleh et al. 2006). While the book does mention that BiH is home to different peoples, this fact appears to carry no particular significance in comparison to the dominance of Islamic images and drawings. Even the illustrations that are given no further description depict primarily mosques, albeit those from the Arab world. Cities such as Travnik (R3, 161f) and Mostar (R3, 163f) are presented in the same way. While the description of the Old Bridge of Mostar does briefly mention the previous older hanging bridge, the text fails to inform the reader from which period the older bridge originated and who had commissioned its construction. Such details would reveal that some cultural assets also originate from the pre-Ottoman period, and that the rulers of the time had been Christians, for example. In this context, however, such knowledge appears irrelevant. Mostar is addressed once again in the fourth year of primary school, and the Ottoman heritage is now accompanied by an emotional portrayal of "Islamic Mostar." The historic part of the city with its Old Bridge is described as a "warm nest," for example, and all that is beautiful is depicted as Allah's gift to mankind (R4, 14).

In the continuing lesson, "The Proud Bosniak," a man by the name of Ali speaks of his pride in BiH with its various (Ottoman) cultural monuments and of having been born as one of his own people (R3, 158). The people were ready and willing, the textbook states, to confront all problems of the past (R3, 157). In this lesson, if not before, it becomes clear that positive experience is closely connected to the idea of a nation of one's own and, above all, one's own religion. There are no notable differences in the "Lesson about our Homeland" for the fourth year. Here too, the book reaffirms love of one's country and emphasizes that "every Muslim loves, protects and defends his country" (R4, 128). How a country should be defended in times of peace remains unclear. An indirect answer, and indeed a further form of positive experience, is offered by lessons that present (male) writers and scientists, exclusively of Islamic faith (R4, 129).

The book for year eight focuses on the construction of the *šeher*: the Ottoman cities (Turk. Şehir, R8, 115). These are held to have had a positive impact on other religious groups, such as—at the time—the Serbian Orthodox, Jewish and Catholic settlements (R8, 116). The importance of good neighbours is emphasized as a principal feature of this past way of life. There is no mention of Serbian Orthodox, Catholic or Jewish neighbours in the present day. In conclusion, it appears that references to the Ottoman Empire are exclusively positive. The book does not address the many other eras of history, such as Antiquity or the Middle Ages. Nor does it mention the Late Middle Ages, the time of the emergence of the Bosnian Church, which some Bosniak historians claim to be the predecessor of Islam (Štimac 2004).

c. Aesthetics, Ecology and Islamic Human Rights
Beauty in general and in particular the beauty of nature plays an important part in the textbooks under analysis. From year one (R1, 38-41), natural beauty is not only described but also associated with ethical and ecological issues. How can mankind care for nature and ensure its continued existence? In what ways does

mankind poison and destroy nature (R1, 41)? In the religious education textbook for year four, some lessons do address the topic of nature, for example with regard to the different seasons, or describe the qualities of various animals, the usefulness of wind, water, sun and clouds for nature as a whole (R4, 25-40). Although these issues are relevant for the whole of society and there are many possibilities for initiating an exchange between different "religions" with regard to cherishing Creation and to ecological sustainability, the book remains focused on a singly Islamic statement: Allah created all this for mankind (R4, 38) and Muslims significantly take care of the natural world (R4, 140ff). This claim is supported by statements and sentences such as "When a Muslim plants a tree …" or "No Muslim plants something or sews [seeds], which are then eaten by birds or people, without his deed being understood as a *zakat* (R4, 140).

In the context of the conservation of nature, issues such as "the Qur'an and human rights" (R7, 46ff) and "universal human rights are equally seen as important elements (R7, 69ff). The first lesson referred to here describes in great detail human rights as laid down by the Qur'an and the Sunnah. The lesson also presents several lines on each of relevant Islamic documents such as the Charter of Medina, the Universal Islamic Declaration of Human Rights (1981), the Cairo Declaration on Human Rights in Islam (1990), the UN Universal Declaration of Human Rights (1948) and the European Convention on Human Rights (1950). The exercises provided primarily address the Islamic perspective (R7, 47). A project requires pupils to provide an overview of all other perspectives—such as that of the UN and the European Declaration on Human Rights, which are only mentioned very briefly in the text (R7, 48). In the second lesson, however, the text deals with children's rights and the responsibilities of parents towards their children solely from the perspective of the Qur'an (quoting various surahs). These rights include the right to life, freedom from gender-related discrimination, the right to nutrition and health care, the right to a "beautiful name," the right to an upbringing, an education, to exercise and the rights of orphans. The UN convention on children's rights is also mentioned in a few lines as a further source (R7, 71), while the universal human rights are not described in terms of content. It becomes clear from the text passages named here that the religion of Islam, alongside its many other qualities, is also considered a source and indeed pioneer of many human rights. The focus of the lessons is always on collective rights, as well as those with a direct connection to Islam.

SOME NEGATIVE EXPERIENCES AND MANY NEGATIVE CAUSES

The textbook for year two addresses an Islamic holiday in BiH—the "Day of War Heroes" (*Dan šehida*, Turk. *Şehîd*) in the context of Ramadan. This is celebrated on the second day of Eid al-Fitr (*Bajram*; Turk. *Bayram*) and presented here as a national holiday. The book specifically states that the Bosniaks—i.e. not only Muslims but also the secular Bosniaks, for instance—visit Islamic graveyards and pray for the soldiers who died in the most recent war, "who [sacrificed] their lives for the dignity and freedom of their homeland" (R2, 113). In the Mosques, too, the day is spent in prayer and reading the Qur'an. Neither the war nor the victims on the other sides of the conflict are explicitly mentioned. This lesson suggests that the children organize themselves to visit a graveyard on this particular holiday (R2, 114). The topic of the graves of Muslim soldiers is addressed again in year three, with the recommendation to say specific prayers at the graveyards and to keep the latter clean and tidy (R3, 160), and again in year seven, this time with a more emotional approach. The young people are asked to talk about their feelings upon reading a poem about the war heroes and, further, to address what it is that inspires these feelings (R7, 63). At this point, if not before, it becomes clear that war as a topic of religious education certainly occupies an important space in the classroom, even if this is not explicit in the textbook contents. We can infer from both the previous positive experiences and from the negative ones described here that the books follow a one-sided perspective on this issue. The pupils are asked to describe what and who these heroes were and are, with the accompanying explanation: "Šehid—someone who sacrifices his life for the lives of others in order to protect the dignity, property, homeland, Islamic values and universal human rights" (R7, 63). It is obvious that both heroes and victims are only supposed to be found on the pupils' own religious and national side.

The book for year eight of primary school teaches the history and present of the Islamic community (R8, 103-109). On the one hand, various negative experiences are mentioned here, such as the isolation of Bosnian Muslims from the Ummah as a result of the annexation of BiH by the Austro-Hungarian monarchy; the negative experience of the Islamic Community with the Kingdom of Serbs, Croats and Slovenes (SHS), with the Kingdom of Yugoslavia and with socialist Yugoslavia. Despite the fact that in all these systems several positive steps were taken within the Islamic Community, the textbook named above laments the prohibition of the Sharia, attendance of religious schools, and religious education in public schools (R8, 104f). The negative experiences are claimed to be the results of differing political systems. The current political system, in which the Islamic Community can indeed flourish, is not described any further; rather the book informs its readers of the structure of the Islamic Community today and of its institutions that are relevant to education (R8, 108). The various aspects of content mentioned here point clearly towards this system also being rather a negative cause. We can therefore conclude that the outline of history sketched here primarily points to politics as the negative cause from the perspective of the Islamic Community.

CONCLUSION

In the following we will discuss two elements: firstly the results of the analysis of the statements on peace and—implicity—also on war (positive and negative experiences) within the textbook contents, as well as their positioning within the religious field. Secondly, we will discuss links between the HabitusAnalysis and the textbook analysis.

Generally speaking, we can deduce that the textbooks portray a kind of Islamic paradise. Here, all aspects of life are determined by religion, and—in the sense of the praxeological square—are experienced as highly positive. The logical consequence is that God is the ultimate cause of all positive experiences. The various positive aspects of life include the practising of religion, all people who participate in it (Islamic family, friends, neighbours, religious community, Ummah), all of nature and the Islam-influenced areas of the state of BiH, its culture, architecture, literature and history. All other possible perspectives and positions are excluded entirely from the texts under examination. The texts equally exclude the possibility of a secularized position within BiH, with the result that the religious group of Muslims are indistinguishable from the Bosniaks, some of whom are highly secularized. Nor is there any mention of a secularization amongst other groups (Christians and Jews, who are also constantly portrayed as minority religions). This is also the case with the ecological issues, where indeed the Christian churches—in the sense of sustainability and preserving Creation—play an important role. There is a clear overlap in the texts of religion, nation and territory (Sundhaussen 1973), and it becomes clear which habitus the young readers are to develop. Diverse strategies are employed in order to shape the habitus of young people: the Islamic religion and people are glorified; history is reinterpreted; historical facts are ignored; facts are emotionalized and romanticized; the worldview is narrowed. All this renders it obvious that the depictions of peace in Islamic religious education textbooks are exclusively linked not only to one religion and its conditions but also to one possible perspective on one religion. If peace is depicted as in the books analyzed here, then the question raises itself—also with regard to the theoretical perspectives introduced here—as to what kind of peace is in question. What is the contribution of the textbooks to the society and is there a new conflict they possibly create?

Once we have ascertained what the textbooks portray as positive experiences and as the causes of negative experiences, the question arises—from the perspective of the praxeological square—as to which negative experiences can be thus counteracted. Another question addresses which strategy could be developed by the Islamic Religious Community in order to prevent new negative experiences arising in a similar manner. These questions can be conclusively answered using the logical relationships with the praxeological square, and the strategy can be reconstructed even in the absence of details of war portrayals in textbooks. Obviously, different political systems of the past are described explicitly as negative causes for all the negative elements that the Islamic Community has previously experienced. However, negative experiences such as war, violence, displacement and their causes feature—as stated earlier—implicitly in lessons from year two onwards that deal with Islamic war heroes, and they will be briefly outlined here. The latter are celebrated, as are all the aspects of Islamic life mentioned above. Poems about the heroes are printed in the textbooks and their emotional impact on the young readers are discussed as part of the prescribed exercises. While this does involve an implicit critique of war, the critique is equally extended to anything that deviates from the Islamic religion. In other lessons, on the other hand, the different political systems that have been in place on the territory of BiH since the collapse of the Ottoman Empire are heavily criticized and portrayed as the root cause of negative experiences for the Islamic Community. Several strategies can be reconstructed from the elements analyzed. One strategy entails, for instance, the condensation of society into the concept of one's own Islamic family, group and people. Another is the focus exclusively on the "Islamic World" and the Ummah. At the same time, the textbooks pursue an usurpation of the country BiH according to Islamic ideas, which suggests that the latter represent the best of all ways of life and indeed are worth fighting for. Such strategies towards peacebuilding are supposed to shape a habitus with a questionable impact on the future of BiH.

The links between the religious field, the HabitusAnalysis and the textbook analysis are diverse. The religious field of a country or of a milieu marks out the area of resonance in which different religious institutions operate and relate to one another. This not only allows for inquiry into how the textbook contents and the position within the religious field correlate with one another, but also into how the content matter shaped by various entities within education relate to—and depend on—one another. Findings relating to the nomos of the religious field in particular might indicate whether a certain form of education is conducive or detrimental to society in the long term if it dramatically deviates from the nomos as in the case of the Islamic Community. We can further clarify how the education concept of various organizations correlates with their social stratification. In other words, a particular concept of education is dependent on the position in the religious field. Interestingly, the field of production of educational media can also—in the broadest sense—be marked out in the same way, as in the case of BiH the religious field and the education field overlap when dealing with religious education in public schools.

From the perspective of the religious field, we can infer that the contents of the Islamic religious education textbooks described here correspond to its position within the field. In other words, this community is not ostensibly defined by the *nomos* of the religious field in BiH, with the effect that an inter-religious content matter, inter-religious dialogue and multiple perspectives apparently appear irrelevant for the textbooks. The narrow understanding of culture, religion and history also clearly illustrates this aspect.

In this context, the concept of the habitus has been constantly applied as a mode of appropriation, with the effect that the HabitusAnalysis must be understood as an analysis of that which is to be developed in the future and not only of those dispositions which are already discernible in the present. The current textbook contents therefore allowed for a reconstruction of the anticipated future as well as of the strategy employed to attain such a future. Following the HabitusAnalysis can consequently be rendered productive for textbook analysis in the following aspects: Firstly, it provides insights into the emic weighting of the content matter, such as the areas of focus, issues subject to controversy, and questions of relevance. Secondly, it provides insights into the subjects that are only implicitly suggested or avoided entirely. The avoided content matter is then not "intuitively" guessed, but—thanks to the different logical relationships—coherently reconstructed. Not only information regarding the contents can be reconstructed from these relationships, but also—and thirdly—a specific strategy for action, which is only rarely explicitly laid out in the textbooks. The underlying message behind the content matter can thus be uncovered. Of course there are several difficulties to be overcome whilst using this approach. How should we evaluate different sources alongside one another, such as images, drawings, maps, etc.? How can we evaluate in an educational context the emotional approach alongside the cognitive? How should we deal with content matter that cannot be clearly categorized into positive or negative experience? How do the textbook contents relate to those in the teachers' books? What is the relationship between textbook contents and their production under different social conditions? Indeed, there is more than enough space and material for further analysis and discussion.

ABOUT THE AUTHOR

Zrinka Štimac is Senior Research Fellow at Georg Eckert Institute, Department of Textbooks and Society. Her research interests include religion and diversity in education and educational media. Her 2010 doctorate was entitled *"Religion and education in Bosnia and Herzegovina. Concepts and strategies of religious and secular stakeholders since 1994"* (Religion und Bildung in Bosnien und Herzegowina. Konzepte und Strategien religiöser und säkularer Deutungsträger nach 1994). Her latest publication is *"Vernetzte Welt - Getrennte Religionen? Verflechtung von Religion und Gesellschaft als Herausforderung der Schulbücher"* (Connected World - Divided Religions? The Interconnections between Religion and Society and Their Challenge to Textbooks). Eckert. Working Papers 2016/1, http://www.gei.de/mitarbeiter/dr-zrinka-stimac.html. Email: stimac@gei.de

REFERENCES

Bourdieu, Pierre. 1987. *Sozialer Sinn. Kritik der theoretischen Vernunft*, Frankfurt am Main: Suhrkamp.
Bourdieu, Pierre, and Loic J. D. Waquant. 1996. *Reflexive Anthropologie*. Frankfurt am Main: Suhrkamp.
Böhnisch, Lothaer, Karl Lenz and Wolfgang Schröder. 2009. *Sozialisation und Bewältigung. Eine Einführung in die Sozialisationstheorie der zweiten Moderne*. München: Juventa.
Bush, Kenneth, and Diana Saltarelli. 2000. *The Two Faces of Education in Ethnic Conflict: Towards a Peacebuilding Education for Children*. UNICEF Innocenti Research Center, Florenz.

Davies, Lynne. 2004. *Education and Conflict: Complexity and Chaos*. London: Routledge.
Höhne, Thomas. 2013. "Der Habitusbegriff in Erziehungswissenschaft und Bildungsforschung." In *Pierre Bourdieus Konzeption des Habitus. Grundlagen, Zugänge, Forschungsperspektiven*, eds. Alexander Lenger, Christian Schneickert and Florian Schumacher. Wiesbaden: Springer.
Haleem, Abdel M. A. S. 2004. *The Quran: A New Translation*. Oxford: Oxford University Press.
Schäfer, Heinrich Wilhelm. 2003. *Zur Theorie von kollektiver Identität und Habitus am Beispiel sozialer Bewegungen. Eine Theoriestudie auf der Grundlage der interkulturellen Untersuchung zweier religiöser Bewegungen*. Berlin: Humboldt-Universität.
Schäfer, Heinrich Wilhelm. 2005. "Identität als Netzwerk. Ein Theorieentwurf am Beispiel religiöser Bewegungen im Bürgerkrieg Guatemalas." *Berliner Journal für Soziologie*.
Schäfer, Heinrich Wilhelm. 2009. "Habitus-Analysis: A Method to Analyze Cognitive Operators of Practical Logic." Conference "Beyond Bourdieu—Habitus, Capital & Social Stratification," Kopenhagen University.
Schäfer Heinrich Wilhelm et al. 2009. Bourdieu's Categories for 'Field' Construction. CIRRuS working paper Nr. 8. Available at: https://www.uni-bielefeld.de/theologie/CIRRuS-downloads/Schaefer-ea_2009_CIRRuS_field-categories.pdf. Last accessed 15.01.2016.
Schäfer, Heinrich Wilhelm. 2015a. *HabitusAnalysis 1. Epistemology and Language*. Heidelberg: Springer VS.
Schäfer, Heinrich Wilhelm. 2015b. *Identität als Netzwerk. Habitus. Sozialstruktur und religiöse Mobilisierung*. Wiesbaden: Springer.
Seibert, Leif. 2010. "Glaubwürdigkeit als religiösen Vermögen." In *Berliner Journal für Soziologie*, Wiesbaden: VS Verlag für Sozialwissenschaften.
Seibert, Leif. 2013. "Religious Credibility Under Fire. A Praxeological Analysis of the Determinants of Legitimacy in Post War Bosnia and Herzegovina." Dissertation, Universität Bielefeld.
Sinclair, Margaret. 2002. *Planning Education In and After Emergencies*. UNESCO International Institute for Educational Planning.
Sobhi, Tawil, and Alexandra Harley. 2004. *Education, Conflict and Social Cohesion*. UNESCO, IBE.
Sundhaussen, Holm. 1973. *Der Einfluss der Herderschen Ideen auf die Nationsbildung bei den Völkern der Habsburger Monarchie*. München: Oldenbourg.
Štimac, Zrinka. 2004. *Bosnische Kirche. Versuch eines religionswissenschaftlichen Zugangs*. Münster: LIT Verlag.
Štimac, Zrinka. 2010a. "Religionsvermittlung in multireligiösen Räumen. Konzepte und Strategien religiöse und säkularer Akteure nach 1994." Dissertation, Universität Jena.
Štimac, Zrinka. 2010b. "Islamische Religionstradierung im Kontext der EU-Integration und Bildungsreform in Bosnien und Herzegowina." In *Islam und Muslime in Südosteuropa im Kontext von Transformation und EU-Erweiterung*, eds. Christian Voß and Jordanka Telbizova-Sack. München: Otto Sagner Verlag.
Štimac, Zrinka. 2011. "Frauenorganisation *Kewser*. Zwischen der islamischen spirituellen Erweckung und der Frauenemanzipation." In *Islam, Frauen und Europa: Islamischer Feminismus und Gender Jihad—Neue Wege für Musliminnen in Europa*, eds. Mualla Selçuk and Ina Wunn. Stuttgart: Kohlhammer.
Štimac, Zrinka. 2017. "OSZE und Bildungsinterventionen. Strategien und Konzepte im Umgang mit multireligiöser Gesellschaft." In *Politische Systembildung nach dem Zerfall Jugoslawiens*, ed. Enver Sopjani. Wiesbaden: Springer.

Textbooks

Begović, Ibrahim. 2005. *Vjeronauka za prvi razred osnovne škole*. Sarajevo: El-kalem.
Grabus, Emina, and Muamer Bašić. 2009. *Vjeronauka za šest irazred osnovne škole*. Sarajevo: El-kalem.
Grabus, Emina, Muamer Neimarlija, Ahmedina Purković and Meliha Zukić. 2011. *Vjeronauka za osmi razred osnovne škole*. Sarajevo: El-kalem.
Nistović, Hazema, Ibro Nistović and Mensur Valjevac. 2007. *Vjeronauka za četvrti razred osnovne škole*. Sarajevo: El-kalem.
Pleh, Mina; Muamer Tinjak and Meliha Nezirovac. 2006. *Vjeronauka za treći razred osnovne škole*. Sarajevo: El-kalem.
Prljača, Mustafa, and Nezir Halilović. 2008. *Vjeronauka za peti razred osnovne škole*. Sarajevo: El-kalem.
Sulejemanović, Šefko, and Safija Husić. 2010. *Vjeronauka za sedmi razred osnovne škole*. Sarajevo: El-kalem.
Tinjak, Muarem. 2006. *Vjeronauka za drugi razred osnovne škole*. Sarajevo: El-kalem.

Endnotes

1. In Bourdieu's theory, the relational, as shown above, refers to the field itself (relationships between different actors). In the context of *HabitusAnalysis*, however, it is obviously a matter of the relationships between the various concepts (cf. Bourdieu/Wacquant: 258–62).

2. Cf. Lothaer Böhnisch, Karl Lenz and Wolfgang Schröder, *Sozialisation und Bewältigung. Eine Einführung in die Sozialisationstheorie der zweiten Moderne*. München: Juventa, 2009. While the deterministic idea of Bourdieu's "habitus" is subject to critique here, the argument nevertheless focuses on the process character of the habitus.

3. For the analysis of an older generation of Bosnian religious textbooks in general, see Štimac (2010a: 273–316). For the analysis of understanding of and interaction with other so-called book religions from the Islamic perspective see Štimac (2010b: 101–26).

4. Sarajevo is portrayed using an Islamic religious school, Mostar using the Old Bridge, Blagaj using the dervish house and Visegrad using the Ottoman Bridge over the Drina.

4. COLONIAL CONFLICTS: ABSENCE, INCLUSION AND INDIGENIZATION IN TEXTBOOK PRESENTATIONS OF INDIGENOUS PEOPLES

Torjer A. Olsen

Indigenous peoples and historical events related to indigenous peoples always have a conflict dimension. Issues of colonization, exploitation, and culture clashes are all at hand in societies in which there are indigenous peoples. You do not need a very broad definition of violence or conflict to understand these as expressions of violence. It may be structural violence, pointing towards discrimination, and it may be indirect or direct violence, through cases of forced conversion, forced relocation, or even genocide. Textbook authors need to relate to these conflicts.

Textbooks most often relate to ideas about common or national culture. This makes them a potential flashpoint of cultural struggle and controversy (Altbach 1991: 257). As schools and education most often are the products of, or at least are governed by, state and majority, textbook representations are always more or less biased. Textbooks seek to anchor the political and social norms of a society, Hanna Schissler states (1989–90: 81). What are the implications of this for the representation of indigenous peoples and minorities? These groups most often will not be seen as the norm of a society. History and geography books contribute to marking the borderlines of a society (Pingel 2010: 7). A way of doing this is to narrate people or groups of people into or out of society.

The case used to discuss the more general topic in this chapter is the representation of conflicts related to the indigenous Sámis of Norway. Is this an issue of colonization? When the Danish-Norwegian state wanted to secure the borders in the beginning of the 18th century, Christian missionaries sent to the Sámis were an important factor. This led to the Christianization of the Sámi. In the middle of the 19th century this had its backdrop through the rebellion in the Sámi village of Kautokeino where people were killed. In the chapter I do an analysis of the textbook presentations of these events as a starting point for a discussion of textbook presentations of colonization and conflicts related to states and indigenous peoples. The assumption made is that textbooks tend to downplay the conflict dimensions of the relationship between states and indigenous peoples. There are three main approaches to the representation of indigenous studies, absence, inclusion, and indigenization.

TEXTBOOK ANALYSIS IN MINORITY STUDIES

Even though the educational systems vary from state to state, textbooks used in schools will relate to commonly shared ideas and values in their respective society, region or culture. Textbook scholar Falk Pingel (2010: 8), points to the emergence of nation states and argues that schoolbooks in general contain statements that glorify their own nation and ruling groups as well as disparage others and minority groups.

Pingel presents two basic questions for textbook analysis with a view of international understanding: "How does a text represent and confirm group identity? How does the fundamental difference between us and them emerge from the portrayal of different groups of humankind in textbooks?" (Pingel 2010: 38). Such questions quite precisely point to the key issues at hand in this article. Going further, I might add that when speaking of indigenous peoples the question could be whether or not they make their way to the pages at all. Indigenous people might not even be *othered*. By othering, I mean the process through which people or groups of people are being categorized as not being "one of us" (Moreton-Robinson 2000: 179).

In textbook representations of indigenous peoples, I argue that there are three main strategies to recognize: Absence, inclusion and indigenization. *Absence* means the way indigenous peoples and issues are omitted more or less on purpose in textbook representations. *Inclusion* points to many ways of adding smaller or bigger parts on indigenous peoples and issues, but from a majority perspective. *Indigenization*, in this setting, means that the representations of indigenous peoples and issues to a bigger or smaller extent add an indigenous perspective, listen to indigenous peoples or even are written by indigenous authors.

Pingel (2010: 39) shows some of the same approaches. Two approaches prevail, he states: Firstly, minorities are included in the textbooks, but not given enough space to be treated properly. Secondly, some governments give minorities the right and chance to make their own textbooks. This is of course a good thing, but it makes it more difficult to include indigenous issues into the mainstream narrative.

Textbook analyses can of course be done in a variety of ways. A choice to make is whether to do concept analysis, content analysis, discourse analysis or didactic analysis, or if you are trying to combine different approaches. In the case studies of this chapter, I will use a content analysis also looking at the concepts used, and a discourse analysis. No matter which approach is chosen, it is important to explore and present the context at hand. This includes both the historical and social context in which a textbook is written and used and the curriculum background and educational system.

INDIGENOUS PEOPLES

The concept of indigenous peoples points towards historical contexts in which a majority group (or groups) is distinguished from a minority seen to have special claims to and belonging to a particular land area.

The concept of "indigenous peoples" has gained a lot of attention and importance during the last decades (Minde 2008). The concept has political, scholarly and linguistic consequences. To be recognized as indigenous can potentially be really important for a group of people when it comes to rights and position. When an ethnic group is talked of as indigenous, it is based on the perception and acceptance of the group as having a particular connection and belonging to a certain geographical area. Another idea concerning indigenous peoples states that the group of people at hand has ethnic characteristics that distinguish them from others. A challenge related to the concept of indigenous peoples is that it is not an objective term. Any group of people can in principle talk of themselves as indigenous. However, states can choose whether or not to accept or recognize this claim. At the same time, the UN has some legitimizing power. Through the *UN Permanent forum for indigenous issues* groups of people can be recognized on an international level as indigenous, securing at least the potential of certain rights. How states in different parts of the world perceive and look upon this varies. Many states hesitate to recognize the claims of ethnic groups to be indigenous.

There is not a single, agreed-upon definition of indigenous peoples. In international conventions, with the UN Declaration on the Rights of Indigenous Peoples (2007) and the ILO 169 (1990) as the most prominent ones, indigenous peoples are talked about as peoples that have been inhabiting an area from a time before the formalization of today's state borders, and that have a culture/way of life and/or a language that distinguishes them from the majority. Hence, the concept of indigenous peoples must be understood and used as relational. This means that the situation that people live and have lived in contributes to the understanding and acceptance of them as indigenous (Minde 2008).

The last three decades have shown the burst of Indigenism, the political movement supporting and working for the rights of indigenous peoples. Education and the right to an indigenous-friendly education is a part of the claims of Indigenism. As an international movement, the idea of indigenous peoples worldwide sharing experiences and culture is important (Niezen 2003: 30).

As pointed to in relation to the function of textbooks, schools and education have the potential to be tools and arenas for colonization. History has clearly shown that this has been the case worldwide. Schools are the state's tools to provide its inhabitants with the knowledge and ways of getting knowledge that are defined as the most important. Thus schools and education are tools for reproduction of ideology and for making policies come into reality. This is obviously a two-edged sword. The experiences of indigenous peoples tell about challenges both on local and global levels. Educational systems tend to be based on the majorities, on the mainstream. To add knowledge on or knowledge based on indigenous peoples to the mainstream curricula is a hard struggle, described as swimming against a strong current (Hays, Bellier and Olsen 2014).

In Norway, history has shown several great changes since the beginning of the public school. The School Act of 1739 made it compulsory for all children to go to school. A main rationale for this was making all citizens able to read the Bible. This coincides with the intensified colonization policy towards the Sámi, the indigenous people of the Nordic countries. A major part of colonization was Christian mission, with school as an important dimension. A century later, the school became the most efficient and important tool for the implementation of the Norwegianization policy that sought to make all minorities abandon their ethnic (and religiously dissident) identity and become Norwegian (and Christian). From the middle of the 19th century the Sámi were one of several minorities who more or less were forbidden to speak their native tongue and learn about their own culture and history in school.

This is an often-told story. In Aotearoa/New Zealand, the period between 1847 and 1960 is a period of assimilation. From 1871, in the many schools that had been established in Maori communities, instruction was only to be given in English. This was part of a bigger assimilation policy aiming towards a radical change of Maori community and culture (Armitage 1995: 143). Social welfare scholar Andrew Armitage (1995) compares the history of aboriginal assimilation in Australia, Canada and Aotearoa/New Zealand. He argues that there are many similarities, and that education clearly is a key factor in the assimilation policies in the respective countries. Education—as a government responsibility alongside health and social welfare—was provided, but in entirely European forms in all countries. This was to a great extent rejected by the aboriginal peoples. However, it was not until 1972 that these countries changed their policies moving away from internal colonialism (Armitage 1995: 230–31).

The sad stories being told, it is important to note that schools and educational systems have the potential and ability to be used in other directions as well, towards decolonization. This can be done in a variety of ways, from indigenous and/or minority groups making their own schools, to states changing their policies both on education and on the rights of indigenous peoples and minorities. Following the same examples, the Norwegian school has radically changed since the times of colonization and Norwegianization. Since World War II, the state policy on the Sámi is changed, making the school an arena for giving knowledge on the Sámi, and articulating this knowledge as nationally important. Of course this was not done in a day.

THE CURRICULAR CONTEXT

The curricular context is of importance when it comes to the analysis and understanding of textbooks. Even though the practice and role of national and/or regional curricula varies, in the majority of cases there are some kinds of guidelines when it comes to what children are supposed to learn in school. In Norway, the national curricula are part of the legislation. This strengthens the position and importance of the curricula.

In Norway, the process of turning the tables when it comes to the situation for the Sámi in school has taken decades. An expression of this is the development and revisions of the national curricula. Hence, from the first national curriculum in 1974 to the most recent curriculum in 2006, the position of the Sámi has been strengthened and the focus on indigenous issues sharpened (Folkenborg 2008: 59). As part of the 1997 curriculum, a Sámi curriculum was made and implemented in Norway.

That being said—a distance and a potential gap remains between curriculum and practice. In between this are the textbooks. As the analysis of the Norwegian textbooks will show, a curriculum stating the importance of knowledge on Sámi and indigenous issues does not in itself warrant textbooks that provide such knowledge.

The curricula relevant for the issues of colonial conflicts are for History and Religious education (RE) in secondary and upper secondary school. In the curriculum for History in upper secondary school, it reads that pupils are supposed to be able to "elaborate on important features of Sámi history and discuss Sámi relations with states having Sámi settlements up to around 1800" (Udir 2016a). The pupils are also supposed to be able to "discuss and elaborate on the policy conducted by the Norwegian national state in relation to indigenous peoples, national and ethnic minorities in the 1800s and 1900s, and discuss some consequences of this policy" (Udir 2016a). In the History curriculum (which is part of Social Studies) for secondary school it states that pupils are to be able to "present the main characteristics of the history and culture of the Sámi people from the mid-1800s up to the present, and discuss and elaborate on the consequences of the Norwegian policy of Norwegianization and the Sámi people's fight for their rights" (Udir 2016b).

These are rather vague statements leaving a lot to teachers and textbook authors. Still, talking of "important features of Sámi history" is easily interpreted as including the colonization and Christianization of the Sámi, especially when relations with states are mentioned and the historical period is defined as up to around 1800. It is striking, however, that the curriculum for secondary school talks of the Sámi culture and way of life up to the Christianization. This leaves the Christianization in itself, as a phenomenon that does not necessarily need a more thorough treatment.

The curriculums in RE both for secondary and upper secondary school also include some Sámi and indigenous issues. The upper secondary school pupils are supposed to be able to "present main characteristics of the diversity of religions and views on life in local communities and the greater society in Norway, including religion and views on life in Sámi communities" (Udir 2016c). Here, knowledge about the Sámi is clearly put in the margins of the curriculum. For the secondary school students, the same issues are put into a mainly Christian context. The students are supposed to be able to "present The Church of Norway, Laestadianism and Sámi church life," to "account for important events in the history of Christianity from the Reformation to today in Norway," and to "account for new religious movements and converse about different forms of new religious and nature religious practice, including the nature religion of indigenous peoples" (Udir 2016d). Both curricula leave quite a lot to textbooks and teachers. How to define "important events" is not easy. The same goes for "main characteristics." Furthermore, what you choose to highlight in a presentation of Laestadianism and Sámi church life can vary. Bengt-Ove Andreassen and Torjer A. Olsen (2015) discuss the curriculum of Religion and Ethics in upper secondary school, arguing that the tendency is that more is now left to the textbooks and the teachers than before.

CASE STUDY 1: COLONIZATION AND CHRISTIANIZATION

A challenge faced by states with a colonial past concerns the need to deal with this past. How should school textbooks tell the story of a state's not so glorious past? Should they tell stories about colonization at all? The experience of colonization is often presented as a shared experience for indigenous peoples. However, the nature of colonization is not univocally the same throughout history and in different parts of the world. Some general characteristics can be made, though. Colonization is always about power and the relation between people. It is about one group of people, or representatives of one group of people, taking control over a geographical area in which other groups of people live, taking and using the surplus of resources for their own benefit. For the matter of simplification, I will distinguish between two main kinds of colonization. The so-called "terra nullius" kind of colonization is the one seen in Oceania, the Americas and parts of Africa and Asia. Here, people coming from the outside, from societies far, far away, landed to "discover" new land and make it their own. The people indigenous to the land were subject to many different kinds of oppression, from being killed, forcibly relocated, and made slaves, to a variety of other ways of exploitation. In northern parts of Europe, most parts of Asia (including Russia) and parts of Africa, the picture and story is different. Here, the distinction between colonizer and colonized is not as obvious. Different groups of people have been living to smaller and greater extent side by side. Through the changing faces of history, the search for and contest for resources and power has turned some groups of people into colonizers.

In a Norwegian/Sámi context, for instance, the Norwegian and the Sámi have been living as neighbors for a long time, making it difficult in some villages to distinguish between who is who. With the emergence of the kingdoms in the first centuries of the last millennium, the power relations became more and more asymmetrical, making the Sámi subject to taxation. Still, it was not until the end of the 17th century that a more outspoken colonization policy started. Now, a main issue was to secure and define the national borders in order to get and defend the control of natural resources. A major part of putting this policy into action was the use of Christian mission towards the Sámi—who had more or less been able to live with what can be termed their indigenous religion. The mission worked: The Sámi became Christians. They learned how to read. They became members of what was to become the national state. And they lost control of parts of their resources.

In the textbooks at hand, the treatment of the colonization and Christianization of the Sámi is not especially thorough. In *Historie vg 2-3* (*History*) (Libæk et al. 2013), a book of some 520 pages written for History in upper secondary school, there are three pages under the heading "Samefolket i Norden" [The Sámi People of the North, my translation]. These pages cover the history of the Sámi up until the beginning of the 18th century. In addition, there are three other pages about the growth of the Sámi ethno-political movement in recent decades. To give an idea of the comparative emphasis, the book includes 40 pages on World War II. The Christianization of the Sámi is described with this statement:

> In harmony with the nature religion, the Sámi worshipped many gods and spirits. But the Danish-Norwegian state wanted to Christen the Sámi, and the Sámi mission was started in the beginning of the 1700s, lead by minister Thomas von Westen. Little by little the Sámis were christened, and the conversed soon looked upon the nature gods as evil powers (Libæk et al. 2013: 168, my translation).

In addition to being rather short cut, this paragraph presents a story about the colonization of the Sámi in which there is little conflict visible. The state has a purpose and goes to action. Little by little the Sámi become Christians. This is an example of a textbook *ignoring* an important aspect of history. The story told is a harmonizing one.

In *Perspektiver: Historie Vg2-Vg3* (*Perspectives: History*) (Madsen et al. 2013), also for History in upper secondary school, there is a quite similar picture presented of the Christianization. The words used are a little different in valor, however. The Sámi and their religion were "put under harder pressure than before" (Madsen et al. 2013: 207, my translation). In spite of this, the mission towards the Sámi is depersonalized in the story: "The Sámi rituals were seen as a dangerous Paganism that had to be extinct. Thus one treated the religious gathering places roughly, burnt the ritual drums and punished those who lead the ceremonies" (Madsen et al. 2013: 207, my translation). To depersonalize those who actually burn drums and punish people is of course a choice made by the authors. To say that "one" did something is to leave out the issue of agency and of state agents putting state policy into life. This way of writing is to downplay and deemphasize the conflict dimension.

Perspektiver. Historie Vg2–Vg3 has an innovative dimension. In addition to the main part of the book, which gives the main history, it includes a set of essays on particular topics. One of these essays has the Sámi as its topic. Written by Sámi historian Bjørg Evjen, this can be read as an expression of indigenization. Evjen is primarily discussing issues of Othering in her essay, arguing that the category of the Other is constantly changing. This meta-perspective on history is challenging and innovative. However, the book as such leaves a rather open picture when it comes to the presentation of Sámi and indigenous history. I will return to the issue of Othering.

The History books for secondary school do not cover the colonization process. It is interesting, though, that they do write about the European colonization of the Americas and Oceania. In the book series *Makt og menneske* [*Power and People*] (Aarre et al. 2010), Colombus is told to have "discovered" the Americas. And the pupils are given the task of discussing positive (the flowering economy) and negative (ethnic cleansing) aspects of the "discovery" of Oceania (Aarre et al. 2010: 41). The book series *Monitor* writes rather extensively on Sámi issues, but starts its presentation of history with the 19th century, that is after the main colonization period.

The RE books for secondary school do not in general cover Sámi and indigenous issues. There is one exception: The book *Under samme himmel* [*Under the Same Sky*] (Wiik and Waale 2006) has a paragraph on the Sámi and Christianity. Here, the Christianization is presented like this:

> In the 1700s the Norwegian minister Thomas von Westen was doing mission amongst the Sámi. He is called the apostle of the Sámi. He said that a personal relation to God was important. Hence he wanted to communicate with the Sámi in their language. He took the initiative to begin language learning for the missionaries and to the translation of books into the Sámi language. Sámi was only an oral language at the time. The missionaries made a big effort to make a Sámi written language (Wiik and Waale 2006: 194, my translation).

The perspective from which this story is told is clearly from the missionaries, and from a Christian perspective. Thomas von Westen is recorded into a Christian grand narrative of apostolic succession being "the Apostle of the Sámi." The motivation and purpose of doing mission amongst the Sámi is presented as part of a Christian rationale (a personal relation to God) and of developing Sámi society (the making of a written language). What is not mentioned or told here is perhaps most interesting: the political dimension is gone. The issue of power and conflicts between states is gone. No conflict is seen. The Sámi perspective and the implication for Sámi society are not talked of. The missionaries are presented as cultural heroes. Religion is described as being about a personal relation to God. This is a striking expression of ignorance and of a majority perspective getting all possible space.

The textbooks for Religion in upper secondary school are equally varied. Most books do not cover very much, however, *I samme verden* (*In the Same World*) presents Sámi and indigenous issues. The book has been published twice, in 2008 and 2013 (Kvamme et al. 2008 and 2013). The changes made from one edition to the other are really interesting. In the 2008 edition, under the heading "Religion and worldview amongst Sámis," the book presents both historical and contemporary aspects of religion in Sámi settings. A part of this is the Christianization:

> The pre-Christian Sámi religion was a religion without writing. The religious traditions were transferred orally. Hence the religion was vulnerable when Christian mission was beginning to make an impact, in Norwegian areas this happened in the 18th century. Norwegian authorities were particularly rough on the most important Sámi tradition bearers, the noaidis, and their drums were confiscated. After a while, only bits and pieces were left from the old storytelling traditions (Kvamme et al. 2008: 378, my translation).

There are (at least) two aspects of this story. First, it is worth noting that the conflict dimension is explicit, making this a completely different story than the one told in *Under samme himmel*. An integral part of the Christianization process, as told in the upper secondary textbook, is Norwegian authorities' rough treatment of the Sámi religious leaders. Secondly, the question of agency is answered with ambiguity and vagueness. Christian mission began "to make an impact." Where and who are the missionaries?

Under the heading/topic "Mankind and Nature," the norms and values of indigenous peoples are explored. The norms and values regarding nature and society are presented as shared by indigenous people globally. In the 2013 edition, it is the only part that is left. The previous one on religion and worldviews among the Sámis has been removed. More correctly, it has been moved to the online resources.

When *Under samme himmel* (Wiik and Waale 2006: 201–205) presents Christian mission it is without any consideration of mission being part of colonization. Mission is told of as connected to the core of Christian faith, to aid-work, and to preaching the gospel of Christ. Hence, mission is presented as totally apolitical.

A term never used in any of the textbooks (neither in history nor in religion) with regards to the representations of the Christianization of the Sámi is "colonization." The term colonization is limited to the European colonization overseas. An analysis of textbook representations of colonization as such deserves a chapter of its own. Nonetheless, it is worth noting that textbooks still make mention of Colombus "discovering" America. Other than this there is great diversity in the representations. Two tendencies are worth pointing towards here. The perspective, from which the story is told, is the majority's perspective. And the religion textbooks do not talk about colonization.

CASE STUDY 2: ETHNO-RELIGIOUS CONFLICTS: THE KAUTOKEINO REBELLION

The second case study concerns representations of more specific conflicts of an ethno-religious kind. In the Norwegian and Sámi context there are a few conflicts that stand out. Regarding religious conflicts, this goes for one particular case: The so-called Kautokeino Rebellion, which is a conflict with religious, psychological, social, cultural, and political aspects. The rebellion is a conflict with a history of its own when it comes to its consequences and representations.

There are several ways of explaining and narrating the Kautokeino Rebellion. Kautokeino is a Sámi village in the inland of Norwegian Sápmi, not far from the borders of Finland and Sweden. In 1852, there was a violent uproar, in which a local police officer and a merchant were killed and several others were hurt by an angry mob. The uproar came as a culmination of a series of events (Zorgdrager 1997).

The background is in part the Christian revival of Laestadianism a few years before in the neighboring village of Karesuando across the border to Finland. The Pietist revival started in 1845 around the Swedish-Sámi minister Lars Levi Laestadius (1800–1861). The movement spread rapidly to neighboring areas, in the beginning mainly amongst the Sámi. Kautokeino was one of the places with a local variation of Laestadianism, with local leaders articulating their own kind of Christianity. The important Laestadian ritual phenomenon termed "rørelse" (Norwegian), "lihkatuus" (Sámi), and literally meaning movement or stirring, caused disturbances at church services. In the services of the church, the "rørelse" caused anger and irritation amongst the ministers and the non-Laestadian churchgoers. This mainly happened in villages with many Sámis. A consequence was distrust and dissatisfaction amongst Sámi Laestadians. In Kautokeino, in addition to the more regional church related conflict, there was a local conflict between the merchant and the local population. A part of this was related to the abuse of alcohol and debt problems. As a religious movement, the Kautokeino Laestadianism became a branch of its own, making their own interpretations of the Bible and of Laestadius' preaching. It seems to have become a rather extreme kind of Christian revivalism enabling its leading figures to see and portray themselves as righteous and having the duty to confront the main sinners, even through violence. Even though the rebels were all Sámi, so were the people coming in to help stop the uproar. In the court case following the rebellion, two of the front men, Aslak Jacobsen Hætta and Mons Aslaksen Somby, were sentenced to death and decapitated. Many others were given prison sentences of different lengths. The heads of those decapitated were taken to Oslo to be subject to research, and were only returned after almost 150 years to be properly buried in an official ceremony in Alta in 1997 (Zorgdrager 1997).

The Kautokeino Rebellion is an important part of Sámi history, and of the social and religious history of the peoples of the north. In 2008, the Sámi filmmaker Nils Gaup, launched his blockbuster movie *The Kautokeino Rebellion* based on stories of the event. On the release of the film, the Norwegian minister of culture, Trond Giske, said in his greeting that the film was more important than a hundred school textbooks. A consequence of Giske's words has, of course, been that teachers choose to screen the film as part of (or instead of) their teaching. However, this is another project. In school textbooks, there is some variation.

In the RE books, neither for secondary nor upper secondary school, no mention at all is given of the rebellion.

The History textbooks for secondary school do not mention the event much either. An exception is *Monitor* (Fagerthun 2008). Here, the complex dimension of the rebellion is presented. I choose to focus more on the upper secondary school books for History. Two books remain silent on the matter. It is, in this context, striking that two other books, *Alle tiders historie* [*History from All Times*] (Heum et al. 2014) and *Mennesker i tid 2* [*People in Time 2*] (Hansen et al. 2012), both tell the story about the Kautokeino Rebellion, and provide an analysis of the causes of the rebellion. *Mennesker i tid 2* (Hansen 2012: 182) emphasizes the complexity of the rebellion, clearly aiming for a representation also of an indigenous Sámi perspective. In *Alle tiders historie* (Heum et al. 2014), the line is drawn even longer. In addition to the discussion about the complex causality, the book sets the context of the Sámi societies being under a lot of pressure in the years leading up to the Kautokeino Rebellion. Furthermore, the book presents the movie about the rebellion and takes this as a starting point of the discussion on representation:

> The action of the movie is based on the historical events. The filmmaker has not hidden the fact that he wished to create understanding and sympathy for the situation of the Sámi. Discuss whether or not the movie can be used as an historical narrative. How can it be used as a remnant? To what degree do you think the movie can contribute to a greater understanding of the Kautokeino Rebellion (Hansen et al. 2012: 241, my translation).

Here, the book emphasizes the reflexive level and moves beyond mere storytelling. The paragraph on the movie can actually be read as an expression of what seems also to be the goal of the book. With the emphasis on the Sámi perspective, the book can be characterized as articulating a kind of indigenizing approach.

An interesting comparison to make is to representations of social and religious uproars of a similar kind. Both the so-called "Thrane Movement" and Christian conservative Haugianism are given treatment in the History textbooks at hand. There is a striking difference, however, when it comes to narrative into which these events are told. When talked of, the Kautokeino Rebellion—and the Laestadian movement as such—is put into a narrative of the Other, a narrative belonging to a different place. The Thrane Movement and Haugianism, having happened in social contexts of southern Norway, are both put into a narrative of Our history. The exception is the book *Monitor* (Fagertun 2008).

A general reading of the textbook representations of Laestadianism and the Kautokeino Rebellion shows that both are mainly told into or within a narrative of the Sámi. This follows along the lines of other representations. In my analysis

(Olsen 2010) of how books on the national history and church history of Norway have presented the Laestadian and the Haugian revivalist movement respectively, I found two main tendencies. First, I found that Laestadianism was depicted as an irrational movement belonging to the "other," to the Sámi and Finnish minorities. Secondly, I found that Haugianism was depicted as "our" movement, as rational and a natural part of Norwegian history.

This means that the textbooks have limitations when it comes to being part of a grand narrative or of grand narratives in plural. Conflicts related to the majority population, or in which the parts turned out to be part of the majority population, seem to be rationalized. In contrast, conflicts related to minorities, especially to ethnic minorities, seem to be deemed irrational or put in the category of the other. The RE books solve the issue of the Kautokeino Rebellion with total absence. The History books, however, show different strategies, from a similar kind of absence to using the conflict as a starting point for a bigger reflection on indigenous issues.

DISCUSSION: ABSENCE, INCLUSION OR INDIGENIZATION

Textbooks relate to national or common culture. The cases considered here clearly show that this implies some challenges when it comes to minorities. Minorities are of course only minorities in relation to majority culture, to common culture. There are also challenges when it comes to the past of national or common culture. A colonial past needs to be put into a narrative. There are many options as to how this can be done.

Conflicts—especially conflicts related to religion—seem to be treated quite differently in the school subjects of History and Religion respectively. Even though this is not the topic as such in this chapter, and even though scholars have not looked into this as far as I know, History seems more eager than Religion to deal with conflicts. In spite of this, the History books talking about the mission towards the Sámi also struggle to deal with the conflict dimension. The lack of conflict perspective in RE (and when it comes to events with a more or less explicitly religious aspect) is in line with the findings of historian of religion Bengt-Ove Andreassen (2008). He argues that scholarly literature within the field of religious education has a general lack of conflict perspectives. The textbooks are inclined to treat and talk about religion as a source of harmony and peace. Thus, conflicts related to religion become something that is on the side of religion, something that religion—through dialogue—can help overcome (Andreassen 2008: 2–4). When the textbook *Under samme himmel* (Wiik and Waale 2006) removes the political aspect and conflict, it is a part of a bigger tendency. Here, there is a confluence of harmonizing textbook religion presentation and of ignorant majority perspectives. The picture painted is of a situation where the missionary as a majority representative brings blessing and progression from the center to the minority in the periphery. Hence, what can be put into the narrative of an ethnic and a religious conflict is put into the narrative of majority and center bringing progress to minority and periphery.

A reading of the many textbooks in History and Religion in the Norwegian school system shows that there is a development and a diversity regarding conflict issues. The tendency is that History books present the whole spectrum from ignorance to indigenization, and that the Religion books struggle to talk of conflicts at all. I would argue that the critique raised by Andreassen is called for. The concept of and approach to religion in educational contexts seems to be harmony-based to the extent that conflicts do not fit in. There is a need for a re-description—to use the term of historian of religion Russell T. McCutcheon (2001)—of mission and of the role of religion in colonialism.

A result of colonialism is that minorities are made and—further down the road—silenced, put into the margins, and even left out. When history is told, and society and culture is described, minorities can quite easily be ignored. The textbooks show the tendency of absence. Historian Håkon Rune Folkenborg (2008: 76–78) argues, in his analysis of History textbooks from the previous national curriculum in Norway, that they can be seen as bearers of a nationalist ideology and the nation building perspective in the most dominant aspect in all books analyzed. The result is that the implicit "We" exclude other ethnic groups in Norway, and that the representation throughout happens on the premises of the majority culture (2008: 76–78). There is a tendency to Othering and silencing. My reading of the textbooks belonging to the current curriculum shows, however, that there is some change. There is a span from total absence shown in some books to an active inclusion and indigenization in other books. From a perspective of indigenous studies and the critical study of religion, nonetheless, it remains important to state and claim the need to tell the story from the minorities' perspectives. The first step is to tell stories wherein minorities actually are allowed to play a part.

Inclusion is an important step. There are different ways of being inclusive. On whose terms will the inclusion happen? An inclusion can on the one hand be done on the terms of the majority. In such a narrative, the grand narrative remains more or less unchanged. A parallel to this is what in gender studies is termed "her-story," pointing towards the importance of telling the story of women alongside the defining stories of men. In an ironic comment, this is called the "add-women-and-stir" approach. The point being: Her-story does not change much, but uses the dominant and traditional perspectives. When it comes to indigenous issues, it is tempting to ask whether the wish to include indigenous peoples in overviews of history or religion, implies an "add-indigenous peoples-and-stir" approach. The parallel to gender studies is interesting and relevant, I would argue. Historian Joan W. Scott (1999: 3) states that feminists share an interest with "[...] those concerned to change the representation of other groups left out of history because of race, ethnicity, and class as well as gender." Seeing and recognizing the similarities is a part of the process. Critical studies of textbook representations should look into the foundation and terms of inclusion. Furthermore, which choices are made when it comes to inclusion? The current case studies show that in textbooks something is included whereas something is left out. When it comes to Sámi and indigenous issues, diversity and complexity tend to disappear or at least to be downplayed.

Indigenization is the next step, moving beyond inclusion. Indigenization is of course also an approach with many and differing starting points. Torres Strait Island scholar Martin Nakata states that in Australia the process of Indigenization has been important. Indigenization of research and of academic work has meant creation of a recognizably indigenous space within universities, a space that works to culturally affirm indigenous people and practices (Nakata 2006: 269). The textbooks explored in the case studies of this chapter are part of mainstream education. Hence, indigenization in such a context would mean something other than indigenous authors writing an indigenized textbook for an indigenous group of readers. One may ask, as does textbook scholar Dan Fleming (1989–90: 7), what are the goals of the textbooks: "Are they to be primarily sources of information, builders of reading, writing and critical thinking skills, purveyors of ethical models, or promoters of patriotism?" Indigenization in a mainstream educational context implies, in my opinion, the move away from promoting patriotism and towards critical thinking and exploring varying ethical models. In contrast to inclusion, indigenization implies a perspective where the voices of the indigenous are seen as important and as something to listen to. This means that colonization cannot be presented only through its consequences for the colonizers. This means that mission cannot be presented only through its consequences or through the concepts of the culture and religion doing the mission. This means that colonial conflicts need to be presented as conflicts with competing parts.

As far as conflict is the case, I claim that the concept of conflict needs to be a dynamic one. Even though indigenous peoples are seen as and spoken of as a group of its own, they are characterized by diversity. Consequently, the dichotomy between "Western" and "indigenous" is not always valid. I do not believe that it is possible to define neither indigenous nor Western in exclusive terms. A strong dichotomy tends to make internal variation and differences blurry (Olsen 2016). Hence, for textbook purposes I would recommend a level of care in facing dichotomies.

CLASHPOINT AND CONTROVERSY

Textbooks are potential flashpoints of cultural struggle and controversy. However, this is more often implicit than explicit in the textbooks themselves. Following the lead from one of the History textbooks, *Perspectives/History*, I would argue towards the end of this text that cultural struggles and controversy can be made explicit. Former colonial states should embrace their colonial pasts as difficult and problematic. Textbooks give governments the possibility to deal with internal struggles. Where does this end? That is perhaps not the most difficult question. Where to begin and on whose terms are more difficult ones.

ABOUT THE AUTHOR

Torjer A. Olsen is Associate Professor in indigenous studies at The Center for Sami Studies, University of Tromsø: The Arctic University of Norway. Olsen holds a PhD in religious studies from the University of Tromsø (2008). His research interests span gender in conservative/fundamentalist religious movements, representations of identity in educational settings, and methodological and theoretical perspectives in research on religious and indigenous issues. Email: torjer.olsen@uit.no

BIBLIOGRAPHY

Aarre, T. and T. Helland. 2010. *Makt og menneske*. Oslo: Cappelen Damm.
Alltbach, P. G., G. Kelly and H. G. Petrie, 1991. *Textbooks in American Society*. New York: State University Press.
Andreassen, B. O. 2008. "Konfliktperspektiver i religionsundervisning og religionsdidaktikk— en bredere og bedre tilnærming til religion?" *Acta Didactica 2 (1)*.
Andreassen, B. O., and T. A. Olsen. 2015. "Religionsfaget i videregående skole. En læreplanhistorisk gjennomgang 1976–2006." *Prismet Forskning* 66(2).
Armitage, A. 1995. *Comparing the Policy of Aboriginal Assimilation*. Australia, Canada and New Zealand, Vancouver: UBC Press.
Fagertun, F. 2008. *Monitor: Historie—grunnbok*, Oslo: Cappelen.
Fleming, D. B. 1989–90. "High School Social Studies Textbooks: Good or Bad Compared to What?" *The International Journal of Social Education* 4(3).
Folkenborg, H. R. 2008. *Nasjonal identitetsskaping i skolen. En regional og etnisk problematisering*. Tromsø: Eureka.
Hays, J., I. Bellier and T. A. Olsen. 2014. "Education, Learning and Indigenous Rights. What Knowledge(s), Skills and Languages for Sustainable Livelihoods?" *Forum for Development Cooperation with Indigenous Peoples—Blog*. Available at: http://site.uit.no/urfolksforum/education-learning-and-indigenous-rights-what-knowledges-skills-and-languages-for-sustainable-livelihoods/
Hansen, S. O., A. Bakkerud, H. Hagen, O. Hamran, T. Heum and A. K. Jacobsen. 2010. *Mennesker i tid 2. Norge og verden etter 1800*. Oslo: Cappelen Damm.
Heum, T., Trond Heum, Kåre Dahl Martinsen, Tommy Moum, and Ola Teige. 2014. *Alle tiders historie*. Oslo: Cappelen Damm.
Kvamme, O. A., E. M. Lindhardt and A. Steineger. 2008 [2013]. *I samme verden. Religion og etikk Vg3*. Oslo: Cappelen Damm.
Libæk, I., K. Fossum and A. Sveen. 2013. *Historie Vg2/Vg3*. Oslo: Cappelen Damm.
Madsen, P. A., H. Roaldset, I. H. Killerud, A. B. Hansen, E. Sæther and E. Sandmo. 2013. *Perspektiver. Historie Vg2/Vg3*. Oslo: Gyldendal.

Minde, H. 2008. "The Destination and the Journey: Indigenous Peoples and the United Nations from the 1960s through 1985." In *Indigenous Peoples: Self-Determination—Knowledge—Indigeneity*, ed. H. Minde. Delft: Eburon.

Moreton-Robinson, A. 2000. *Talkin' Up to the White Woman: Indigenous Women and Feminism*. Queensland: University of Queensland Press.

Nakata, M. 2006. "Australian Indigenous Studies: A Question of Discipline." *The Australian Journal of Anthropology* 17(3).

Niezen, R. 2003. *The Origins of Indigenism. Human Rights and the Politics of Identity*. Berkeley, CA: University of California Press.

Olsen, T. A. 2016. "Responsibility, Reciprocity and Respect. On the Ethics of (Self-) Representation and Advocacy Indigenous Studies." In *Ethics in Indigenous Research, Past Experiences—Future Challenges*, ed. A.-L. Drugge. Umeå: Vaartoe-Center for Sámi Research.

Pingel, F. 2010. *UNESCO Guidebook on Textbook Research and Textbook Revision*, 2nd revised and updated edition. Paris/Braunschweig: Georg Eckert Institute for International Textbook Research.

Schissler, H. 1989–90. "Limitations and Priorities of International Social Studies Textbook Research." *The International Journal of Social Education* 4(3).

Scott, J. W. 1999. *Gender and the Politics of History*. New York: Columbia University Press.

Utdanningsdirektoratet [Udir]. 2016a. *History—Common Core Subject in Programmes for General Studies*. Oslo: Directorate of Education.

Utdanningsdirektoratet. 2016b. *Social Studies Subject Curriculum*. Oslo: Directorate of Education.

Utdanningsdirektoratet. 2016c. *Religion and Ethics—Common Core Subjects in Programme for General Studies*. Oslo: Directorate of Education.

Utdanningsdirektoratet. 2016d. *Curriculum for Religion, Philosophies of Life and Ethics*. Oslo: Directorate of Education.

Wiik, P., and R. B. Waale. 2006. *Under samme himmel 2*. Oslo: Cappelen.

Zorgdrager, N. 1997. *De rettferdiges strid. Kautokeino 1852: Sámisk motstand mot norsk kolonialisme*. Oslo: Vett og viten.

5. TALKING ABOUT CONFLICTS IN PURSUIT OF THE COMMON GOOD, OR HOW TO HANDLE SENSITIVE TOPICS WHILE LEARNING ABOUT RELIGIONS: THE APPROACH OF THE ETHICS AND RELIGIOUS CULTURE TEXTBOOKS IN QUÉBEC

Sivane Hirsch

Québec is still predominantly Catholic — at least nominally — but Catholic religious belief and affiliation are on the decline (in 2001,[1] 83% of Quebecers identified themselves as Catholics, whereas a decade later, this figure fell to 75% according to the National Households Survey, which also showed a general decline in religious belief and practices), while the presence of religious minorities is growing in Québec. The number of Muslims living in Quebec more than doubled in the first decade of the 21st century, increasing from 1.5% of the population in 2001, to 3.2% of the population in 2011. The presence of other religions, especially Hinduism and Buddhism, is also on the rise. And last but not least, atheism is rapidly increasing from 5.8% of Quebecers in the 2001 survey, who said they had no religious affiliation, to 12% in the latest survey. A number that is much more significant (44 %) among young adults.

It is in this general context that the Ethics and Religious Culture Program was implemented in all of Québec's elementary and secondary schools. The Program, which recognizes and even values this apparent pluralism, presents Québec's religious diversity, but seems to avoid any mention of conflict that may emerge in this context. Moreover, since the Program also aims to contribute to the value of "living together" in a secular society, broaching these conflicts may almost appear to run counter to its goals. And indeed, as we will see in this chapter, most of the more popular textbooks or workbooks avoid any issues of conflict of a religious nature, whether they be local or international. But some of the sensitive topics, recently in the headlines in Québec, are to be found in this teaching material. Analyzing how these are dealt with will allow us to better understand the reasons why conflict is, for the most part, absent from this Program and its textbooks, and will demonstrate not only the difficulties that surround discussing this subject in a secular society like Québec's, but also why it is important to do so.

1. CONFLICTS AND RELIGIONS IN THE ETHICS AND RELIGIOUS CULTURE PROGRAM

The Ethics and Religious Culture (ERC) Program has been implemented in all of Québec's schools since 2008. The three competencies of the Program, which are to learn to reflect on ethical questions, to demonstrate an understanding of the phenomenon of religion, and to engage in a dialogue, aim to achieve its two main objectives: the recognition of others and the pursuit of the common good, defined as "the search [...] for common values; the promotion of projects that foster community life, and the respect for democratic principles and ideals specific to Québec society"(Ministère de l'Éducation, du Loisir et du Sport 2008: 2). Discussion of any conflict, and even more so of religious conflict, is, therefore, not an easy task. Not only does talking about what divides us make the process of finding common ground longer and more complicated, but the Program requirement for teachers to be "imbued with objectivity and impartiality"[2] makes it almost impossible. Teachers prefer to avoid all "dangerous" topics, as the consequences of dealing with them in class are unknown (Hirsch and McAndrew 2016).

Nevertheless, inherent in each of these three competencies is the risk of raising conflictual issues: between different values and different beliefs or because of the wish to share them with others. And in fact, the Program recognizes that these are delicate, if not divisive subjects, and dealing with them with students needs considerable forethought. Thus, the Program clearly specifies the teachers' role in the classroom that requires that they adopt a particular professional stance:

> Since the ethical questions raised in the contemporary world are complex, teachers must be able to pinpoint the corresponding issues and use care when handling such issues in class. Forms of religious expression must also be handled with tact in order to respect the freedom of conscience and of religion of each person. In this context, it is important that teachers maintain a critical distance regarding their own world-views especially with respect to their convictions, values and beliefs. [...] Teachers intervene, and emphasize the aims of the Program, in the event that an opinion that is expressed in class attacks a person's dignity or that actions that are suggested compromise the common good (Ministère de l'Éducation, du Loisir et du Sport 2008: 12).

The primary concern is therefore not that a religion will be misrepresented, but that some students will see their personal beliefs, religious or not, dismissed or, on the other hand, that teachers will find themselves accepting any idea or belief in the name of a misunderstood relativism (that some will define as "absolute relativism"). This is why it is explicitly asked of ERC teachers:

> Throughout the learning process, teachers help students go from simply expressing their opinions to clarifying and analyzing points of view in order to assess whether they are relevant and coherent. In this way, teachers help students develop a critical sense that will enable them to understand that not all opinions have the same worth. In this context, teachers do not have a monopoly on right answers; rather they use the art of questioning in order to encourage their students to learn to think for themselves (Ministère de l'Éducation, du Loisir et du Sport 2008: 13).

Indeed, the Ethics and Religious Culture Program makes every possible effort not to create or even bring up any matter of religious conflict in the classroom. However, this is not so different from any other official curriculum (Tutiaux-Guillon 2006) that chooses to avoid "socially charged questions." For religion is indeed a social question. Subject of a recurrent debate in society, particularly concerning the place it should have in it, it is also the subject of numerous debates among experts and over the values and the social representations of both teachers and students alike (Legardez 2006). The heated debates around the Program's implementation in schools in 2008 and the cases referred to the Supreme Court[3] demonstrate this well.

Taking all this into consideration (and the fact the Program was approved by all religious communities before its implementation), one can better understand the effort to avoid any controversial issues and to not include any "explosive" material in the Program. Religious conflict is therefore not a main focus and is barely mentioned at all. Rather, the Program, considered as the culmination of the "process of deconfessionalization of all aspects of the public school system" (Ministère de l'Éducation, du Loisir et du Sport 2008: preamble), focuses on the ethical and religious diversity and pluralism of Québec's society, and the great value this has for the common good.

> Like many democratic societies, Québec society is characterized by growing pluralism. Evident in the diversity of values and beliefs held by individuals and groups, this diversity contributes to shaping Québec culture. An important factor of enrichment, diversity can also be a source of tension. Living together in today's society requires that we collectively learn to build on this diversity. It is therefore important to develop an awareness of this diversity and to reflect upon and take actions that foster community life (Ministère de l'Éducation, du Loisir et du Sport 2008: 1).

Therefore, the Program aims not so much to teach the history of religions or, even less so, their theology, but rather to "take into account the students' environment" (Ministère de l'Éducation, du Loisir et du Sport 2008: 8), to allow students to better apprehend the reality they live in, or as it is clearly stated in the Program, to better understand "the main components of religions that is built on the exploration of the sociocultural contexts in which they take root and continue to develop" (Ministère de l'Éducation, du Loisir et du Sport 2008: 1). Family celebrations, local architecture, street names, and the contribution of religious institutions (schools, hospitals, etc.) to today's society are some of the examples put forward. However, since the Program emphasizes the importance of religious (among others) diversity in Québec society, one must also take into account a more diverse environment somewhat foreign to the students' culture, and therefore also more controversial.

An analysis of the second competency, through which the student should "demonstrate an understanding of the phenomenon of religion" allows us to identify several themes that could trigger debate, especially as they are currently at the heart of a social debate. Here are some examples of the most sensitive topics that came to the fore in 2014.

The first theme of the Program in Secondary Cycle One (first two years) is "Québec's religious heritage," and features the contributions of religious groups to Québec's society, such as the founding of its health and education institutions, or the traces (mostly architectural, but also ethical) of religious influence in Québec's contemporary culture. But it can also allow for more controversial issues to be raised, such as the "traditional" collective prayer before council meetings in Saguenay (a judgment on the matter was rendered by the Supreme Court of Canada on April 15, 2015) or about the crucifix that still hangs at the *Salon bleu* (Blue Hall) in Québec's National Assembly. The highly publicized refusal of some municipalities to allow construction of new Muslim places of worship (mosque, cemetery, etc.), and the less known solution that was later found,[4] can also be brought up while discussing architectural heritage and the numerous churches around the province.

The second theme, "Key elements of religious traditions," discusses stories, rites and rules, and explains their origins, characteristics and roles. However, it also includes some sensitive issues that made headlines in Québec this last year. Among these headlines was the much debated Muslim veil and other religious practices, for instance the religious labelling of food (Halal and Kosher), and rituals that had wider social consequences, notably the construction of a temporary hut (sukkah) for the Jewish holiday of Sukkot, or the "refusal" by observant Jews to move their parked cars from the streets for snow removal on a Saturday.

International religious conflicts (ISIS being the most "infamous," but certainly not the only one) can also find their way into the classroom. Some may come up during discussions on "Religions down through time" (the first theme of Secondary Cycle 2 or Secondary 4 and 5), given its different geo-historical elements. Others, like the Paris terror attacks in January 2015 (against Charlie Hebdo and the Jewish supermarket), may be broached when discussing "Representations of the divine and of the mythical and supernatural," or, in the case of Muslims, their prohibition.

All these examples clearly show that, in spite of the attempt to circumvent any mention of religious conflict, teachers may stumble on numerous controversial issues that touch one or more religions. Moreover, since the ERC Program invites teachers to take into account the students' environment, it can also give rise to numerous debates concerning religion's place in modern society, subjects that are often front page stories in Québec. The teaching of and about religions in schools, the presence of religious symbols in the public space, and modern society's accommodation of religious rules and rites, have all been subjects of fierce debate over the last decade. By ignoring the possibility that these socially charged questions could be brought up in the classroom, the Program not only sends the message that these subjects are better not dealt with at school, but also fails to recommend respectful ways of handling them, if and when they do come up. Indeed, teachers are not well-prepared enough to tackle the issues that could arise while teaching and, since they do not want to cope with them in their classroom, often try to avoid them all together (Hirsch and McAndrew 2016).

2. ETHICS AND RELIGIOUS CULTURE TEXTBOOKS AND SENSITIVE SUBJECTS

Considering the absence of mention of any kind of conflicts in the Ethics and Religious Culture Program, the failure of textbooks to deal with these delicate subjects is hardly surprising. Even more so, since textbooks must be approved by the Minister of Education, Higher Education and Research, their editors may prefer to avoid these topics to ensure that the process for government approval is not hindered.

It is quite a different story for the workbooks that do not have to be submitted for ministerial approval. In fact, they have an altogether different mandate, i.e. to offer teachers a turnkey lesson for each of the Program's themes. Thus, each chapter introduces students to a different subject through the presentation of short texts, followed by questions and other teaching exercises (for example, small group discussions) designed to have students examine their knowledge and sometimes deepen it even further. Given this mandate, and given the growing popularity of these workbooks among teachers, especially as this Program requires knowledge about a wide variety of subjects, one can easily understand why publishers prefer to reedit this material rather than the textbooks, which are used by teachers mostly as reference tools (Hirsch and McAndrew 2016).[5] In fact, three new or reedited workbooks (from 2012 and 2014) are now on the market, while all of the textbooks are from 2008, or before. This probably explains why the workbooks are more likely, albeit seldom, to deal with current affairs, including controversial ones. The following are three examples from these workbooks that clearly demonstrate how delicate religious questions are treated differently.

2.1. Religion in School

The debate around the Ethics and Religious Culture Program, and its' implementation in all elementary and secondary schools in the province of Québec, is mainly centred on the second competency: Demonstrates an understanding of the phenomenon of religion. The Program's opponents, religious and non-religious alike, disputed the acknowledgement of religious pluralism within society in the classroom, questioning whether or not religion should have a place in schools (Morris 2011). Once the Program was implemented, fairly successfully, the debate subsided, although it does reignite from time to time. The most recent example is of the judgment rendered by Canada's Supreme Court in favor of Loyola High School mentioned earlier. However, other news items, or even anecdotes, bring this issue back in the headlines and illustrate the wealth of opinion surrounding these teachings in Québec society. One such example is of a recent (March 2015) complaint from a father who was "shocked" when looking over his son's homework to discover that he was learning about Islam, and a new petition was launched to demand the abolition of the Program. The fact that only one workbook (*Vivre ensemble 4*, 2014) openly discusses the question of religion and education in Québec should not therefore be taken lightly. The chapter examines the history of religious education in the province, as well as the social changes that Québec has experienced over the last few decades (for instance, in the proportion of different religions in the population, or the place religion has in the life of Quebecers). The workbook also broaches controversial issues concerning religion in Québec society: the crucifix hanging in the *Salon bleu* in the National Assembly, the debate on wearing the Muslim veil in the public space, and a discussion about an individual's right to believe in and practice their religion. On the same page, it gives a definition of secularism, which is simplified enough not to be the cause any dissension. In this way, students are invited to consider the question of religion from an ethical point of view. The notion of "tolerance" is also presented in this same context.

In a sense, this workbook discusses Québec's pluralism. It should also be mentioned that it is the only one that dedicates such an important place to this subject, although it is this same pluralism that not only explains the Program's approach, but also, as we saw earlier, its' *raison d'être*. Indeed, each competency of this Program develops this awareness by its' recognition of a variety of world visions (ethics) and religious beliefs and practices (religious culture), and by developing the capacity to live with these differences and accord them a place in open dialogue.

That is not to say that pluralism is considered a value by all. When the majority is a "fragile" one (McAndrew 2013), as is a majority that is the minority of another society, like Québec with its Francophone majority being a minority within a continent of Anglophones, pluralism is seldom considered to be a threat to national or cultural identity. In fact, the main criticism of this Program is about this specific aspect of it (Maxwell and Hirsch 2016).

Most textbooks or workbooks do not treat pluralism as a theme, but incorporate it in other themes, mainly by presenting a variety of rituals, narratives or rules, places of religious worship (synagogues, mosques) and representations of the divine. In other words, they show diversity in Québec's society without discussing the effects of it. Sometimes, though, workbooks actually ignore any other religious presence or their contribution to Québec's society. This is true, for example, of the section entitled "Society is changing" (*Acteurs du monde* 2012: 74) that refers only to the Christian values and norms that contributed to this change, or were influenced by it.

The previous example plainly shows how not talking about something, in this case the influence of other religions on society and of contemporary society on other religions, can create a certain misunderstanding. Indeed, if it were only Christianity that changed with society, all other religions would be frozen in time ... On the contrary, inviting students to openly discuss the ERC Program, its history and its goals, as the other workbook suggests, would make what they are learning meaningful. This lesson may help them to realize that in order to appreciate the transformation of Québec society, it is essential to not only better understand the heritage of Catholicism, but also of religious phenomena in general, and to know a little of their history and practices. Moreover, a delicate subject seems to present a good opportunity for engaging in dialogue, not to discuss the religions themselves, but rather to understand why it is important to learn about them.

2.2. Rules: Islamic Veil, the Image of God and Religious Diet
Some religious rules, mostly those that require no "accommodation," whether they are more or less "reasonable," pass unnoticed. Others frequently provoke social debate among "common sense" Quebecers. This is particularly true for the Islamic veil, Jewish and Muslim dietary rules, and Jewish Sabbath rules that forbid working, driving a car or turning on the power, among others. Indeed, all these rules often seem to "offend" many Quebecers, who feel that their values and customs are being criticized: how else can they explain why some members of religious minorities choose not to adopt these when they settle in the province.

The Muslim veil is a good example of how a sensitive subject is dealt with. More often, it is presented as the wearing of symbolic religious clothing, alongside others, such as the chasuble and the alb worn by priests, the monk's habit and the Jewish skullcap. The various books do not actually attempt to address the sensitive issues that surround this custom, but rather present it in a very specific circumstance that appears to associate it with its religious context, and which plays down its political and social connotations: "For Muslims, the garment can have a religious significance in everyday life. It should reflect the modesty of duty of the men as well as women." However, some bias still appear in the texts, as, following the line of text quoted here, the book goes on to explain that "some women wear the hijab (veil or headscarf) as a sign of piety and modesty, but other Muslim women choose not to wear it." Indeed, this sentence seems to suggest that while Muslim women must wear the hijab sometimes, others out of choice, decide not to do so. This small paragraph is followed by a description of the kippah that "certain men [...] are only for prayer, while others prefer [...] wear at all times." In this case, the choice is to wear a kippah (and thus affirm one's Jewishness all day, for all) while in the case of Muslim women, the choice seems rather to remove it (*Vivre ensemble 1*).

The approach to dealing with both the Islamic and Judaic prohibition on representing God is similar in many respects. Under the title "Defending the image" (*Living Together 2*), the text explains the rule's origins in these two religions: first in the Jewish tradition (to "end practices [idolatry]"), then in the Islamic (Muhammad "wanted believers to avoid the temptation of any god but Allah"). It also explains that such prohibitions have led Muslims to represent God otherwise, such as through calligraphy, which is a highly developed art in Islamic lands. However, this ban has recently raised tensions (the Danish cartoon affair has been a watershed event of the last decade).

The treatment of dietary rules, an issue raised from time to time in Québec society, leaves more room for debate. In a textbook (*Living Together 4*), a section, entitled "à Table!" (Let's Eat!) starts by dealing with the topic of requests for accommodation for food served in public institutions. A discussion around "controversial food" is clearly addressed by bringing to mind that "everyone [is] on his plate!" Moreover, this book not only explains the rules of the various religions, but it also reflects on the meaning we give to food, including other types of diets based on contemporary ethical values (veganism, vegetarianism, etc.). This case clearly shows that there is an interest in discussing sensitive topics with students, and in raising the debate from the outset to address the issue. This helps not only to motivate students to deepen their learning, but also to establish their own views on the question by examining its most problematic elements. Given the context of the ERC Program, this is somewhat significant.

3. AVOIDING CONFLICTS WHILE TALKING ABOUT RELIGIONS

Presenting sensitive issues without giving any consideration to their conflicting aspects remains the current practice in textbooks and workbooks devoted to the ERC Program. They generally avoid conflict of any kind, violent or not. I will try here to put forward some possible explanations for this to better understand what seems to be an editorial preference.

In Québec, religion is a sensitive topic. While Québec's society is clearly a secular one, religion is very often at the heart of its social debates, especially on the place it should have in the public space. It is also the subject of controversy between experts (for example, on the issue of wearing ostentatious religious symbols in the public space or about the political and social significance which certain symbols, including the Muslim veil, may have) and, undoubtedly, it touches the values and the social representations of both teachers and students alike. Even in today's Québec, the question of teaching about religion is a socially charged one.

As is the case for other socially charged questions, the legitimacy of talking about this is not yet accepted. However, it is more surprising in this case since the Ethics and Religious Culture Program clearly broaches these topics, and even requires that they be dealt with in the context of students' own environment and the wider society. Still, as we have shown elsewhere, specifically the way in which the Jewish community is treated in the curricula (Hirsch and McAndrew 2014) causes teachers not only to question whether they can legitimately discuss these questions, but also to feel helpless before the task that this represents.

Textbooks, often considered as reference tools, probably encounter greater difficulties in putting forward these topics for discussion, since they are faced with two other important constraints. The first is to include current affairs in a book with a shelf life of several years and not have their relevance and legitimacy questioned in the long run. The second constraint seems to me to be even more important. As the experts themselves are still divided over these issues, how can a reference tool maintain a critical distance from the knowledge it imparts — crucial to the proper treatment of these issues — and, at the same time, propose that students deal with them? In other words, how can a textbook handle these "hot" subjects, so different from the "cooled knowledge" schools mostly teach (Legardez 2006).

These difficulties are easy to understand, but they also bring to the fore the relevance of how they are dealt with. These questions cannot be circumvented when teaching about religion in a pluralistic environment, even though the Program itself does so. Indeed, the very fact that the Program insists on treating these social phenomena (religion in general) from the students' own social environment, lends itself directly to these socially controversial issues. The void left by the Program and its textbooks cannot be easily filled by the teachers, who are just as much in a position of disadvantage in this situation. They have no tools to connect these conflicts to specific disciplinary themes, which would have been more than helpful on these occasions and lent legitimacy to the entire Program. The examples discussed here clearly illustrate that. Although the way they treat conflicts is not perfect, these workbooks do offer tools, knowledge, examples and references to the teacher who does not want to ignore the reality students live in.

CONCLUSION

The importance of dealing with conflicts between and with religions in contemporary society in the Ethics and Religious Culture Program is twofold. Firstly, it allows students to fully use the competencies they are developing, especially those that concern dialogue and the ability to express their own viewpoints. Secondly, it provides them with an opportunity to discuss the reality they live in, in which religion is frequently a source of conflict, or at least controversy. Thus, the challenges that this creates are also those that make this Program relevant to Québec's society.

It is extremely important to prepare teachers on how to deal with such subjects, so that they can judiciously consider different points of view without assuming any one right answer to a question, maintain a critical distance from the information available and the "common sense" that is so culturally ethnocentric, and avoid using emotion as a pedagogical tool, etc.

However, it is even more important to understand why these conflicts should be dealt with. In fact, the answer lies in the knowledge that by dealing with them in the classroom, we contribute, at the same time, to a better understanding of the phenomenon of religion (Competency 2 of the ERC Program), to the development of one's own point of view (Competency 1), and to learning how to engage in a dialogue with those you don't agree with or maybe do not even understand (Competency 3). In a way, it is these kinds of topics that make the Ethics and Religious Culture Program relevant.

ABOUT THE AUTHOR

Sivane Hirsch, a Professor at the Department of Education at the University of Québec at Trois-Rivières (UQTR), holds a dual PhD in Sociology (Paris-Descartes) and education (Laval University, Québec). Her thesis analyzes the perception university students in Québec, France and Israel have of contemporary spirituality as well as the way they integrate it in their daily lives. She further studied the role of religion in education as part of her postdoctoral research at the University of Montreal, within a larger project that analyzed the role of education in the relations between the Jewish community and other Quebecers. This included, on the one hand, the representation of the community, its history and its culture in the curriculum, and on the other hand, the articulation of Québec's Education Program with the specific educational project of Montreal's Jewish schools. Her current research concentrates on the treatment of religious and cultural diversity as well as other acute issues regarding religious markers in classrooms, studying mostly the challenges and opportunities associated with these teachings and its contribution to the relations between ethnic communities within schools. Email: Sivane.hirsch@uqtr.ca

REFERENCES

Hirsch, S., and M. McAndrew. 2014. "To Learn about the Other and to Get to Know Him: Judaism and the Jewish Community of Quebec as represented in Ethics and Religious Culture Textbooks." In *Textbook Gods. Genre, Text and Teaching Religious Studies*, eds. B.-O. Andreassen and J. R. Lewis, 86–97. Sheffield: Equinox Publishing.

Hirsch, S., and M. McAndrew. 2016. "L'enseignement de l'histoire des communautés juives au Québec: le traitement curriculaire et les besoins des enseignants." In *Judaïsme et éducation: enjeux et défis pédagogiques*, eds. S. Hirsch, M. McAndrew, J. Ipgrave, and G. Audet. Québec: Presses de l'Université Laval.

Legardez, A. 2006. "Enseigner des questions socialement vives. Quelques points de repères." In *L'école à l'épreuce de l'actualité. Enseigner les questions vives*, eds. A. Legardez and L. Simnneaux, 19–32. Issi-les-Moulieneaux: esf éditeur.

McAndrew, M. 2013. *Fragile Majorities and Education. Belgium, Catalonia, Northern Ireland, and Quebec*. Montreal: McGill-Queen's University Press.

Ministère de l'Éducation, du Loisir et du Sport. 2008. *Québec Education Program. Ethics and Religious Culture*. Quebec City: Ministère de l'Éducation, du Loisir et du Sport.

Morris, R. W. 2011. "Cultivating Reflection and Understanding: Foundations and Orientations of Quebec's Ethics and Religious Culture Program." *Religion and Education* 38(3): 188–211.

Maxwell, B., and S. Hirsch. (2016). Religion in National Systems of Education: Quebec. In B. Gates (ed.), *Religion in National Systems of Education: Insider and Outsider Perspectives in Religious Education in England*. Tübingen: Mohr Siebeck.

Tutiaux-Guillon, N. 2006. "Le difficile enseignement des 'questions vives' en histoire-géographie." In *L'école à l'épreuve de l'actualité. Enseigner les questions vives*, eds. A. Legardez and L. Simnneaux, 119–35. Issy-les -Moulineaux: esf éditeur.

List of Studied Textbooks

Brière, D., C. Mainville and M. Méthé. 2012. *Acteurs du monde A—B. Cahiers d'apprentissage*. Anjou: CEC.

Dubreuil, M., and S. Farley. 2014. *Vivre ensemble 4. Cahier de savoir et d'activité. 2e édition*. Montreal, ERPI.

Dubreuil, M., and S. Farley. 2014. *Vivre ensemble 5—Cahier d'activités et de savoirs. 2e édition*. Montreal: ERPI.

St-Onge, P.-L., M. Ladouceur and M. Paradis. 2015. *Libre accès—1er cycle (2e année)*. Montréal: Chenelière.

Tessier, J. 2014. *Vivre ensemble 2. 2e édition*. Montreal: ERPI.

Tessier, J., M. Dubreuil and S. Farley. 2014. *Vivre ensemble 1 (2e édition)*. Montreal: ERPI.

Endnotes

1. The complete data of the 2001 censure is available at: http://www.statcan.gc.ca/eng/start; and data of the 2011 National Household Survey here 2011 National Household Survey: Data tables.

2. This might be a response to those critics who consider that the ERC curriculum indoctrinates. However, it is an extremely difficult stance for teachers who want to broach more than just the general cultural manifestations of the different religions (as textbooks do, for example, by exploring religious patrimony through the images of churches and other architectural vestiges).

3. A recent favorable judgment to one school's claim to teach the Program in a "catholic perspective" was rendered on March 19, 2015.

4. http://montrealgazette.com/news/quebec/opposition-puts-pressure-on-government-to-act-on-values-after-shawinigan-refuses-mosque-permit

5. In this study we interviewed ERC teachers on their use of textbooks when teaching Québec's Jewish community's history. We realized that when they feel they know their subject well or when they are motivated to teach it, they prefer creating their own material, and seldom use the textbooks, other than as references tools. And when they broach a subject they have not mastered as well, they prefer to use the workbooks and one of its turnkey lessons.

6. REPRESENTATIONS OF ANTI-SEMITISM AND THE HOLOCAUST IN RE TEXTBOOKS FOR NORWEGIAN UPPER SECONDARY SCHOOL

Suzanne Anett Thobro

In recent years, there has been a public debate about the reoccurrence (or increasing occurrence) of anti-Semitism in Europe and Norway. This debate has been followed by a demand for more focus on anti-Semitism and the Holocaust in the Norwegian school system generally and in RE more specifically. Hoffman et al. (2012) found that 12.5 % of the Norwegian population could be said to have significant prejudice against Jews. The same research group recommends, on the basis of this report, that knowledge about Jewish history and anti-Semitism be strengthened in the Norwegian education system (Hoffman et al.: 10). Eidsvåg et al. (2011), in a report on anti-Semitism and racism in education, point directly to RE in their recommendations, saying that the subject is well suited as a context for counteracting religiously-motivated harassment.[1]

An alternative perspective on this is that the topic of anti-Semitism is not necessarily a natural part of teaching about Judaism as religion. In a report from 2014, Døving and Moe found that although there are differences between generations, the history of anti-Semitism was not the most significant building block in the formation of Jewish identity among Jews in Norway (2014: 11, 28). In England, according to Wintersgill (2014: 110), Jewish communities want less focus in RE textbooks on the topics of anti-Semitism and the Holocaust, and more on living religious practice. Døving and Moe found some similarities to this in their report on Jewish identity in Norway: younger Jews were more inclined than the older generations to point to positive aspects within Judaism — instead of the Holocaust — as the basis for Jewish identity (2014: 26). This alternate perspective is another good reason to examine how anti-Semitism and the Holocaust are and have been treated in RE textbooks.

During my research on maps in RE textbooks for upper secondary school (see Thobro 2014a, 2014b), I have noticed a change in the religions that are considered interesting from the Norwegian perspective. From the end of the 1930s until today, fewer and fewer religions have been presented in the RE textbooks, and in the most recent years there seems to be a tendency towards treating just three religions[2] as "important" enough to be included in all textbooks: Buddhism, Islam and Christianity. Judaism as well as Hinduism are no longer included in all of the newest textbooks for the RE course in upper secondary school.[3] This can in part — but only in part — be explained by the fact that Judaism is no longer a mandatory part of the RE curriculum. There has never been a one-to-one relationship between curricula and textbooks, so external factors are bound to have an impact. Whatever the reason for this narrowing of religion topics in the textbooks, it is nevertheless interesting, particularly considering the ongoing expressions of the wish for more of a focus on anti-Semitism and the Holocaust in RE.

My analysis will examine textbooks published between 1970 and 2014.[4] It is important to be aware that during this period a change took place in Norwegian society regarding the World War II (WWII) and the Holocaust, from having direct communication with these historical events, to one of indirect representations left in the collective/cultural memory (Lenz and Nilssen 2011a: 11–12). The further one goes into the period, the less the chance that the pupils will have living family members or others who can communicate direct experiences from WWII to them. Collective memory, as found in, for example, textbooks, therefore becomes more important as a mediator of knowledge about the Holocaust. This does not mean that textbooks are the only, or, for that matter, the most important influence on pupils' understanding of the Holocaust and anti-Semitism. Collective memory and discourses are formed in many social practices, but textbooks "constitute a genre in which established truths are conveyed [...]" (Andreassen 2014: 1). Examining how textbooks represent these topics is thus important, but it is necessary to be aware of the limits of this kind of analysis. One cannot conclude what pupils learn just by analyzing the textbooks they read.

In this chapter, I will look at how topics on anti-Semitism and the Holocaust are described in Judaism chapters in Norwegian RE textbooks for upper secondary school. My starting point is 1970, when Judaism first appeared as a separate religion category in an RE textbook, and the analysis will end with the latest published book (2014) for the school subject. I will not present a detailed analysis in this chapter of every book published during this period, but will provide an overview which will include examples of books published in the 1970s, the 80s, 90s, and the decades following the turn of the century. I will particularly focus on iconography in the second half of this chapter.[5]

RECENT RESEARCH ON ANTI-SEMITISM AND THE HOLOCAUST IN NORWEGIAN RE TEXTBOOKS

In a national research project on descriptions of ethnic and religious minorities in Norwegian teaching materials, Midtbøen et al. (2014) examined textbooks in the subjects of History, Social Studies and RE for lower and upper secondary school. All the analyzed books are from after the year 2000, and are the latest editions published. Among their findings is that anti-Semitism, in contrast to racism, is barely mentioned in the textbooks as a whole (Midtbøen et al. 2014: 83). In some books, however, the topic is described without the use of the *term* anti-Semitism, where, for example, a term such as "hatred of Jews" is used instead. History books highlight the topic more than books in the two other subjects, and for the most part anti-Semitism is described as something belonging to the past. However, RE textbooks differ in two interesting ways: (1) Midtbøen et al. found that "anti-Semitism" is mentioned twice as often as "racism" (10 to 5) in upper secondary textbooks, and that (2) it is treated in both lower and upper secondary textbooks as a topic relevant for contemporary Norway (Midtbøen et al. 2014: 82–113).

The textbooks in Midtbøen et al.'s analysis are, at the time of writing this chapter, the latest editions published. For the RE course in upper secondary school, that means three books (Gyldendal 2008; Cappelen Damm 2013; Aschehoug 2014).[6] These three textbooks are the "endpoint" in my data, while the starting point is 1970. Considering Midtbøen et al.'s findings in the most recent books, it will be interesting to see if the same patterns are evident in older textbooks. I will, however, not look at the prevalence of the term and topic of anti-Semitism in contrast to racism or other terms and topics, as Midtbøen et al. have done, but I will analyze how anti-Semitism is represented in the textbooks published all the way back in the 1970s. I will also go into a more detailed analysis of iconography. The reason for the focus on iconography will be explained below.

TEXT ANALYSIS

After working with textbooks as data for some years for my ongoing PhD project about cartographic representations of religion(s) (see Thobro 2014a, 2014b), I had hypothesized that Judaism chapters had large sections set apart for the treatment of anti-Semitism and the Holocaust. However, my analysis proved my original hypothesis to be incorrect. My findings resonate with the findings of Midtbøen et al. described above; anti-Semitism and the Holocaust are topics that are mentioned and elucidated in relatively small sections of textbooks' Judaism chapters. Additionally, anti-Semitism is seldom defined, and it is violent actions, not ideology, that are brought into focus.

In an article on teaching about the Holocaust in the subject of History after 2006, Harald Syse (2011: 41) raises an interesting question: in the classroom, is it practically possible to separate knowledge about anti-Semitism from collective memory about the Holocaust? What I have found in my data is that an analytical distinction between anti-Semitism and the Holocaust is not discussed in the textbooks. Neither are the terms anti-Semitism or the Holocaust used consistently, and, just as Midtbøen et al. found in their material, other terms and descriptions are used interchangeably. Why violence and violations against

Jews are committed is never thoroughly explained to the readers (the pupils).⁷ Anti-Semitism researchers often differentiate between different kinds of anti-Semitism. Eriksen et al. (2005: 7–9), in their substantial book about the history of anti-Semitism, employ Wolfgang Benz' (2004) distinction between four types: (1) anti-Judaism, which is primarily religiously motivated; (2) "modern" anti-Semitism, which is (was) based on the "scientific truths" of race and biology; (3) secondary anti-Semitism, which occurred after WWII, with role reversals between victims and perpetrators of the Holocaust; 4) anti-Semitism masked as anti-Zionism. These distinctions rarely find their way into the textbooks. This applies to the entirety of the period from 1970 to 2014. Because of this, my use of the term anti-Semitism in this chapter refers primarily to anti-Semitic actions or the consequences of some form of anti-Semitic ideology.

The text analysis is conducted with a special focus on intertextuality. Based on a rough idea of this volume's topic — violence — I have taken the terms anti-Semitism and Holocaust as starting points, nesting the description of these and other terms used in these descriptions from textbook to textbook. As part of this, I have not read the textbooks in any particular order, but have gone back and forth between books, trying to capture relevant text and voices, as well as significant absences (Fairclough 2003: 47). I have not limited the analysis to a predefinition with clear boundaries, but I have also explored possible borderline cases.

A Naturalized Part of the Discourse
It was, as mentioned, in 1970 that Judaism was represented for the first time in a textbook for upper secondary school on the topic of religions other than Christianity. From the very beginning, a clear discursive decision was made that chapters on Judaism in RE textbooks should focus on violence and violations against Jews. The terms being used are often "hatred of Jews" and "persecutions," not "anti-Semitism." The same pattern applies to the Holocaust as well, which seems to be a natural part of Judaism chapters with the effect from the 1970s, but not described by the term "Holocaust" until later.⁸

Short descriptions, such as this one repeated in Dreyer's and Gyldendal's textbooks from 1972 to 1989,⁹ are common, especially for the first part of the analyzed period:

> In the 15th Century Spanish Jews were exposed to great persecutions, but the worst of all persecutions Jews have experienced took place in Germany in 1930–1940's. It is believed that about six million Jews died during the Nazi regime in Germany.¹⁰

This discursive approach of non-elaborated information, which is characteristic for the textbook corpus in general, is heavily dependent on prerequisite knowledge on the part of the reader. As will be demonstrated below, this also applies to the textbooks' use of the iconography of atrocities and violent acts.

It should be noted that the Holocaust — though not by that name — is geographically limited to Germany in the quote. This is a very artificial limit, and is an expression of typical Norwegian discourse on the Holocaust as an atrocity happening *somewhere else*. I will explore this tendency below.

In the late 1980s, there was a change in the way anti-Semitism and the Holocaust were represented in textbooks. First, the actual terms start being used. Second, elaborations that are more substantial do occur. For example, in 1976 and 1982, Aschehoug publishes books in which the sections on these topics contain short formulations in the same style as the passage quoted above. Five years later, in 1987, both the headlines and the text body are markedly different and longer. Under the headlines "Diaspora—anti-Semitism—ghetto"[11] and "From Auschwitz to their own land"[12] fairly detailed descriptions are given about how Hitler attempted to destroy the Jewish population. Additionally, the term Holocaust is also both used and briefly explained. To quote a part of the longer section:

> The Jews were sent to concentration camps, among others Majdanek, Auschwitz, Treblinka and Bergen-Belsen where most died of hunger and other causes. Worst of all: They were annihilated in gas chambers. For this gruesome annihilation of Jews, we now use the Greek/English noun: Holocaust (= whole offering, burnt offering). When the war was over, 6 million of Europe's 9.7 million Jews had suffered death.[13]

However, in subsequent books from the same publisher, the sections on anti-Semitism and the Holocaust are shortened. Ten years later, in 1997, the details provided in the 1987 edition have vanished. The Holocaust is no longer mentioned by name,[14] but anti-Semitism is now said to be "anti-Jewish racism."[15] This reference to *race* is uncommon in the textbook corpus. In the article "Confronting Holocaust in Religious Education", Geoffrey Short points to erroneous links between religion and the Holocaust when describing pitfalls in teaching about the Holocaust in relation to Judaism. One pitfall is the assumption that the Holocaust was "essentially an expression of religious intolerance" (Short 2001: 41), another that "the Jews murdered during the Holocaust were necessarily committed to Judaism" (Short 2001: 42). It is likely, according to Short, that students will not have enough prerequisite knowledge to avoid making these assumptions when the Holocaust is represented as a part of education about Jewish *religion*.

Short's focus is on RE in England and Wales, but his observation is also relevant for Norwegian RE textbooks. In none of the books I am analyzing do the Judaism chapters clarify or elaborate on why Jews were persecuted, nor do they explain that religious behavior was irrelevant to the category "Jew" during the Holocaust. Even the above-mentioned book that speaks of "anti-Jewish racism," does not explain it further. The typical pattern is a representation that blurs the distinction between anti-Semitism based on race, and anti-Semitism (or anti-Judaism) based on religion. An example can be found in Cappelen's 2002-edition, where two full pages are devoted to the topic(s). Towards the end of the section, the Holocaust is described with reference to racial theories and nationalism. It is, however, summed up in the claim that "Judaism in Europe was almost eradicated,"[16] followed by a description of how Jews later refused to accept the idea of a God (i.e. stopped being religious) or "held on to their faith in God [and] tried to find various kinds of meaning in the sufferings, in the Jewish tradition."[17] This representation thus gives an impression that the Holocaust ultimately was about religion. Anti-Semitism in WWII is in some of the newer textbooks' sections on philosophy and ethics explained as having to do with race, but no connection is made between these sections and the Judaism chapters. The complexity of anti-Semitism is never revealed to readers of the textbooks.

It can be said that there is a slight tendency in successive textbooks towards longer and more detailed sections, but then one finds a return to relatively shorter descriptions by the end of the analyzed period.[18] As I will discuss later, only one of the three most recently published textbooks has a chapter on Judaism (Cappelen Damm 2013), and in that book the topics are placed in a textbox and thus separated from the rest of the chapter.

From Inclusion to Exclusion from Jewish History
Anti-Semitism, the Holocaust and Pogroms are described in textbooks from the 1970s, 1980s and 1990s as being *part of Jewish history*, culminating in the foundation of the state of Israel. There is no mention of anti-Semitism as a problem after WWII, prior to textbooks published after the year 2000. In, for example, Aschehoug's books from 1976 and 1982, the Holocaust and anti-Semitism are treated in the beginning of the Judaism chapter, in two sections called "A wandering people"[19] and "Ghetto, Zionism, their own land."[20] In this way the story of anti-Semitism, which in the textbook representations culminated in The Holocaust and the creation of Israel, are portrayed as the fulfilling of "an almost two thousand year old dream,"[21] and is thus represented as one of the most important aspects of Judaism.

Another example is Cappelen's 1992-edition, in which the section "Persecutions of Jews,"[22] which includes a synopsis of the history of anti-Semitism, is the last section under the heading "The Jews and history."[23] In the introduction to that segment, it is said:

> History is very important to the Jews. All their religious celebrations have their background and explanation in historical events. [...] Some claim that one of the reasons for the strong unity among the Jews is precisely their ability to cherish and remember their history.[24]

This stands in contrast to editions of textbooks published by the same publisher[25] in 2008 and 2013 where the topics on Anti-Semitism and the Holocaust are presented in a textbox and thereby thematized as history partly distinguished from the history of Judaism. The story of anti-Semitism is separated from the rest of the Judaism chapter, and therefore represented as being of less importance to the *religion* of Judaism.[26]

Other conflicts after WWII are rarely touched upon in the textbooks, but Gyldendal's 1975 book stands out. Instead of ending the history of Judaism section with the foundation of Israel — which, as I have mentioned, is common during the largest part of the analyzed period — the chapter begins with it. It is atypical that the establishment of Israel as a state is *not* contextualized in terms of anti-Semitism and WWII. The textbook in question also highlights that the foundation of Israel has been a source of conflicts between Jews and Arabs, mainly because of "the huge refugee problem that the foundation [...] created."[27] Such a political statement is rarely made in textbooks, both from the 1970s and later. It is, rather, typical for the period I am analyzing that no violent conflicts after 1948 are mentioned, either internal or external, political or religious.

This can however be found in more recent books, as in the above-mentioned editions from Cappelen Damm. The conflict between Israel and "the Palestinian population and the states bordering the country"[28] is treated in about half a page. Both today's settlements and Palestinian refugees after 1948 are stated as reasons contributing to an ongoing conflict. Secular Zionism and "Judaism's religious and cultural heritage"[29] are linked with the establishment of the state of Israel, but as in Gyldendal's textbook from 1975, it is not presented as the end point of a history of persecutions.

Anti-Semitism in the Norwegian Context
As mentioned above, Midtbøen et al. (2014) found that both History and Social Studies textbooks describe anti-Semitism as a thing of the past, but that RE textbooks relate it to the current Norwegian situation. My analysis shows that this is quite new for RE textbooks. In the 1970s, there was no mention of anti-Semitism in Norway. Anti-Semitism is something that has happened elsewhere, in addition to being something historical in the textbooks from this period. Later books do note anti-Semitism in Norway, but still only as a historical phenomenon "a long time ago." Often, the only relation to Norway are references to the so-called "Jew paragraph." Sometimes the writer and poet Henrik Wergeland's (1808–1845) struggle against the constitutional prohibition against Jews is highlighted. The focus is then not on the Jews or implications for Jews, but on the famous Norwegian writer and his compassion. This resonates with what Midtbøen et al. found in their research about today's history and social studies textbooks.

Det Norske Samlaget's textbook from 1992 is a typical example:

> The Norwegian law of Kristian V from 1687 establishes that no Jew can reside in the country without a special permit. The constitution from 1814 simply stated that 'Jews are still banned from the realm'. This so-called 'Jew paragraph' was not abolished before 1851.[30]

Nothing is said about the Norwegian situation after 1851, plus there is no mention of what happened to Norwegian Jews during WWII. Although anti-Semitism is presented as a Norwegian (historical) reality, the Holocaust is not. In "The

Norwegian Holocaust: Changing Views and Representations," Bruland and Tangestuen (2011: 593) describe the Norwegian perception of the Holocaust immediately after WWII as "a tendency to quietly forget." The Norwegian part in the Holocaust was never discussed in either public schools or the universities. The history of World War II was a "consensus history" in which internal differences and contradictions in Norwegian society during the war were left out (Lenz and Nilssen 2011a: 20), and this conventional-memory construction of the Norwegian community excluded Norwegian Jews from the narrative about WWII (Reitan 2011: 55).[31] The annihilation of Norwegian Jews first came into focus in the 1990s (Lenz and Nilssen 2011a: 20, Bruland and Tangestuen 2011: 596). I suggest that the longstanding omission of the Holocaust in Norway from the RE discourse on anti-Semitism is a part of this tendency to quietly forget.

A substantial change occurs in Det Norske Samlaget's 1997 edition. It includes a one-and-a-half page long section on Judaism in Norway which had not existed in the older (by five years) edition. A significant part of this new section highlights anti-Semitism and the Holocaust in Norway:

> When the Second World War started in 1940, there were a little over 1800 Jews in Norway. Anti-Jewish propaganda and legislation soon made the situation unbearable for them. In 1942, the old constitutional provision that Jews should not have access to the territory, was reintroduced. Arrests and deportations increased. Many fled to Sweden, but 795 Jews ended up in German concentration camps. Only 25 of them returned. In 1945, the Jewish congregation had only 559 members.[32]

Such an extensive elaboration in textbooks is rare. However, this description does not mention that *Norwegians* played a role in effecting the arrests and deportations — though, as mentioned, Norwegian public discourse started focusing on this theme in the 1990s (Bruland and Tangestuen 2011: 597). The same applies for Holocaust descriptions in books published after the year 2000, though it should be noted that in Cappelen 2002, it is noted that arrests of Norwegian Jews in 1942 were effected "with good help from Norwegian police."[33]

It is not until after the year 2000 that *contemporary* anti-Semitism in Norway is thematized in RE textbooks. Just as Midtbøen et al. pointed out (see above), references to Norway are found in the newest RE textbooks. However, it has to be remembered that only one out of the latest textbook editions on the market today from the three publishers Gyldendal (2008), Cappelen Damm (2013), Aschehoug (2014) includes a chapter on Judaism. This is part of the tendency I noted in the beginning of the chapter that fewer and fewer religions have been deemed important enough for pupils to learn about.[34]

Of the books from the three publishers mentioned, only Cappelen Damm has a separate chapter on Judaism. Cappelen Damm's 2013 edition has a section that is almost identical to their 2008 edition. Under the headline "Anti-Semitism"[35] a short synopsis of its history is given. The Holocaust is mentioned in only one sentence, and is, just as in older textbooks, represented as the end result of a longer history. It is asserted that "[t]oday, violent anti-Semitism in Europe is responded to sharply."[36] What distinguishes this synopsis from earlier ones, though, is the addition of a "but": "But that doesn't mean that anti-Semitism has vanished completely,"[37] followed by some examples. There are, however, some very interesting differences between the 2008 and 2013 editions. Firstly, in both editions, anti-Semitism is said to be a continuing problem, but in 2013 the phrase "also in Norway"[38] is added. This explicit relation to the Norwegian context does not exist in the previous edition. Second, in 2008 the reader is informed that "[a]nti-Semtisim is also a growing problem in Muslim countries and among some Muslims in Europe." The word "also"[39] indicates that although only Muslims and Muslim countries are mentioned explicitly, anti-Semitism is not a problem exclusive to them. In the next edition, though, "also" is taken out of the sentence, which makes Muslims the only contemporary group associated with anti-Semitism. The book does not explicitly say that anti-Semitism is limited to Muslims, but represents Muslims as the only group where the problem is growing.[40] These two changes result in a situation in which only one of the textbooks after 2010 addressing anti-Semitism in a chapter on Judaism, describes it as a relevant topic for the current Norwegian situation, but at the same time limits the responsibility for it to a certain group.

ICONOGRAPHIC ANALYSIS

In a paper from 1997, David D. Perlmutter conducted a study of images of the Holocaust in American secondary school History textbooks. He claims that:

> [o]ne of the most direct ways to understand the current social conception of the Holocaust is to look at its portrayal, particularly how it is pictured in visual images [...] The locus in which this display can best be measured as reflecting current social and cultural struggles and norms is the school textbook (Perlmutter 1997: 151).

Textbooks can be considered "power texts" that provide authorized stories and normative claims[41] (Andreassen 2014). Thus textbook images can be said to be "power images" that have the potential to have a great impact on readers (pupils).

As mentioned, before I began analyzing how anti-Semitism and the Holocaust have been represented in Norwegian textbooks, I had the impression that there were chapters on Judaism in many which included large sections devoted to these topics. However, my analysis proved my impression wrong; there are, as we have seen, mostly just a few passages in each textbook. Why, then, had I formed an impression that these treatments were larger? The answer is probably iconography. As Mary Hayward (2014: 140) remarks in her analysis of image use in textbooks, with reference to Pingel (2010: 49) and David (2000: 243), visual text has primacy over written text in memory. Prominent illustrations thematize violent acts against Jews in many of the RE textbooks I have analyzed, and even though these illustrations are few, considering the total number of pictures and photographs in chapters on Judaism, they draw attention to themselves.

The illustration motifs are diverse; there clearly is no common expectation in the RE textbook genre of what images of anti-Semitic violence should be used. Considering that there is a fairly large number of books that do not employ visual representations of the topics in question, this lack of discursive expectation becomes clearer. As stated above, there is evidently a discursive expectation in the period I am examining that textual representations (in the narrower sense) of anti-Semitism, or anti-Semitic acts, should occur in Judaism chapters, but visual representations appear optional. This means that not all pupils have had textbooks containing these kinds of images, and that the iconographic impact from that perspective can be said to be less than the impact of the relevant textual discourse.

In addition to diversity in the kind of motifs used, there is also variation in how violent they are. The less violent ones are, for example, portraits of Jews (named or anonymous) and an image of a Holocaust memorial; the most violent ones are of emaciated people and/or dead bodies.

In my analysis, the images are treated as visual text, and in relation to the written text. As in the text analysis (see above), I have not sharply predefined what kind of illustrations to include, but also looked at borderline cases. In this chapter I will present select samples, not a thorough analysis of every image.

General Tendencies
In his material on images of the Holocaust in textbooks, Perlmutter (1997) found six tendencies:[42] all Holocaust images had motifs from concentration or death camps, and other aspects of the Holocaust were thereby excluded; all non-Jewish non-victims were either German soldiers or liberators (the Allies); the Holocaust was primarily represented by photographs, with a few exceptions (art/sculpture); all but one photograph was black and white; only two images were of dead bodies, and these were emaciated corpses;[43] and collaborationists were absent from all images. Perlmutter's interpretation of these findings is that textbooks tend to avoid controversy by making an easily recognizable distinction between "good" and "bad."

In my data, I found some similarities to Perlmutter's findings, but also some differences. As in Perlmutter's study, photographs are mostly employed; other types of illustrations are exceptions. Photographs are mainly used when illustrating the Holocaust and WWII, whereas other types of illustrations are used to represent earlier expressions of anti-Semitic ideologies. The photographs in the RE textbooks are also in black and white, which is to be expected, considering both the age of the photographs and that colour print in textbooks did not become common before the 1990s. As I will discuss below, the use of black and white photos, though it might be expected given that they refer back to the first half of the twentieth century, probably contributes to an impression of authenticity and heightens the expectation that the photographs are showing atrocities.

Illustrations of dead bodies are rare in Norwegian RE textbooks, but the ones that do occur are some of the most violent images. While mostly Jewish victims are portrayed in the illustrations, there are also a few images with non-victims. Although German soldiers are shown in some photographs, liberators are not represented. Despite the differences from Perlmutter's findings in American History textbooks, I will also claim that the use of illustrations in Norwegian RE textbooks makes a clear distinction between "good" and "bad" that is easily detectible for readers (pupils).

Illustrations Stand for Themselves
It is typical for most textbook illustrations — not just in chapters on Judaism — that few have captions which explain or elaborate on what they are showing. The meaning of the illustrations must therefore be constructed in large part by the reader, based on the cotext[44] and context, and many of the textbook illustrations of violent acts against Jews draw heavily on an expectation of the reader's (pupil's) prior, prerequisite knowledge.[45] Two examples can be taken from Cappelen's 1992 edition. A whole page is set aside for two illustrations related to the Holocaust and WWII. They are both expressionist paintings from, respectively, 1945 and 1943.

The first is the painting "Sult" ("Hunger") by the Norwegian artist Kåre Øijord. The caption mentions that the artist painted it in the Neuengamme concentration camp, and that it shows "exhausted and hungry prisoners in a line for soup."[46] In the painting we see bareheaded people with unnaturally hollow eyes and thin faces, in striped garments. Nowhere else in the chapter are concentration camps and the atrocities going on inside them mentioned or elaborated on, but it is said in the section "Persecutions of the Jews"[47] that persecutions are what "we today first and foremost associate with the horrors that happened during the Second World War."[48] This is all that is explicitly said about WWII in the body of the text, and it is up to the reader to connect the visual statement in the Øijord painting and the information in the illustration's caption to the Holocaust and WWII.[49]

The second illustration is also a painting; "Jødene" ("The Jews") by the Norwegian artist Henrik Sørensen. It is printed on the same page as and just below "Sult," and shows only two women, who both, in contrast to the emaciated people in "Sult," appear normal. The caption says that "'The Jews' was painted in 1943, and is one of few paintings from this period with a clear political sting."[50] To me, this illustration is much less instinctively understood than the Øijord painting, because of the lack of signs of atrocities. Readers of the textbook have to either already be familiar with the painting, or have to use their imagination to make meaning out of the painting. The caption implies that it has to do with WWII and the Holocaust, but no information on how to interpret the illustration is given. The use of Norwegian painters hints at the fact that atrocities against Jews also happened in Norway during WWII, but nothing else in the Judaism chapter is said about this. The only reference to Norway in the section "Persecutions of Jews" is to the "Jew paragraph" in the Norwegian constitution and that it was taken out in 1851.

The expectation of the readers' capacity to make the connection is enhanced by the placing of the two paintings, not in the section about persecutions, but in a section on an unrelated topic. It is clear that a substantial prerequisite knowledge about anti-Semitism and especially WWII and the Holocaust is expected of the readers when these two paintings are used as illustrations in the 1992 textbook from Cappelen.

In textbooks where just short mentions of Anti-Semitism and the Holocaust are found, image use can be seen to function as an elaboration on these topics. In the aforementioned books published by Dreyer and Gyldendal, where the same phrasing is used in subsequent books from the beginning of the 1970s to the end of the 1980s, violent illustrations start being used in the 1980s. A black and white photograph covering half a page (but with no caption) of what can be interpreted as an arrest or preparation for an execution of several men, is used in the 1982 edition. In 1989, another black and white photo is included, along with the caption "Jews in a German concentration camp during the last World War. Prisoner next to his dead friend."[51] What we see is a man who seems to be crying sitting on a crate; beside him lies a half-naked, dead body that looks considerably starved. A barbed wire fence runs around them. It gives the reader a poignant example of "the worst of all persecutions."[52] However, as with the expressionist paintings described above, the reader has to be able to make the connection between anti-Semitic persecutions and concentration camps and the atrocities being carried out in them. These images function as, in the words of Isabel Wollaston (2010: 439), "visual shorthand for the Holocaust." The RE textbooks are dependent on reader familiarity with the discourse on the Holocaust and anti-Semitism from WWII.[53]

The Importance of Framing
In the following, I will compare three photographs being used, respectively, by Aschehoug (1996), Gyldendal (1997) and Cappelen (2002), to discuss how the framing — the cotext — of the illustrations are shaping how they are perceived (see for example Fairclough 2003: 53). These three photographs are all black and white. Two of them are directly linked to WWII in their captions, but the third one (Gyldendal 1997) is not. It is not even a violent image, but the reason I am including the photograph here is to point out the importance of framing and prerequisite knowledge in the reader to be able to make meaning of the illustrations, by comparing it to the two other illustrations. It is also an example of the fact that a clear distinction between images that illustrate violence and violations and images that do not is difficult to draw. It all depends on the cotext, context and the reader.

The photograph in Aschehoug's 1996 edition shows two women walking down a street. The situation looks quite "everyday"; the only thing remarkable is that one of the women is wearing the Star of David on her coat. The caption says: "The Jewish star was used as a symbol for the hatred of Jews during World War 2. Street image from Paris."[54] There are several aspects of this that are interesting.

The photograph is placed in the section "Anti-Semitism,"[55] but to see the headline to which the photograph belongs, one has to turn the page back. Because of this, there is no headline on the same page that could give an indication as to what kind of cruelty this "everyday" picture is meant to illustrate. The caption under the image does not explicitly link what we see to the atrocities done to the Jews, nor is there a description about what happened during WWII and the Holocaust in the text body in the Anti-Semitism section, except a mention of Hitler's racial doctrine and the claim that "We also know the ghettos from incidents under the Second World War (the Warszawa-ghetto)."[56] To make a larger picture out of the information given, both iconographic and textual (in the narrower sense), the reader has to apply substantial prior knowledge.

The photograph in Gyldendal's 1997 textbook shows a group of men walking towards the viewer. There are trees in the background, but that is all that can be seen apart from the group. The men are of different ages, and at least one (fairly old) child can be seen. In the foreground, an older man is carrying what is presumably a scroll. Some of the men appear to be talking, some are smiling, and others look serious. It seems like a diverse group in many ways, even though they apparently walk together as a group. The illustration does not have a caption, and even though the photograph is printed under the heading "Persecutions and genocide",[57] it is difficult to see anything in the image that points to violence or to atrocities. Based on the clothes the men are wearing, it is likely that the image is from the time around WWII, but, once again, there is nothing else, apart from the placement in the section thematizing anti-Semitism and the Holocaust, that links it to the theme. The reader never gets an explanation of what we see in the photograph. There is a possibility that it was originally taken in a situation where the consequences of anti-Semitic ideology took place, but in the textbook, there is no explanatory information.

The section in which the photograph is placed, however, thematizes anti-Semitic violations committed against Jews from the Middle Ages until WWII. The section is, as in most of the other textbooks I have analyzed, a short outline where the Holocaust, although not by that term, is mentioned in three sentences.[58] What makes the use of the photograph as an illustration interesting is that the framing — the section in which it is printed — probably will colour the reader's perception of it. On the page in question, the image and the heading are probably the first elements a reader will notice. Because the heading, "Persecutions and genocide," is about atrocities, it is plausible that the reader will perceive the photograph as illustrating just that.[59]

In Cappelen's 2002 edition, we also see a street motif, but it is significantly different from the photograph in Aschehoug 1996. The image is very dark, and in the background there are apartment buildings. It is likely a scene from a larger city (which the caption confirms). In the middle of the street there is a group of civilians, facing towards the viewer, walking with their hands raised. They are mainly adults, but one child can also be seen. On the side and behind them are soldiers. Some of the soldiers seem to be focused in other directions, but at least one looks

Figure 1. Photograph used in Cappelen's 2002 edition. In the textbook the image printed is dark and of poor quality, so the details are difficult to see. Public property.

like he is watching the group of civilians. There is a weapon in his hands. In the background, which is very dark, there might be flames and smoke, but it is difficult for the viewer to say for sure. The image in itself is violent. Whereas the photograph in Aschehoug's book, described earlier, is a more indirect statement of atrocities, Cappelen's is a more direct account. By this I do not mean to say that there is not a violation happening in Aschehoug's photograph, but that the viewer has to have another kind of prerequisite knowledge about the Holocaust to see the violation. It is easier — more intuitive — to recognize the motif in Cappelen's photograph as violence. No special knowledge about WWII, anti-Semitism or the Holocaust is needed to understand that the photograph documents and illustrates violence. It is clearly a war scene.

The framing of Cappelen's illustration enhances the violent appearance of the photograph. The illustration's caption is: "Jews are driven out of the ghetto in Warsaw in 1943,"[60] and it is printed in the section "Isolations and persecutions."[61] This section takes up two full pages of the Judaism chapter. The image, the caption, the size and the title of the section, and the textual representation in it, all work together to increase the overall expression of violence and violations.

The three illustrations described here are all used in textbook sections on anti-Semitism and the Holocaust, and they can be placed on a scale from showing a very violent scene to not depicting any violence or violations at all (seemingly, at least). In *Eyewitnessing; The Use of Images as Historical Evidence* (2001: 22), Peter

Figure 2. Woodcut from Hartmann Schedel's Nuremberg Chronicle (Die Schedelsche Weltchronik), printed in black and white in Det Norske Samlaget's 1992 and 1997 editions. Public property.

Burke notes, with reference to Sarah Graham-Brown (1988), that the texture and colour of a photograph also expresses a meaning. A black and white image can give the viewer a feeling of "harsh reality." Even though it is expected that the photographs are in black and white, as stated above, I would say that it is likely that the fact that they are heightens the expectation that they are showing atrocities, even when this cannot be explicitly seen in the image. It is also likely that this effect has increased over time, as illustrations in black and white stand out after colour printing in the textbooks becomes the norm in the second half of the period analyzed.

Illustrations Not Related to World War II
World War II is a topic Norwegian pupils do learn about, on several levels and in several subjects in school, and the Holocaust is a potent symbol in Norwegian culture (see for example Lenz and Nilssen 2011b). This could be a reason why the Holocaust is represented, both iconographically and textually, in a way that relies heavily on intertextuality and the reader's own knowledge about the topic. It is, however, not a fully satisfactory explanation, considering that the same applies to other illustrations of violent acts against Jews, unrelated to World War II.

For example, a woodcut print from 1475 "which shows how Jews are subjected to torture"[62] is used in Gyldendal's 1982 edition. In Det Norske Samlaget's 1992 and 1997 editions, the section "Anti-Semitism and New Wanderings"[63] is illustrated with a woodcut print of a similar type from 1493 (see figure 2).[64] The caption says "massacring of Jews in Europe,"[65] and shows people being executed by being burned alive. As with other illustrations, these are not explained further, and it is less likely that the reader will have the same degree of prerequisite knowledge about European persecutions of heretics in the fourteenth, fifteenth and sixteenth centuries to be able to place it in a context themselves — in contrast to the knowledge they probably have about World War II.

In some editions, Gyldendal prints a photograph of the relief on the Titus Arch in Rome (also used in other textbooks). The caption says: "A relief on the Titus Arch by the entrance to Forum Romanum in Rome. Emperor Titus brought, among other things, the seven-pointed candlestick and 97,000 Jewish prisoners to Rome."[66] There is no further explanation in the text, except the statement that "[a]fter the Romans destroyed Jerusalem and the temple in 70 AD, most Jews have lived dispersed in many parts of the world."[67] In the 1989 edition of the textbook, this illustration is placed on the opposite page to the photograph from the concentration camp. Although the last quoted statement is not printed in the section "Persecutions," but in the previous section, the image can be perceived as thematizing the same situation as the illustration next to it. Both images are, in their captions, said to illustrate Jewish prisoners. The relief will probably be perceived as an image of violence *because of* the caption, while the black and white photo on the opposite page to a greater extent "speaks for itself." The placement of the photographs, however, gives an impression of a timeline and that both are illustrations of the same phenomenon.

Anti-Semitism Illustrated Cartographically
There is only one publisher employing cartography as part of the visual representation of anti-Semitism. This is in the aforementioned book published in 1997 by Det Norske Samlaget. It is an unusual, but interesting way of highlighting the topic. Placed in the section "Judaism in Norway,"[68] which is about the historical development of demography and numbers of followers of the religion, the map is said to show "The first Jewish immigration to Norway."[69] On the map, information on where Jews emigrated from, why and when they emigrated, and the numbers of immigrants are given. Immigration in the periods 1852–1880 and 1880–1920 is compared in a textbox on the map, showing a substantial increase after 1880 (25 immigrant Jews before, 1200 after). The map, with its many arrows and scattered textual information, has a most uncommon discursive expression for textbook maps, and is therefore not necessarily easy to understand for readers.[70] It is unclear how the different pieces of information on the map are connected to each other. However, the visual effects give an impression of persecution, that a people has moved (or been moved) from one place to another on a large scale, first to an internal Russian/Polish area, and then to Norway. Texts on the map also enhance

this by the use of the terms "deported,"[71] "driven out"[72] and "pogrom waves."[73] The atrocities of the persecutions are underlined by their mention on the map, that when, in 1891, 2000 Jews were deported from St. Petersburg, "many [were] in shackles."[74] The map visually focuses on immigration to Norway, where the numbers were relatively small, but it is stated on the map that "[f]rom this town [Brody], in 1880 emigration began of over 2 million Jews from the Russian territory to USA, England, Europe, South-America and Palestine."[75] This again accentuates the violations the map is seeking to illustrate.

The map is cotextualized, as mentioned, by the section "Judaism in Norway." About a third of this section is about the situation for Norwegian Jews in WWII. Two facts are mentioned: that Jews had to flee the country, and that a little less than half of the Jewish population was deported to concentration camps. The textual representation (in a narrower sense) conveys a sense of Norway as both a place where Jews could flee to from anti-Semitic acts, and as a place where Jews were subjected to them. The cartographic representation shows that violence and violations happened *outside* of Norway, and Norway is represented as the country to which Jews flee. The textual and the cartographic representations therefore diverge; the map only depicts anti-Semitic violence as something that happened "somewhere else," while the textual representation conveys the notion "it also happened here."

Different Expressions Essentialized into One Phenomenon
Many of the images illustrating anti-Semitism in the textbooks are placed in time, by references to production year or to the situation in which they were made. The lack of contextualization, however, gives them an aura of interchangeability — that all images of violence or violations against Jews are expressions of the same phenomenon. As mentioned, definitions and the complexity of anti-Semitism are never thoroughly explained to readers, and this contributes to an understanding that time and space may give the expressions specific appearances, but that it is essentially the same. In this way, anti-Semitism acquires its own identity. According to Claudia Lenz (2011: 16), identity in Western thinking has been perceived as a phenomenon with an essence that remains the same despite changes in time or in perspective. In the textbooks, then, expressions of essentializing "the Jew" — that is, concrete situations of persecutions of, and violations against Jews because they are Jews — are themselves essentialised to *a* or *the* phenomenon (of anti-Semitism).

THREE INTERTWINED STRATEGIES FOR MARKING A DISTANCE FROM ANTI-SEMITISM

I would like to end this chapter by highlighting how the Norwegian RE textbook representations in general convey a distance from the problem of anti-Semitism. As mentioned in the beginning of the analysis, the topics of anti-Semitism and the Holocaust are naturalized as a part of Judaism chapters in the RE textbooks during the whole period. It is clear that learning about these topics in school has been deemed relevant for Norwegian pupils. Nevertheless, there are three intertwined strategies to be found in the textbook corpus for marking a distance between "Norwegian-ness" and anti-Semitism: temporal distance, spatial distance and distance to "the others."

The temporal distance is evident in both textual and iconographic representations, where anti-Semitic actions are epitomized as a historical phenomenon—something that happened "in the old days" — ending with the Holocaust. Very few of the textbooks mention conflict, violence or violations after WWII. The use of images and illustrations underlines this. Even when anti-Semitism is mentioned as a contemporary problem, as in the books from Cappelen Damm 2008 and 2013, the topic(s) are nonetheless illustrated by a black and white image from WWII.[76]

Although several of the textbooks mention that Jews were banned from Norway until 1851, violence and violations are, with some exceptions, represented as something happening elsewhere. This is the spatial distance, which is also evident in that the majority of images are, or at least appear to be, from outside of Norway. In a large study conducted by UNESCO and the George Eckert Institute (2015), *The International Status of Education about the Holocaust: A Global Mapping of Textbooks and Curricula*, Norway was found to supply the context for teaching about the Holocaust in secondary school History and Social Studies curricula, but not to say anything explicit or specific about it. The UNESCO study did not look at the curriculum or textbooks for RE. Even though it is noted that explicit references to the Holocaust are to be found in Norwegian History and Social Studies textbooks, these are not analyzed in the report. The international findings in the report are nevertheless interesting in comparison with my findings. Textbooks from 26 countries were analyzed, and were found to provide narratives not about the Holocaust, but about the Holocaust*s* (in plural). This is in part due to local historical concepts and narrative traditions, but also differences from textbook to textbook in the same country or region (UNESCO 2015: 160). The representations of anti-Semitism and the Holocaust found in my material must be understood as the Holocaust (or *a* Holocaust) *seen* from Norway. This Holocaust is something that happened *somewhere else*, not in Norway.

The last strategy for marking a distance is that when anti-Semitism is represented as both a contemporary and a Norwegian problem, it is linked explicitly only with Muslims. I have found that in the RE textbooks in general, Muslims have been, and to a certain degree still are, represented as "others." As one of only three religions that have an "obvious" status of importance in the most recent textbooks, and as one of two in the current curriculum,[77] Islam can be understood as being less "other" than Judaism.[78] However, Islam is still represented as "other," and it is remarkable that this group is the only one being explicitly mentioned when the growth of violence and violations against another "otherized" group is focused on in one of the most recent textbooks. In this way, anti-Semitism can be said to acquire a discursive function in a continuing othering of Muslims in the Norwegian society.[79]

The use of these three strategies can be understood in relation to the identity-forming project of the school system. That identity-formation is a main goal in the school system is made clear by the objects clause in the education law. Although the objects clause (and the education law) has changed during the period I have examined, from a clear focus on a Christian identity and values to more focus on "secular" values like democracy and human rights, the school system, religious education and textbooks have always communicated what it is to be *Norwegian* (see for example Thobro 2008; Iversen 2012; Døving 2011: 235). The marking of a distance to the phenomenon of anti-Semitism in the textbooks can be read as an expression of a normative claim: anti-Semitism and anti-Semitic violence and violations are (and should be) un-Norwegian. At the same time, however, the representations also result in a descriptive claim: that anti-Semitism and anti-Semitic acts have nothing to do with "us," and are somebody else's problem — either (1) the Norwegians of "the old days," (2) people outside the country, or (3) "the others" within the Norwegian realm. The first two can be found during the larger part of the analyzed period, the third is very new.

CONCLUSION

Although changes and differences in representations of anti-Semitism and the Holocaust have taken place, several overarching tendencies can be found in the RE textbook corpus during the period 1970–2014. There is a discursive expectation that anti-Semitism and the Holocaust should be addressed in Judaism chapters, but image-use appears optional. The topics are nevertheless given little space, with minor contextualization and explanation. Anti-Semitism is typically not defined, and it is violence and violations, not ideology, that are in focus. This applies to both text (in the narrow sense) and images. Although anti-Semitism is addressed in Judaism chapters in textbooks for religious education, the distinction between violations based on religion and violations based on race is not made clear to readers (pupils). All representations, both textual and iconographical, are heavily dependent on intertextuality and prerequisite knowledge by the reader. The forming of a Norwegian identity occurs in the textbook corpus through three strategies for marking a distance from anti-Semitism and the Holocaust, two of which can be found in the larger part of the analyzed period and a third which can be found in one of the most recent books.

ABOUT THE AUTHOR

Suzanne Anett Thobro was recently a Ph.D student at the Department of History and Religious Studies, University of Tromsø. The topic for her PhD project was cartographic representations of religions in textbooks used by the Norwegian upper secondary school system. Her latest publication is "Cartographic

Representations of Religion(s) in Norwegian Textbooks," in B.-O. Andreassen, and J. R. Lewis (eds) *Textbook Gods* (Equinox, 2014). Email: suzannethobro@gmail.com

SOURCE MATERIAL (BY PUBLISHER AND YEAR OF PUBLICATION, EDITION OR PRINT)

Aschehoug
Ribsskog, R. 1942. *Religionshistorie for gymnaset*. Oslo: Aschehoug.
Strøm, H. 1970. *Religionskunnskap og religionshistorie*. Oslo: Aschehoug.
Strøm, H. 1973. *Religionskunnskap og religionshistorie*. Oslo: Aschehoug.
Strøm, H. 1976. *Hinduismen, buddhismen, religioner i Kina og Japan: Religion for videregående skoler*. Oslo: Aschehoug.
Strøm, H. 1976. *Jødedommen, kristendommen, islam: Religion for vidaregåande skolar*. Oslo: Aschehoug.
Strøm, H. 1976. *Religionskunnskap: Afrikanske naturfolks religioner: Religion for videregående skoler*. Oslo: Aschehoug.
Strøm, H. 1976. *Religionskunnskap: Religionar i dag: Religion for vidaregåande skolar*. Oslo: Aschehoug.
Strøm, H. 1982. *Religioner i dag: Religionskunnskap for den videregående skolen*. Oslo: Aschehoug.
Strøm, H. 1987. *Religioner i dag*. Oslo: Aschehoug.
Elseth, E., B. Myhre, L. Akslen, J. Opsal, T. B. Pettersen and A. Østnor. 1996. *Veier og visjoner*. Oslo: Aschehoug.
Heiene, G., B. Myhre, J. Opsal, H. Skottene and A. Østnor. 1998. *Mening og mangfold: religion og etikk for den videregående skolen*. Oslo: Aschehoug.
Heiene, G., B. Myhre, J. Opsal, H. Skottene and A. Østnor. 2006. *Mening og mangfold: religion og etikk for den videregående skolen*. Oslo: Aschehoug.
Heiene, G., B. Myhre, J. Opsal, H. Skottene and A. Østnor. 2008. *Tro og tanke: religion og etikk for den videregående skolen*. Oslo: Aschehoug.
Heiene, G., B. Myhre, J. Opsal, H. Skottene, S. Tinderholt, K. A. Tysse-Hostad and A. Østnor. 2014. *Tro og tanke: religion og etikk for den videregående skolen*. Oslo: Aschehoug.

Cappelen/Cappelen Damm
Strøm, H. 1947. *Religionshistorie for gymnaset*. Oslo: Cappelen.
Strøm, H. 1948. *Religionshistorie for gymnasiet*. Oslo: Cappelen.
Strøm, H. 1956. *Religionshistorie for gymnaset*. Oslo: Cappelen.
Strøm, H. 1960. *Religionshistorie for gymnaset*. Oslo: Cappelen.
Strøm, H. 1968. *Religionshistorie for gymnaset*. Oslo: Cappelen.
Strøm, H. 1971. *Religionshistorie for gymnaset*. Oslo: Cappelen.

Dreyer
Hellern, V., H. Notaker and U. H. Stubbraaten. 1970. *Verdens religioner: Kristendomskunnskap for gymnaset*. Lærebok 1. Oslo: Dreyer.
Hellern, V., H. Notaker and U. H. Stubbraaten. 1972. *Verdens religioner: Lærebok med tekstsamling for videregående skoler*. Oslo: Dreyer.

Hellern, V., H. Notaker and U. H. Stubbraaten. 1975. *Verdens religioner: lærebok og tekstsamling.* Oslo: Dreyer.
Hellern, V., H. Notaker and U. H. Stubbraaten. 1976. *Religionane i verda: Lærebok og tekstsamling.* Oslo: Dreyer.
Hellern, V., H. Notaker and U. H. Stubbraaten. 1977. *Religionane i verda: Lærebok og tekstsamling.* Oslo: Dreyer.

Fabritius
Aasland, R. 1941. *Religionshistorie for gymnasiet.* Oslo: Fabritius.
Aasland, R. 1953. *Religionshistorie for gymnaset.* Oslo: Fabritius.
Aasland, R. 1956. *Religionshistorie for gymnaset.* Oslo: Fabritius.
Aasland, R. 1961. *Religionshistorie for gymnaset.* Oslo: Fabritius.
Aasland, R. 1966. *Religionshistorie for gymnaset.* Oslo: Fabritius.
Aasland, R. 1967. *Religionshistorie for gymnaset.* Oslo: Fabritius.
Aasland, R. 1971. *Religionshistorie for gymnaset.* Oslo: Fabritius.

Gyldendal
Jor, F. 1975. *De store spørsmål og de store svar: Religionskunnskap.* Oslo: Gyldendal.
Jor, F. 1976. *Dei store spørsmål og dei store svar: Religionskunnskap.* Oslo: Gyldendal.
Hellern, V., H. Notaker and J. Gaarder. 1984. *Verdens religioner.* Oslo: Gyldendal.
Hellern, V., H. Notaker and J. Gaarder. 1989. *Religionsboka.* Oslo: Gyldendal.
Hellern, V., H. Notaker and J. Gaarder. 1997. *Religionsboka : Religion, livssyn, etikk.* Oslo: Gyldendal.
Gaarder, J., V. Hellern and H. Notaker. 2000. *Religion og etikk: For den videregående skolen.* Oslo: Gyldendal.
Aronsen, C. F., L. Bomann-Larsen and H. Notaker. 2008. *Eksistens: Religion, etikk, livssyn, filosofi.* Oslo: Gyldendal undervisning.

Nomi/Luther
Skjerpe, O. 1973. *Religionskunnskap for videregående skoler.* Oslo: Nomi.
Skjerpe, O. 1974. *Religionskunnskap for vidaregåande skolar.* Oslo: Nomi. Luther).
Skjerpe, O. 1977. *Religionskunnskap for vidaregåande skolar.* Oslo: Luther.
Skjerpe, O. 1980. *Religionskunnskap for videregående skoler.* Oslo: Luther.

Det Norske amlaget
Christoffersen, S. A., T. Rasmussen and N. R. Thelle. 1992. *Mennesket og mysteriet.* Oslo: Det Norske Samlaget.
Christoffersen, S. A., T. Rasmussen and N. R. Thelle. 1997. *Mennesket og mysteriet: religion og etikk VK 2.* Oslo: Det Norske Samlaget.

Tanum
Jansen, H. L. 1941. *Religionshistorie for gymnasiet.* Oslo: Tanum.
Jansen, H. L. 1948. *Religionshistorie for gymnaset.* Oslo: Tanum.
Jansen, H. L. 1965. *Fremmede religioner.* Oslo: Tanum.
Jansen, H. L. 1968. *Fremmede religioner.* Oslo: Tanum.
Jansen, H. L. 1971. *Fremmede religioner.* Oslo: Tanum.

REFERENCES

Andreassen, Bengt-Ove. 2014. "Introduction: Theoretical Perspectives on Textbooks/Textbooks in Religious Studies Research." In *Textbook Gods: Genre, Text and Teaching Religious Studies*, eds. B.-O. Andreassen and J. R. Lewis. Sheffield/Bristol: Equinox Publishing.

Benz, Wolfgang. 2004. *Was ist Antisemitismus?* München: C. H. Beck.

Bruland, Bjarte, and Mats Tangestuen. 2001. "The Norwegian Holocaust: Changing Views and Representations." *Scandinavian Journal of History* 36(5): 587–604.

Bueie, Agnete Andresen. 2002. *Lærebokvalg—en formalisert og systematisk prosess? En undersøkelse av valg av lærebøker for norskfaget i den videregående skolen*. Rapport 11/2002. Tønsberg: Høgskolen i Vestfold.

Burke, Peter. 2001. *Eyewitnessing: The Use of Images as Historical Evidence*. Ithaca, NY: Cornell University Press.

Corell, Synne. 2007. "Hva er historien om krigen? Historiografien om den tyske okkupasjonen av Norge under annen verdenskrig." Fortid 2.

David, Robert G. 2000. "Imagining the Past: The Use of Archive Pictures in Secondary School History Textbooks." *Curriculum Journal* 11: 2: 225–46.

Døving, Cora Alexa. 2011. "Formidling av annen verdenskrig i et flerkulturelt klasserom." In *Fortiden i nåtiden: Nye veier i formidlingen av andre verdenskrigs historie*, eds. C. Lenz and T. R. Nilssen. Oslo: Universitetsforlaget.

Døving, Cora Alexa and Kraft, Siv Ellen. 2013. *Religion i pressen*. Oslo: Universitetsforlaget.

Eidsvåg, Inge et al. 2011. "Det kan skje igjen: Rapport fra Kunnskapsdepartementets arbeidsgruppe om antisemittisme og rasisme i skolen." Oslo: Kunnskapsdepartementet.

Eriksen, Trond Berg, Harket, Håkon and Lorenz, Einhart. 2005. *Jødehat: Antisemittismens historie fra antikken til i dag*. Oslo: Damm.

Fairclough, Norman. 2003. *Analysing Discourse: Textual Analysis for Social Research*. London and New York: Routledge.

Flottorp, Vigdis. 2002. *Forlagenes rolle i lærebokutvikling: En casestudie av arbeidet med to matematikkverk for grunnskolen*. Rapport 9. Tønsberg: Høgskolen i Vestfold.

Graham-Brown, Sarah. 1980. *Palestinians and their Society, 1880–1946: A Photographic Essay*. London: Quartet Books.

Hayward, Mary. 2014. "Visual Engagement: Textbooks and the Materiality of Religion." In *Textbook Gods: Genre, Text and Teaching Religious Studies*, eds. B.-O. Andreassen and J. R. Lewis. Sheffield/Bristol: Equinox Publishing.

Hoffman, Christhard et al. 2012. *Antisemittisme i Norge: Den norske befolkningens holdninger til jøder og andre minoriteter.* Oslo: HL-senteret.

Institute for the Study of Global Antisemitism and Policy. 2015. "Antisemitic Attitudes among Muslims in Europe: A Survey Review." ISGAP Occasional Paper Series 1.

Iversen, Lars Laird. 2012. *Learning to Be Norwegian: A Case Study of Identity Management in Religious Education in Norway*. Münster: Waxmann.

Lenz, Claudia. 2011. "Konstruksjon av den andre—teoretiske og historiske perspektiver." In *Forestillinger om jøder: aspekter ved konstruksjonen av en minoritet 1814–1940*, eds. V. Moe and Ø. Kopperud. Oslo: Unipub.

Lenz, Claudia, and T. R. Nilssen. 2011a. "Innledning: historiekultur, historiebevissthet og historisk kompetanse." In *Fortiden i nåtiden: Nye veier i formidlingen av andre verdenskrigs historie*, eds. C. Lenz and T. R. Nilssen. Oslo: Universitetsforlaget.

Lenz, C., and T. R. Nilssen, eds. 2001b. *Fortiden i nåtiden: Nye veier i formidlingen av andre verdenskrigs historie.* Oslo: Universitetsforlaget.

Midtbøen, Arnfinn H., Julia Orupabo and Åse Røthing. 2014. *Beskrivelser av etniske og religiøse minoriteter i læremidler.* Oslo: Institutt for samfunnsforskning.

Perlmutter, D. D. 1992. "The Vision of War in High School Social Science Textbooks." *Communication* 13(2): 143–60.

Perlmutter, David D. 1997. "Re-visions of the Holocaust: Textbook Images and Historical Mythmaking." *Howard Journal of Communications* 8(2): 151–59.

Pingel, Falk. 2010. *UNESCO Guidebook on Textbook Research and Textbook Revision.* 2. ed. Paris: Braunschweig: UNESCO/George Eckert Institute for International Textbook Research.

Reitan, Jon. 2011. "Nazileirene i den norske historiebevisstheten." In *Fortiden i nåtiden: Nye veier i formidlingen av andre verdenskrigs historie,* eds. C. Lenz, and T. R. Nilssen. Oslo: Universitetsforlaget.

Short, Geoffrey. 2001. "Confronting the Holocaust in Religious Education." *Journal of Beliefs & Values: Studies in Religion & Education* 22(1): 41–54.

Skarsem, Bjørn. 2007. "Andre verdenskrig i lærebøker for gymnaset/den videregående skolen." Master thesis, Norwegian University of Science and Technology. NTNU.

Store norske leksikon. "Holocaust: Folkemordet på jødene under andre verdenskrig." https://snl.no/Holocaust%3A_folkemordet_p%C3%A5_j%C3%B8dene_under_andre_verdenskrig (accessed 11.08.2015).

Syse, Harald. 2011. "Historieforståelse og holocaust i Kunnskapsløftet." In *Fortiden i nåtiden: Nye veier i formidlingen av andre verdenskrigs historie,* eds. C. Lenz and T. R. Nilssen. Oslo: Universitetsforlaget.

Thobro, Suzanne Anett. 2014. "Cartographic Representations of Religion(s) in Norwegian Textbooks." In *Textbook Gods: Genre, Text and Teaching Religious Studies,* eds. C. Lenz and T. R. Nilssen. Sheffield/Bristol: Equinox Publishing.

Thobro, Suzanne Anett. 2014. "Hva uttrykker kart?." *Religion og livssyn: Tidsskrift for religionslærerforeningen i Norge* 26(3): 41–45.

Thobro, Suzanne Anett. 2009. "Endringer i representasjoner av buddhisme: En analyse av norske lærebøker i perioden 1948–2006." *Dīn: tidskrift for religion og kultur* 4: 4–29.

Thobro, Suzanne Anett. 2008. "Representasjoner av buddhisme og hinduisme: En diskursanalyse i postkolonialt perspektiv av lærebøker i religionsfaget for gymnas/videregående skole." Master thesis, The University of Bergen.

UNESCO and George Eckert Institute. 2015. *The International Status of Education about the Holocaust: A Global Mapping of Textbooks and Curricula.* UNESCO.

United States Holocaust Memorial Museum, "Neuengamme," http://www.ushmm.org/wlc/en/article.php?ModuleId=10005539 (accessed 31.08.2015).

Wintersgill, Barbara. 2014. "Researching Materials Used to Teach about World Religions in Schools in England." In *Textbook Gods: Genre, Text and Teaching Religious Studies,* eds. C. Lenz and T. R. Nilssen. Sheffield/Bristol: Equinox Publishing.

Wollaston, Isabel. 2010. "The Absent, the Partial and the Iconic in Archival Photographs of the Holocaust." *Jewish Culture and History* 12(3): 439–62.

Endnotes

1. It is the RE subject for primary and lower secondary school that Eidsvåg et al. specifically mentions. The subject for upper secondary school, which is the focus of this chapter, has nevertheless been mentioned in the public debate.
2. In this chapter, I will not go into a discussion about the definition of "a religion," but follow the conventional categorization employed by the textbooks I analyze. See Thobro (2014a: 160) for more on this.
3. My data includes only printed books, not online resources. Although textbook publishers in recent years have provided online resources for use in RE, printed books are still the primary source of information.
4. Textbooks from the 1930s until 1970 have also been examined and found not to cover Judaism. These are also listed in the References at the end of this chapter.
5. I extend my thanks to everybody who has read and commented on earlier drafts of this chapter.
6. I will refer to the publisher's name and year of publication/edition/print to distinguish between the books, and not use the name of the authors except in references (see the References section for the full list of publishers). I have during my research noticed that publishers have more impact than authors on the textbooks. This is evident for example in the fact that even when authors are replaced by new ones, the textbooks remain very much the same. In a report from 2002, Bueie found it likely that the same reason explains why many teachers in the subject of Norwegian (the subject on Norwegian language, grammar and literature) do not choose textbooks on the basis of knowing the authors (2002: 33–34). With reference to Flottorp (2002), Bueie claims that the author is just one of many factors that contribute to a textbook, and that it is publishers that both choose the authors and make final decisions about the textbooks. With regard to discourse analysis, it can, from an ethical point of view, also be argued that it is problematic to "pin" discourses to specific authors, and I think both my findings and Bueie's claim strengthen this argument.
7. Pupils are not the only readers of textbooks, but also teachers, parents and so forth.
8. The Holocaust as a term for the WWII genocide of the Jews first came into use in the 1960s, and into regular use in the 1970s (Store norske leksikon, snl.no, accessed 11.08.2015, see References for full webpage reference). That the textbooks from the 1970s and beginning of the 1980s do not employ a specific term, but just descriptions, can be understood as a reflection of this, as textbooks tend to have a certain inertia in the internalization of external changes in discourses.
9. From 1982 and onwards, Gyldendal published subsequent editions of textbooks that were earlier published by Dreyer.
10. Norwegian text: "På 1400-tallet ble de spanske jøder utsatt for store forfølgelser, men de verste av alle forfølgelser som jødene har fått oppleve, fant sted i Tyskland i 1930–40-årene. Det antas at omkring seks millioner jøder døde under nazi-regimet i Tyskland" (Hellern et al. 1972: 18). All translations of quotes are my own. In the translations I have tried to stay as close to the Norwegian formulations as possible.
11. "Diáspora—antisemittisme—getto" (Strøm 1987: 63).
12. "fra Auschwitz til eget land" (Strøm 1987: 64).
13. "Jødene ble sendt til konsentrasjonsleirer, bl.a. Maidanek, Auschwitz, Treblinka og Bergen-Belsen der de fleste døde pga. sult og andre lidelser. Verst av alt: De ble tilintengjort

i gasskamre. Om denne grusomme tilintetgjørelsen av jøder bruker vi nå det gresk/engelske substantivet: holocaust (= heloffer, brennoffer). Da krigen var over, hadde 6 millioner av Europas 9,7 millioner jøder måttet lide døden" (Strøm 1987: 64, parenthesis in original). It is unclear whether the word "lidelser," which I have translated to "causes," is used as in the general meaning "sufferings" or as in "sickness" or "causes of death."

14. "Holocaust" is mentioned once in the textbook, but not in the chapter on Judaism. The term can be found in a suggested assignment in the back of the book, "The Holocaust as a theological problem," but it is neither explained nor further elaborated.

15. "antijødisk rasisme" (Heiene et al. 1997: 82).

16. "Jødedommen i Europa ble nærmest utryddet" (Kvamme et al. 2002: 59).

17. "holdt fast på sin gudstro [og] forsøkte i den jødiske tradisjonen å finne ulike former for mening i lidelsene" (Kvamme et al. 2002: 59).

18. I have not done a word count, so I cannot therefore determine whether the sections on these topics have more or less in relation to the total number of words in the Judaism chapters. A word count requires a clear-cut line between what counts and does not count as being text about the topic(s), but that line is difficult to draw.

19. Norwegian: "Et folk på vandring" (Strøm 1976: C1).

20. Norwegian: "Ghetto, sionisme, eget land" (Strøm 1976: C2).

21. "en nesten to tusen år gammel drøm" (Strøm 1976: C2).

22. "Jødeforfølgelser" (Grande and Myklebust 1992: 60).

23. "Jødene og historien" (Grande and Myklebust 1992: 57).

24. "Historien er svært viktig for jødene. Alle deres religiøse fester har sin bakgrunn og forklaring i historiske hendelser. [...] Noen hevder at en av årsakene til det sterke samholdet blant jødene nettopp er deres evne til å ta vare på og minnes historien" (Grande and Myklebust 1992: 57). As Harald Syse at The Center for Studies of the Holocaust and Religious Minorities (Oslo, Norway) has pointed out to me, this claim reproduces a myth about Judaism, and can therefore itself, because it lacks contextualization and explanation, be characterized as an anti-Semitic notion. This is an interesting aspect with several of the textbooks' Judaism chapters, and I would recommend this as a topic for further research on textbooks.

25. Now called Cappelen Damm.

26. It is of course still thematized in the Judaism chapter, and therefore more a part of Judaism than separated.

27. "det enorme flytkningproblemet som opprettelsen [...] skapte" (Jor 1975: 57).

28. "den palestinske befolkningen og statene som grenser til landet" (Kvamme et al. 2013: 159).

29. "jødedommens religiøse og kulturelle arv" (Kvamme et al. 2013: 159).

30. "Kristian 5.s norske lov av 1687 slår fast at ingen jøde må oppholde seg i landet uten spesiell tillatelse. Grunnloven av 1814 slo ganske enkelt fast at 'jøder er fremdeles utelukket fra riket'. Denne såkalte 'jødeparagrafen' ble ikke opphevet før i 1851" (Christoffersen et al. 1992: 98).

31. Reitan refers to Corell (2007) and Skarsem (2007).

32. "Da andre verdenskrig brøt ut i 1940, var det litt over 1800 jøder i Norge. Antijødisk propaganda og lovgivning gjorde snart situasjonen uutholdelig for dem. I 1942 ble den gamle grunnlovsbestemmelsen om at jøder ikke skulle ha adgang til riket, innført på nytt. Arrestasjonene og deportasjonene økte i omfang. Mange flyktet til Sverige, men 795 norske jøder endte

i tyske konsentrasjonsleirer. Bare 25 av dem vendte tilbake. I 1945 hadde den jødiske menigheten bare 559 medlemmer" (Christoffersen et al. 1997: 102f). What is meant by "den jødiske menigheten" is unclear. I have translated it to "the Jewish congregation," but it is possible that "menighet" is meant to refer to "community."

33. "med god hjelp fra norsk politi." (Kvamme et al. 2002: 60).

34. In later years, this seems to change from a narrowing to a shift in which religions are considered interesting in the Norwegian context. Sikhism is, for example, on the verge of being included. Even though this religion is still not represented with a chapter in any of the latest textbooks, Cappelen Damm now has a downloadable chapter on Sikhism following the same layout as other chapters in their printed book.

35. "Antisemittisme" (Kvamme et al. 2008: 189, 2013: 161).

36. Norwegian text: "I dag blir voldelig antisemittisme i Europa slått hardt ned på" (Kvamme et al. 2013: 161).

37. "Men det betyr ikke at antisemittismen har forsvunnet helt" (Kvamme et al. 2013: 161).

38. "også i Norge" (Kvamme et al. 2013: 161).

39. "også."

40. In a survey review from the Institute for the Study of Global Antisemitism and Policy (2015) it was found that anti-Semitic attitudes are higher in the Muslim population in many European countries. This, however, does not justify linking the problem exclusively to that group.

41. Before 2001 all Norwegian textbooks had to be officially approved, and thereby the authority was also national.

42. All the examined textbooks in Perlmutter's study are from the 1980s and 90s.

43. In an earlier study of images of war, Perlmutter (1992: 155) found that death was almost always being shown as a result of combat, with the exception of these Holocaust images.

44. Cotext (not context) refers to surrounding text (both in a narrow and wide sense) on the same and following pages.

45. This is in different degrees true for every kind of illustration.

46. "utslitte og utsultede fanger i suppekø" (Grande and Myklebust 1992: 62).

47. "Jødeforfølgelser" (Grande and Myklebust 1992: 60).

48. "Jødeforfølgelser forbinder vi i dag først og fremst med de grusomhetene som skjedde under annen verdenskrig" (Grande and Myklebust 1992: 60).

49. Something that underlines the interchangeability of the images being used to illustrate anti-Semitism (see more below), is the fact that very few of the prisoners in the Neuengamme were Jews. According to the United States Holocaust Memorial Museum, about 13,000 out of 104,000-106,000 prisoners, during the period 1938-1945, were Jews (www.ushmm.org, accessed 31.08.2015, see References for full webpage). I would like to thank Harald Syse at the Norwegian Center for Studies of Holocaust and Religious Minorities for pointing this out to me.

50. "'Jødene' ble malt i 1943 og er et av de svært få maleriene fra denne perioden med en klar politisk brodd" (Grande and Myklebust 1992: 62).

51. "Jøder i tysk konsentrasjonsleir under siste verdenskrig. Fange ved sin døde kamerat" (Hellern et al. 1989: 97).

52. See above for full quotation.

53. In the last quote it is said that the men we see are Jews. However, as touched upon in note

49, Jews were not the only ones being detained in concentration camps. This fact is underexposed in the textbooks, and claims like the one in the quote probably contribute to a misunderstanding about the difference between concentration camps and death camps.

54. "Jødestjernen ble brukt som et symbol på jødehatet under 2. verdenskrig. Gatebilde fra Paris" (Elseth et al. 1996: 80). The claim in this quote is rather odd, as it is more correct to say that the Star of David was used as an identifying symbol separating Jews from other citizens.

55. "Antisemittisme." (Elseth et al. 1996: 79).

56. "Gettoene kjenner vi også fra hendinger under den annen verdenskrig (Warszawa-gettoen)" (Elseth et al. 1996: 80, parenthesis in original).

57. "Forfølgelser og folkemord" (Gaarder et al. 1997: 94).

58. The terms anti-Semitism and the Holocaust are not used in the text body surrounding the illustration. Anti-Semitism is used and elaborated on in a different part of the book, "Life Stance, Philosophy and Ideology," which is separated from religion both in terms of the layout of the book and thematically. This resonates with the curriculum. I have not included this in my analysis because it is how these topics are represented in the Judaism chapters in textbooks which is my interest.

59. When working with these textbooks, but not directly on Judaism chapters, I have always thought about this image in Gyldendal 1997 as illustrating violence and violations against Jews, and it therefore surprised me to find, when I looked closer, that it does not. It would have been interesting to, for example, interview pupils and teachers on how they perceive this image. Even without having done that, I still think it is fair to say that because of its placement in the textbook, it is a picture that is easily "misunderstood" to illustrate persecutions and genocide.

60. "Jøder drives ut av gettoen i Warszawa i 1943" (Kvamme et al. 2002: 58).

61. "Isolasjon og forfølgelser" (Kvamme et al. 2002: 58).

62. "som viser hvordan jøder utsettes for tortur" (Hellern et al. 1982: 36).

63. "Antisemittisme og nye vandringer" (Christoffersen et al. 1997: 87).

64. The woodcut is from Hartmann Schedel's *Nuremberg Chronicle (Die Schedelsche Weltchronik)*. This information is not given in the caption.

65. "Massakrering av jøder i Europa" (Christoffersen et al. 1997: 87).

66. "Et relieff på Titusbuen som står ved inngangen til Forum Romanum i Roma. Keiser Titus brakte blant annet den sjuarmede lysestaken og 97 000 fanger til Roma" (Hellern et al. 1989: 96).

67. "Etter at romerne ødela Jerusalem og tempelet i år 70 e Kr, har de fleste jødene levd spredt over store deler av verden" (Hellern et al. 1989: 96). It is interesting that this is mentioned as the last sentence in the section under the headline "The Judaism Forms" ("Jødedommen blir til"), and is not thematized further as violence/atrocities against Jews.

68. "Jødedommen i Norge" (Christoffersen et al. 1997: 102).

69. "Den første jødiske innvandringen til Norge" (Christoffersen et al. 1997: 102).

70. See Thobro 2014a and 2014b for more on textbook maps.

71. "Deportert."

72. "Fordrevet."

73. "Pogrombølgene."

74. "mange [var] i lenker" (Christoffersen et al. 1997: 102).

75. "Fra denne byen [Brody] begynte i 1880 utvandringen av 2 millioner jøder fra det rus-

siske området til USA, England, Europa, Sør-Amerika og Palestina" (Christoffersen et al. 1997: 102).

76. This black and white image is of Ruth Maier, who died during the Holocaust — or to be more precise, it is the cover of the 2007 publication of her diary (Aschehoug). This illustration has two "layers," both an historical layer and a contemporary layer, but I see it as likely that it is the historical layer that will be noticed by readers of the textbook as it is the most prominent.

77. The others being Christianity and Buddhism in the textbooks, and Christianity in the curriculum. As Cora Alexa Døving and Siv Ellen Kraft (2013: 83) have pointed out, "othering" of every religion apart from Christianity can also be found in the objects clause in the educational act from 2008.

78. Muslims can also be said to be less "other" than other religions in earlier textbooks, see for example, S. Thobro 2008: 51–53 and Thobro 2009: 10.

79. By this I do not mean that textbook publishers or writers do this deliberately.

7. ANICONISM AND IMAGES IN NORWEGIAN RELIGIOUS EDUCATION TEXTBOOKS: REPRESENTATIONS AND HISTORICAL CHANGE[1]

Sissel Undheim

INTRODUCTION: TEXTBOOKS AND RELIGIOUS EDUCATION IN NORWAY

As interpretations and concretizations of local or national curricula, textbooks play a substantial role in religious education. The integrative Religious Education (RE) subject in Norway has passed through a number of revisions since 1997, being known by the acronym KRL, presently KRLE, with a significant period between 2008 and 2015 when the subject was known as RLE.[2] Given the topical range as well as the historical controversy of the subject, teachers, particularly in primary and middle school, appear to have been and still be rather dependent on textbooks in their teaching.[3] Norwegian RE textbooks consist of highly multimodal texts, where images, texts and symbols combine in meaning making.[4] As for all textbooks, the aim is to convincingly present the subject matter by means of establishing trustworthy and authoritative voices. As Bengt-Ove Andreassen has convincingly pointed out, the selection of subject matter and representations of this subject matter thus carry political implications.[5] In the encounter with teachers and pupils in the classroom, the choices made and presented by authors and editors consequently contribute to shape not only individual, but also collective, conceptions and understandings of religion and religious traditions.[6] While many recent studies have focused on textual representations of Islam in textbooks,[7] less attention has been given visual or multimodal representation. By comparing two "generations" of textbooks written for Norwegian integrative RE,[8] it is possible to trace change in how textbook authors and publishers have used images, and particularly visual art, as part of the subject matter in the period since mandatory and integrative RE was introduced in Norway in 1997. The analysis will focus on visual representations of Islam in textbooks for pupils aged 10-12. As material for comparison, I will use sections that thematize Judaism in the same books or textbook series. I will then discuss some of the changes that are visible in the material in light of some of the contemporary research on Islamic figurative and non-figurative art.⁹

In 1997 the Royal Ministry of Church, Education and Research (as it was then named) launched a completely new curriculum for the Norwegian school subject then known as "Knowledge of Christianity" (*Kristendomskunnskap*). As signaled in this new curriculum, both the name of the subject and its content was renewed and expanded by adding to the name "Knowledge of Christianity" the following specification: "— with Orientation in Religion and Philosophies of Life" (*—med religions- og livsynsorientering*, abbreviated *KRL*). This new subject was intended to replace the earlier, separative and confessional subject that had been the main option for the majority of Norwegian school children.¹⁰ The inclusion of "Other Religions" as well as "Philosophies of Life" was justified in a lengthy and detailed curriculum, where competence aims for each school year from 1-10 were outlined. In the 343 page-long and richly art studded national curriculum that was published in 1997, KRL was presented as the first gem of the subject collection that succeeded the core curriculum. Perhaps unsurprisingly, the new subject turned out to be quite controversial. With the start of the new school year in August 2015, Norwegian teachers faced the fourth curriculum revision/name change since 1997, indicating some of the controversies that in turn have brought changes along the way.¹¹ The Press Release following this last curriculum change of 2015 stated however that there was no need to revise or publish new textbooks, despite the rather substantial skewing of subject matter which quantitatively favors Christianity over other topics.

The main focus of this specific study will be textbooks written for the curricula of 1997 (KRL) and 2008 (RLE). The aim is to detect changes in visual representations of Islam and Judaism in these two "generations" of Norwegian RE textbooks. The main body of the material will be books written for pupils in grade 3-6, that is pupils aged approximately 9-12. There are several reasons for this selection of material. Firstly, these textbooks are the ones that most closely answer to the curriculum changes, and thus may be said to clearly belong to two different textbook generations. Revised and new textbooks for secondary school have also been produced, but do not follow the curriculum revisions as closely in time as the ones for primary school do.¹²

The subject matter is largely organized in terms of seven seemingly equal and clearly demarcated units, based on five world religions,¹³ with the addition of Secular Humanism and Philosophy and Ethics. These seven categories are often demarcated by organization into chapters dedicated to each "religion," a thematic structure which is particularly evident when it comes to the parts of curriculum originally phrased as "other religions" (i.e. other than Christianity). This "world religion" structure, combined with organization loosely corresponding to Ninan Smart's "dimensions," thus also lay the ground for comparative perspectives in this textbook analysis.

"THE AESTHETIC DIMENSION"

With a recognizable nod to the dimensions of Ninian Smart,[14] the "aesthetic dimension" became a prominent feature of the new subject *Knowledge of Christianity with Orientation in Religion and Philosophies of Life*. In the curriculum of 1997, it is stated that:

> The aesthetic dimension has throughout all of history been a central part of religious expression. It is obvious then that this relationship ought to be part of the education through emphasis on visual arts, architecture, music, drama and literary texts.[15]

On the previous page of the document, however, it was stated that "the same pedagogical principles shall found the basis for working with Christianity and other religions and philosophies of life."[16] This could potentially lead to a didactic dilemma, as parts of the subject may exclude certain methods for working with religious aesthetics, while others may depend on it. In the debates that followed the RE subject of 1997, it was argued that working with religious aesthetics on the one hand might be problematic because it could be experienced as involvement, and thus subjectively be considered religious practice or participation, or, on the other hand, be deemed as blasphemous and/or disrespectful behavior towards what some considered most sacred. Such subjective assessment of teaching methods as conflicting with individual religious views could in turn be a reason for parents to take their children temporarily out of class.[17] The Norwegian researcher, Geir Winje, has pointed out that RE represents fundamental didactic challenges because the curriculum so insistently states that "[c]lassroom teaching shall not include preaching, proselytising or religious practice," while the material the pupils work with in class in fact consists of texts and images that are originally made in order to "preach" and "proselytise."[18]

The 2008 curriculum thus also holds this tension between on the one hand attending to different religious "insider perspectives," — that is, an emic understanding of religion that aims at representing the adherents' own world views — and on the other hand upholding an outsider perspective that is objective, critical and pluralistic.[19]

> Religion, Philosophies of life and Ethics is an ordinary school subject intended to bring all pupils together. The Norwegian Education Act demands that the teaching of this subject be objective, critical and pluralistic. [...] The principles of equivalent education shall be the basis for teaching in the subject. This involves treating all religions and philosophies of life in an academic and professional manner based on the distinctive characteristics and diversity of all religions.[20]

The 1997 and 2008 curricula's emphasis on the aesthetic dimension are reflected in amply illustrated textbooks. The books published in 1997, as well as those released in connection with the revision of 2008, are all strikingly adorned with colorful photographs and art historical treasures from all over the world and across time periods. In 2003 Geir Winje published a report assessing the art used in the KRL textbooks. His criticism of the 1997 generation was that some of the art that was selected and reproduced in the books was not representative of the majority within certain religious groups. He argued that the manner of illustrating Christian narratives, including Old Testament narratives shared by the three Abrahamic traditions, by the use of central work from the Western art historical canon was highly problematic, particularly with respect to the aniconic traditions of both Islam and Judaism.

PROHIBITED IMAGES? IMAGES, ANICONISM AND ICONOCLASM

If much of Islam and Islamic traditions were quite unknown to the majority of the Western world throughout most of the twentieth century,[21] the media coverage of the so-called Cartoon controversy of 2005 and 2006 brought Islamic aniconism to everybody's attention. It has been frequently argued that the anger aroused by the cartoons printed in the Danish newspaper *Jyllandsposten* was caused by what was deemed blasphemous depictions of the prophet Muhammad, and thus not necessarily having anything to do with so-called aniconism. However, the motivation for the publication of the cartoons was presented by the editor, Flemming Rose, as a response to what was seen as self-censorship among Danish artists, referring to a planned Muhammad biography for children that allegedly had been discarded because the author had not been able to engage an illustrator for the project.[22] Despite otherwise seemingly obvious distinctions between art produced to provoke, art produced for devotion, and what might here be called pedagogical children's book illustrations, media coverage of the cartoon controversy nevertheless seems to have conflated all combinations of "image" and "Islam" under the rubric of "Islamic aniconism." The aggressive iconoclastic assaults launched by the Taliban in Bamiyan and the even more recent so-called Islamic State in Palmyra in Syria have further contributed to a mass mediated general image of Islam and figurative art as incompatible, an impression so much more strengthened by the terrorist attack on the French satirical cartoon magazine *Charlie Hebdo* on January 7th 2015. Although the images said to cause these violent attacks, as well as the specific context and religious justifications given by the attackers, were indeed very different, they all thus eventually seem, in the eyes of Western media consumers, to be understood in terms of "Islamic aniconism" or "prohibition of images" (Bildeforbud/Bilderverbot).[23] More general knowledge of so-called Islamic aniconism among non-Muslims was therefore, at least in Norway, seemingly tied to the cartoon controversy. But what does such "prohibition" against images imply? What cannot, according to Islam, be rendered in image? Humans? Animals? The prophet

Muhammad? Allah? In which circumstances are figurative images problematic? Always and forever, or only in certain contexts and settings? What is often called "aniconism" is in fact a bewildering span of variations within (and outside of) the boundaries set by norms and religious laws that state, or even negotiate, what can be visually represented when, where and in what form. So-called aniconism and iconoclastic movements are found within several religious traditions at different historical periods, while other groups, even within the same religious traditions, assign pivotal cultic roles to figurative images and sculptures.[24] As norms and rules are constant subjects of negotiation among different groups in a society, the same will apply for various religiously founded prohibitions against use and fashioning of images. The media coverage of the cartoon controversy of 2006 appears to have caused a political polarization where "Islamic hostility towards images" was presented as a characteristic feature of Islam. However, it also gradually seems to have re-opened for discussion more nuanced views of Islamic art by bringing figurative traditions within Islam to the fore again. A number of Muslims publicly voiced plurality within Islam in response to religious authorities and others who argued for stricter interpretations.[25] Many scholars will point to the fact that the Qur'an itself contains no prohibition against making images. Some passages in the Qur'an have however been put forth as support for Islamic aniconism, particularly the description of Abraham's cleansing of the Ka'ba by throwing the pagan idols out.[26] The Hadiths, on the other hand, contain a number of narratives about the life of the prophet and his family where the fashioning, as well as display of images, are not approved of.[27] Officially, hadiths do not have status and authority as sacred scripture like the Qur'an has. These texts are however very important in Islam as part of Sunnah ("tradition"), and are as such considered to be authoritative sources in Islamic jurisprudence (*fiqh*) and thus for Islamic law (*sharia*). There are several schools of Islamic law, and hadiths are interpreted differently according to different schools and traditions. The dissemination of some of these hadiths also indicates variations that may be understood in terms of geographical and cultural contexts. This in turn implies that there will be quite a lot of variation, both historically and geographically, when it comes to Muslims' own interpretations of so-called aniconism.[28] Ingvild Flaskerud has pointed out that, considering the large amount of visual figurative expressions that we already know from different Muslim traditions, it is impossible to speak of a general aniconism or prohibition against images in Islam, neither in theological nor in a practical sense.[29]

With this plurality of Islamic visual expressions in mind, the selection and rendering of images in Norwegian textbooks becomes an interesting topic to investigate as expressions of how Norwegian publishers and textbook authors have interpreted and rendered Islamic aniconism. To the extent that the subject material the students encounter ought to be representative of religious traditions that are neither homogenous nor constant, while the classroom at the same time is to provide a space for encounters between individuals that identify with a wide variety of religious majority and minority groups, images and visual art may certainly represent some fundamental didactic challenges for publishers, authors and teachers alike.

TEXTBOOKS — SELECTION AND MATERIAL FOR THE ANALYSIS

In the curriculum of 1997, the competence aims are very specific, and the learning outcome detailed for every year from 1-10. For middle school, topics concerning Islam and Judaism (translated into "chapters" in the textbooks) were placed on year 5 (Islam) and 6 (Judaism).[30] The analysis of the 1997 books therefore focus on the books for these years, published by four different publishers. In addition, a rather large two-volume "Source Collection" (*Kildesamlingen*) was published by the National Centre for teaching aid (then a center under the Ministry of Church, Education and Research) as a resource for teachers when the new subject was introduced in 1997. For the textbooks published around the time of the 2008 revision, the topics (still organized mainly in terms of "world religions"), are spread over all years, and not assigned to a specific age group as in 1997. The material analyzed here will therefore also be from books for pupils for year 3-5, where there will be chapters on Islam and Judaism in all books. At the time of the name change and curriculum revision of 2008, three Norwegian publishers chose to write completely new textbooks. A forth publisher had started on a new textbook series for all ten years as early as in 2006, and later volumes have been adapted to the new curriculum.[31] The publisher Gyldendal also introduced an illustrated "Book of Narratives" (*Vivo-Fortellingsbok*) which, although of a much lesser scale than the 1997 source collection, may still contribute in the analysis as a reference for comparison. This very specific link between curricula and textbooks, and the time span between the publications corresponding so neatly to the curriculum revisions of 1997 and 2008 make it possible to speak of two "generations" of textbooks that it makes sense to compare also in a historical perspective.

TEXTBOOKS OF THE 1997 GENERATION

A review of the chapters on Islam in all the textbooks for year 5 from 1997 demonstrates that various sources were used in the selections of illustrations and images. Although photographs by far constitute the dominating form of visual representation,[32] there is also use of maps[33] and specifically appointed illustrators in addition to reproductions of existing visual art. Among the reproductions of art historical material, there are examples provided by photographs of architecture, calligraphy and geometric and botanical ornamental art as well as reproductions of art with anthropomorphous and zoomorphous figures. A telling example is the Persian miniature attributed to Aqa Mirak which covers a whole page (A4) in the Source Collection.[34] In this image,[35] perhaps best known as Mi'raj, the viewer is presented with the ascent of the prophet Muhammad, riding on Burak and surrounded by angels. The prophet and Burak are placed in the center of the image, and the prophet is encircled by an aureole of golden flames. The prophet also differs from the other anthropomorphic figures (the angels) by the fact that his face is covered by a white veil, and thus not rendered. The text that accompanies the image specifies that this is not representative of traditional Sunni Islam:

> Illustration from a 16th century Persian manuscript made for Shah Tahmasp. In the Persian tradition, one has been less reluctant with depictions than in Islamic culture in general. The prophet's ascent has been a favored motif. Traditional sunni-Islam prohibits these kinds of images.[36]

A very small version of this motif is also found in the textbook *Reiser i tid og tro* ("Travels in Time and Faith") for 5th grade, where it is placed in the margins on page 134. The colors of this reproduction differ quite a bit from the one in the Source Collection, and this version is so small that the details are difficult to make out, but apart from that, the two motifs are similar, and obviously belonging to the same tradition.[37]

We also encounter visual representations of the prophet Muhammad in some of the other textbooks of the 1997 generation. The book *Broene 5* ("Bridges 5"), renders a miniature accompanied by the following text: "The angel Gabriel appears before Muhammad."[38] As in the Aka Mirak miniature, the prophet's face is covered, while that of Gabriel is not. Returning to *Reiser i tid og tro 5* ("Travels in Time and Faith 5"), there is another miniature rendered, with the text "Muhammad with the four caliphs." In this image, Muhammad sits enthroned with the golden, flame-like aureole around his body, as in the other two examples. Once again, the face is covered, apparently by a white veil, but it is turned towards Gabriel (Jibril) who approaches the prophet from above in the left corner. The four caliphs are seated in front of Muhammad in the lower right hand corner of the image. The face of the angel, like those of the caliphs, are rendered, in contrast to that of the prophet (*Reiser i tid og tro 5*: 138.)

On page 118 of *Broene 5*, we find an image that seems to illustrate the main body of text on the page. This text is arranged under the headings "The wives of Muhammad" and "The family of Muhammad." The painting depicts 27 kneeling women, while a fully covered figure sits in front of them, on a richly decorated and elevated chair. By the chair are also two women standing beside her on the right hand side, and one man kneeling on her left. They are all turned towards the covered person. The caption is brief, but indicates the motif by the following text: "The prophetic flame of Aisha."

Fortell meg mer 5 ("Tell Me More 5") introduces prohibition of images explicitly in the very last pages of the chapter on Islam. On page 130, the reader encounters one page dominated by two equally sized photographs rendering a minaret decorated with colorful, geometrical mosaics and a carpet with geometric pattern respectively. The caption reads: "Islamic art often avoids depicting living creatures, specifically when for example mosques or prayer carpets are being fashioned. Instead, they use all kinds of patterns, flower motifs and colors to create a work of art. Such art is called ornamental." The following page expands on this in the main body of text:

> Muslims also developed their own art forms. The Qur'an prohibits depiction. Some interpreted this as if one could not depict any living beings at all. Others meant that the prohibition only applied to images of deities (idols). At any account, the result is an art without images of living creatures in the mosques. The particular forms of this art we call calligraphy and ornamental art, a form of art that uses colors and figures.[39]

Fortell meg mer 5 is, together with *Under samme himmel 5*, two of the total five textbooks from the 1997 reform that do not render any examples of visual depictions of the prophet Muhammad. All of the five textbooks, however, reproduce one or more examples of figurative, anthropomorphous and zoomorphous art in the chapters where Islam is the topic. These reproductions are in the main miniature paintings that depict scenes with various secular motifs. A telling example of these kinds of illustrations is the one that is found on page 100 in *Under samme himmel 5*, accompanied by the following caption: "This old painting depicts astronomers working with instruments to study the sun, moon and stars. In this manner, they could find the right way to Mekka."[40] The exact same illustration is reproduced in *Broene 5*, and we encounter several similar images in the other textbooks.[41]

To sum up at this point, we have seen that, although photography is by far the dominating visual form of representation in the chapters on Islam, it is not the only figurative visual mode that is used. All of the 1997 textbooks convey other types of illustrations, and the general impression is that the volumes in their entirety are characterized by rich and varied visual expressions. Several of the publishers have hired one or more illustrators, predominantly to visualize scenes from the narratives, but also in order to develop smaller symbols and vignettes that appear at various places in the book. In the chapters that present Islam, the reader encounters a number of colorful examples of calligraphy and ornamental art, alongside some reproductions of miniature paintings, used both as illustrations to texts about more secular aspects of Arabic culture, like trade and science, and, most notably perhaps, by a handful of miniature paintings and manuscript illustrations depicting the prophet Muhammad and his family. In addition to these historical examples from specific periods in Islam's history, it is thus the appointed illustrators that may be said to challenge any kind of prohibition. None of the books render images where the prophet's face is visible, a tradition that, although not particularly widespread, is found within certain communities of Shia as well as Sunni Muslims.[42] Nevertheless, in three of the five 1997 textbooks, the students could encounter depictions of the prophet Muhammad with the face covered. Less noticeable, but no less relevant, is the fact that all of the textbooks of the 1997 generation contained various kinds of figurative representations of animals and humans (i.e. living creatures).

RLE POST-2008

Leaping 11 years or more ahead from 1997 to the textbooks published in the wake of the 2008 curriculum-revision, the most noticeable change is that the reproductions of miniature paintings are now no longer there. Photography is still the predominant mode of visual representation, but the appointed illustrators of each textbook series have also to a much larger degree been given the opportunity to put their personal imprint on the visual design. An example of this may be seen in the illustrations that accompany the narrative of Muhammad's escape from Mekka to Medina, which is described in all of the four 2008 textbooks. The same scene is also depicted in words and drawings in *Fortell meg mer* from 1997, which thus provides an interesting example for comparison across the span of 11 years.[43]

Starting with the 1997 version from *Fortell meg mer 5*,[44] we find that the illustrator, who has provided illustrations in the same style for the entire volume, depicts a central scene from the narrative. Hostile persecutors chase Muhammad and his close companion Abu Bakr, but the two men find a cave, where they are able to hide from their persecutors. According to the narrative, a tree spontaneously grows in front of the cave's entrance, a spider spins a web across it, and a bird makes a nest and lays eggs in it. When the persecutors arrive at the cave, they are led to believe that no one may be able to hide in it. In *Fortell meg mer 5*, the scene is illustrated with three men, all depicted frontally, approaching the cave. The one in the foreground bends towards the cave's entrance, which is covered by the tree, spider web and bird in her nest.

Inn i livet 4 from 2008 also makes use of an illustrator to visualize the scene with the cave. In this illustration, three simple, almost naïvely drawn figures illustrate the point of the story: a tree, a spider in a web and a bird in her nest. *Vi i verden 4* from 2006 has the following heading "Muhammad leaves Mecca" on page 137, but unlike the other corresponding textbooks of this generation, it does not render the narrative of the cave and the miracle. Instead of an illustration, the more factual text is visually supported by a map and photography. We do however encounter the narrative of the cave again in *Vivo 3-4*. On the two-page spread with the heading "Muhammad flees to Medina" the reader is met with a variety of visual modes in map, photography and illustration. As the illustrator here is one of two illustrators that have contributed throughout the volume, the distinct drawing is recognizable as part of the more general visual design of the book as a whole. In comparison with the other chapters in the volume, the illustrations in the chapter on Islam thus stand out, in that humans in this chapter only are depicted from behind. In the illustration of this particular story, the persecutors are rendered moving away from the cave, while the covered entrance of the cave is depicted in the foreground.

The last of the "flight from Mecca to Medina" illustrations is found in *Du og jeg 5*. In this version too, we see one of the persecutors approaching the cave's entrance. The tree is not depicted, but the nest and the spider web that covers the opening are visible behind a human figure shown from behind. When seen together, and in comparison with the images from the 1997 textbooks, these five different versions and visualizations of the same narrative, evidently demonstrate a change in the choice of visual representations. The 2008 illustrations not only avoid depicting the face of the prophet (there are no contemporary depictions of the prophet's face in the 1997 books either), but they also seem to avoid rendering human faces at all and, to a lesser degree of consistency, also animals. To the extent that the bird and the spider are depicted in the 2008 illustrations, the drawings are stylized, while all the humans are depicted with their backs towards the reader.

VIVO-FORTELLINGSBOK

Moving to *Vivo-Fortellingsbok* ("Vivo–Book of Narratives"), published in 2010, we likewise find photography as the characteristic visual mode in the chapter on Islam. Illustrations by the three recurring illustrators of the volume do however accompany four of the stories. All three illustrators have distinct visual characteristics, by which they all add to the visual expression of the chapter and volume in general. The same artist has illustrated two of the narratives: "Muhammad's night journey" (page 151) "the verdict of Sulaymans" (page 165), while two others have provided one each: the stylized drawings that accompany "The leper, the bald and the blind" (pages 166-67), and the dog that illustrates the story of "Muhammad and the dog" (page 164). The different illustrators and their distinct styles thus contribute to the varied visual expression of this book, and provide contrast to the more homogenous, yet somewhat exotifying photographs in the remaining part of the Islam chapter. The illustrations render a dog, a sheep, a camel and a cow, in addition to a male character (in all likelihood to be identified by the readers as the angel in the story about the "The leper, the Bald and the Blind"), and two women with heads covered and the visible face of an infant in "The verdict of Suleyman." In addition, the text rendering the Night Journey and Burak are illustrated with three Pegasus-like animals and a ladder that iconographically may remind readers of traditional Christian representations of Jacob's dream. In *Vivo-Fortellingsbok* the reader thus encounters representations of both humans and animals, in the same characteristic style of the illustrators as in the other chapters of the volume. Despite the fact that the illustrations to other chapters in this book may be both larger and more in terms of number, the contrasts between the visual expressions of the different chapters are not necessarily so striking as in the "ordinary" textbooks of the 2008 generation.

The examples discussed so far demonstrate a tendency to move from the frontal depiction of human faces in the 1997 generation books, to the averted and covered human figures in the illustrations of the 2008 books. This applies most notably to the "custom made" illustrations made by appointed illustrators who are represented throughout the volumes. The tendency, however, is supported by the absence of other figurative representations of human beings in these particular chapters that deal with Islam. Also in the depiction of animals, it seems we may trace a more careful approach by means of stylizing and omissions, as in *Vivo 3-4*, where the bird from the story is left out of the visual image.[45] This omission may certainly be due to a number of other factors than those discussed here, but nonetheless when all the books are taken together, the tendency is still evident. The exception to this change seems to be the *Vivo-Fortellingsbok*, published two years after the curriculum revision, and thus as the new subject had perhaps "settled" down.

In terms of visual representations of Islam, the readers of the 2008 books are presented with a range of photography of ornamental art, architecture, landscape sceneries and human beings. To pupils in Norwegian classrooms, several of these photographs may appear strange as they often depict exotic and geographically distant contexts. It should also be noted that the artistic illustrations used are mainly made by contemporary Western illustrators/artists. Examples of figurative, historical Islamic art are thus conspicuously absent.[46] Contemporary figurative expressions are equally scarce. One single exception is found on page 10 in *Du og jeg 4*. Here, we encounter a reprint of a photo of what seems to be an embroidery depicting Burak. There is no caption explaining or contextualizing the motif, and the list of illustrations merely state that the image is found at Photos.com. The motif is however similar to the one presented in the source collection (*Kildesamling*) of 1997 at page 232, where the caption reads as follows: "Burak is a common motif in popular art. This example is a poster from Pakistan." In the 2008 generation of textbooks, the embroidered Burak in *Du og jeg 4* is thus an exceptional example of contemporary expressions of Islamic figurative piety.

REPRESENTATIONS OF JEWISH ANICONISM

Judaism is also often said to be aniconic[47] and prohibitions and regulations regarding images have varied greatly throughout history and among different groups of Jews. Consequently, an obvious next step in the analysis would be to compare the development in use of images in textbook presentations of Islam with those sections of the books presenting Judaism to the pupils. A review of the very same books and series as the ones analyzed above, demonstrates that a move towards fewer figurative representations is less evident in the sections on Judaism. As already stated, the textbooks of 1997 are in general characterized by a large and diverse selection of images, both those that are custom made for the particular textbook, and also for the art historical examples, and this also applies to the chapters that present Judaism. *Fortell meg med 6* for example, renders images by Gaugin (page 79), Edward Poynter (page 80), an un-attributed fresco in modern Greek-Orthodox style with the caption: "Moses leads the Israelites through the split waters" (page 81) and Marc Chagall (page 82), i.e. four very different visual expressions on four succeeding pages. Elsewhere in the chapter, the reader encounters a Pre-Raphaelite (Herbert G. Schmalz, page 86), a German woodcut from 1492 (page 91) and yet another Chagall (page 92). The visual design of the chapter thus aligns with the remaining chapters in the book, although the Western art historical canon takes up a striking amount of space. Geir Winje has pointed out how this dominance of Western European (i.e. Christian) art mainly is due to the fact that images in these textbooks first and foremost serve as illustrations to the religious narratives. As many of the Old Testament/Tanakh narratives are shared by Judaism and Christianity, it seems to have been easy to reach for already familiar art when finding illustrations for (to the authors at least) familiar stories. When Jewish narratives are richly illustrated by images from Christian art history, the images have thus been used despite not being particularly representative of Jewish art.[48] The remaining chapters from the 1997 generation of textbooks leave the same impression, although visual examples are more likely to be provided from the religious and cultural context described in the verbal texts of the various sections.

Turning to the 2008 generation of books, there appears to be little change in the visual expression. In *Vivo 5-7*, an entire page is dedicated to the reproduction of the first page of a Late Medieval Tanakh from 13th century Germany. Forty-six roundels, symmetrically placed around the title of the book, depict central scenes and figures from the Tanakh narratives. Among the scenes represented are Eve and Adam with the snake and the tree, and Abraham lifting his sword above Isaac (Bondevik et al. 2010: 65). There is also a photo of the famous marble relief from the Arch of Titus in Rome, which, although by no means considered representative for Jewish art, functions as an example of how art may provide historical documentation. Marc Chagall has been and still is a recurrent figure in Norwegian RE-textbooks, and the artist's works are often presented in relation to chapters on Judaism or the Christian Old Testament, since his paintings often portray the Abrahamic patriarchs. *Vivo 5-7* introduces the reader to a brief text in the margins, beside the reproduction of one of Chagall's stained glass works. This text explains how Chagall managed to circumvent the so-called prohibition of images. "because of the Jews' prohibition of images, it is not common to depict human beings in a synagogue. For this reason, Chagall gave the figures in his art three, four or six fingers, so that he could say they were not humans."[49]

Du og jeg 5 from 2008 renders illustrations by the appointed illustrator of the books and reproductions of Gustave Doré's Bible illustrations. Since the same artist provided illustrations for all the chapters in the volume, as well as the chapter on Islam, the contrast between the two chapters is perhaps more evident too. In the chapter concerning Islam, discussed above, the humans are depicted with their backs turned towards the viewer, so that no faces are visible. The frontally depicted human figures in the remaining sections of the book, including the one that thematizes Judaism, thus bring out the differences in visual expression.

If there is a noticeable change from 1997 to 2008 when it comes to the choice of art and visual representation of Judaism, it is the fact that the art in the most recent textbooks to a much lesser extent is taken from "Christian" representations of Old Testament narratives. This is in accord with the recommendations put forth by Geir Winje, who has argued that the art that is used as illustrations in RE textbooks ought to be representative, meaning it is to be found in the religious tradition that is the topic for the verbal text and chapter.

REPRESENTATION AND REPRESENTATIVENESS

Some of the most crucial issues in RE didactics concern representation and representativeness. Both relate to questions of how to select material for an education unit, it being texts, images, music or religious artefacts. It is important that the teacher has knowledge about how different aspects of religion have been and still are presented in different media and historical contexts, i.e. different representations of religion. Representativeness, on the other hand, implies that the representations that the pupils encounter are recognizable by the adherents of that particular religious tradition. Representativeness can be thought of as determined by global as well as local concerns.

The Norwegian curriculum simultaneously stresses that RE is to be diverse and reflect religious plurality across religious traditions as well as within them.[50] In his report on Norwegian RE textbooks from 2003 Geir Winje pointed out that,

> The subject matter includes topics such as angels, prayer, birthing rites and religious festivals. It may be tempting for textbook authors and art editors to illustrate the narratives [of Islam] in the same manner as when illustrating the narratives in Christianity and Eastern religions. Such a solution is however not in accordance with dominant aesthetic though in Islam.[51]

Much has happened since 2003. The Norwegian subject KRL was ruled by The European Human Right Court, as well as the Human Rights committee in Geneva, to conflict with parents' religious freedom and right to choose religious upbringing for their children (Alberts 2011; Lied 2008). The controversies eventually led to the name change and curriculum revision of 2008. "Christianity" was removed from the name of the subject, and replaced with "ethics" as the last joint of the three-word chain (Religion, philosophy of life and ethics = *Religion, livssyn og etikk*, or RLE). On December 5th 2008 the education act was also changed. The role of Christianity in the prior principal aim — that the public school was to "assist in providing pupils with a Christian and ethical upbringing" — was now toned down and values found across religious and non-religious traditions were emphasized instead.[52] The connection between the so-called "Christian education act" and the school subject that its critics had stressed, was now less flagrant.

According to Ingvild Flaskerud, the focus on the aesthetic dimension in the 1997 curriculum was one of the aspects that aroused the criticism which in turn lead to the Human Rights Court in Strasbourg. Drawing as a student activity was deemed particularly problematic, as Muslim organizations argued that representations of prophets were blasphemous. Parallel stories and shared religious figures would lead to dilemmas for Muslim children, when faced with such assignments as "draw Jacob and his ladder" or "draw baby Jesus in the manger."[53] However, the main challenge related to images in the court proceedings that followed in the wake of KRL 1997, was, as highlighted by Borchgrevink, drawing as a learning activity, and to a lesser extent the images printed in textbooks.[54] In an article from 2006, describing the process of preparation of the RE textbooks from the publisher Aschehough, one of the textbook authors, Jan Opsal explains the decision to leave out images depicting Muhammad and other prophets in the chapters presenting Islam to the students. According to Opsal, the decision was not due to self-censorship, but,

> [...] was made from a pedagogical assessment based in the KRL-curriculum's aim to acknowledge the identity of Muslim students. One thus has to represent the religion in question based in its Norwegian contextual form. It would then not have been right to present to the students art which would be considered foreign in relation to their own religious traditions. Had Muslims in Norway had their provenience in traditions where such images were naturally accepted, our assessment would have been different."[55]

When we compare textbooks from the 1997 generation with those adapted to the revision of 2008, there is thus, as indicated in Opsal's quote, a rather eye-catching change in the visual representations of Islam. Both generations are dominated by often large and colorful photographs, depicting humans, as well as architecture and ornamental art. Historical and/or contemporary examples of Islamic figurative art, such as the miniature paintings reproduced in all of the 1997-books, are however completely absent from the 2008-generation.[56] This applies to scenes depicting the prophet Muhammad with his face covered, as well as to other, secular motifs then used to illustrate Arabic science and cultural history.

Another noticeable change is that most publishers of the 2008 generation have one or more illustrators who to a larger degree contribute to the visual design of the volume(s) as a whole. In cases where humans indeed are depicted by these illustrators in the chapters on Islam, they are predominantly shown with their backs turned towards the reader, so that no faces are rendered (most notably in *Vivo 3-4* and *Du og Jeg 4*, with *Vivo, Storybook*, being the exception, depicting both humans, angles and animals *en face*). When the same illustrator is used repeatedly throughout a volume, contrasts between different topics and chapters become more apparent.[57] This is for instance evident in the beautiful collages that introduce each chapter in *Vivo 3-4*. In the chapters dealing with the three Abrahamic traditions, the reader repeatedly encounters the patriarchs in the illustrator's distinguishing pen in the chapters dedicated to Judaism and Christianity. They are also part of the two-page spread with the collages introducing these chapters.[58] The artist's line is also very recognizable in the chapter about Islam. Here, however, is there no man-made (drawn, painted or otherwise) representation of humans in the chapter collage, and in the chapter itself, the illustrator's human figures are all depicted from behind. When these three chapters immediately succeed one another in the book, the contrast between the visual designs also becomes more attention-grabbing. This indicates that the publishers and the authors must have thought of Islamic prohibition of images, not only in the selection of visual art to be reproduced in the books, but also when working with the illustrations that are "custom made" for the textbooks. Considering that the cartoon controversy originally was presented as a response to the failure of producing illustrations to a Muhammad biography for children, the absence of such illustrations is perhaps not so unsurprising after all. This development in the RE textbooks seems, however, to be contrary the changes traced by Torsten Janson in a study of British-Muslim picture books for children. Janson here identifies a range of visual strategies. Although not identifying images depicting the prophet Muhammad or other religiously significant persons, Janson's preliminary study indicates that it is "untenable to conceptionalize the contemporary norms of representation of Sunni Islamic children's literature in terms of any fixed set of visual rules and regulations."[59] The material analyzed in Janson's study reveals instead how norms are negotiated and reinterpreted within the frames of new culturally defined notions of pedagogical, artistic and communicational aims, allowing for varied representations of zoomorhic as well as anthropomorphic images. Likewise, the German textbooks *Sahir* (Behr et al. 2008), written for separative Islam education, reproduce many of the historical, figurative miniatures found in the 1997 generation of Norwegian textbooks. Although genre, cultural and social contexts may only indicate a fragment of the potentially innumerable reasons for these very different choices in visual representations found in these books, it is still interesting to note how very differently the so-called Islamic prohibition of images is interpreted.

DIVERSITY OR DISTINCTIVE CHARACTERISTICS?

The analysis of these selected textbooks thus indicates that authors and publishers have been more cautious in their choice of images for the books of the 2008 generation than in the earlier textbooks. This caution may be understood as an expression of tolerance and respect towards Muslims' own insider perspectives. As such, the changes follow the recommendations for choosing art work for RE that were put forth by Geir Winje in 2003. Here, he advised art ought to be representative, i.e. in line with majority views, and should not go against the Islamic "prohibition of images."[60] On the other hand, both national and global development in recent years has perhaps more than ever demonstrated that "Islam" by no means is a fixed or homogenous entity. Insider struggles over the authority to define what is "right" Islam is certainly relevant to a school subject aiming to teach pupils about religion. Taking a stand, or making hierarchies over insiders' truth claims, however, is much more problematic. Through the selection of material used in RE textbooks, the 2008 generation implicitly draws some demarcations that may be seen as favoring one specific majority perspective within Islamic tradition.[61] Seeing that "aniconism" may imply a whole range of different practices and interpretations, also in the Muslim world, these demarcations may then be drawn at the expense of minority groups and pupils who also identify themselves as Muslims, and who may interpret and express their understanding of the role of figurative images quite differently. Aspects of Islamic cultural history which was made known (although undoubtedly somewhat uncritically conveyed) to previous generations of Norwegian pupils, are now no longer represented in the textbooks. Pupils with a family background and/or cultural ties to Muslim communities where images play a different role in religious practice, such as piety and education, may thus experience that respect and tolerance is only limited to a majority among Muslims, a group that they themselves do not necessarily identify with.[62] These pupils' cultural history and visual (religious) expressions, the ones they know from home, are thus presented as nonexistent, marginal or deviant. As pointed out by Bengt-Ove Andreassen: "What is not mentioned or included in the text appears to be secondary and ultimately unimportant — something the reader does not need to know."[63] The same argument certainly also applies to the images of multimodal texts.

This is a dilemma that perhaps is unavoidable, given the objectives of the RLE subject, and its intentions, historical background and profile. In a subject that is meant to attend to "diversity" as well as "distinctive characteristics" — in this case a diversity of different insider perspectives — and at the same time prepare the students to learn respect, tolerance and pluralism, there are necessarily difficult choices to be made when different insider perspectives so obviously exclude each other and do not agree on what the "distinctive characteristics" may be. Consequently, in a globalized society where there in fact are many different majorities and minorities, and new minorities within groups of minorities, the RE teacher has to maneuver with comprehensive subject knowledge and skills if everyone is to be included and "seen" in the learning processes anticipated in the RLE curriculum. It is needless to say an impossible task to fully represent plurality, complexity and nuances of "religion" within the covers of a textbook. Simultaneously, or perhaps exactly because of this, it is nevertheless important not to forget that textbooks themselves, by their fundamental position as providers of subject material in Norwegian public schools, achieve authoritative status as a kind of state-initiated "canonization" based on the curriculum, that is, as a normative selection of religious traditions where the selection of texts and images contribute in defining boundaries for what is inside and what falls outside, what is "correct" religion — and thus, by omission — what is wrong. As pointed out by Cristiane Gruber and Avinoam Shalem in their 2014 anthology *The Image of the Prophet between Ideal and Ideology*:

Purposefully or not, these many [scholarly] discourses on so-called Islamic iconoclasm have the net result of eclipsing the visual material, most especially paintings of Muhammad and religious imagery within Islam — which falsely reasserts their position as rare or exceptional. Marginalized as anathema, such images become increasingly vulnerable to repudiation, censorship, erasure, and eradication.[64]

If this is the case, Norwegian RE textbooks may also contribute to a larger development where academic and educational representations of Islam eventually end up reifying the attributed significance of Islamic prohibition of images, and thus, assumingly inadvertently, eventually shoring up some insiders' normative assessments at the cost of the practices of others.

ABOUT THE AUTHOR

Sissel Undheim is Associate Professor, Department of Archaeology, History, Cultural Studies and Religion, University of Bergen, Norway. Her research interests include Multimodality, Lego, Late Antiquity, Art and RE textbooks. Among her most recent publications are "RLE-religion. Religionsbegrepet i RLE-læreverkene for småskoletrinnet," *Prismet* 64.4 (2013),"The Sacred Power of Lego-Chi. Mediatized Spirituality in Lego, Legends of China," *Young* 25.1 (2017). Email: sissel.undheim@uib.no

REFERENCES

Aarflot, Anne-Kristin, Jan Olav Aarflot and Jan Opsal. 1997. *Fortell meg mer 5*. Oslo: Aschehoug.
Alberts, Wanda. 2007. *Integrative Religious Education in Europe: a Study-of-Religions Approach*. Berlin: Walter de Gruyter.
Alberts, Wanda. 2011. "Religious Education in Norway." *Religious Education in a Plural, Secularized Society*, eds. Leni Franken and Patrick Loobuyck. Münster: Waxmann.
Andreassen, Bengt-Ove. 2010. "Bruk eller misbruk? Ninain Smarts dimensjonsmodell I tilnærmingen til religion I norsk religionsdidaktikk." *Religionsvidenskabeligt tidsskrift* 55: 55–73.
Andreassen, Bengt-Ove. 2012. *Religionsdidaktikk: en innføring*. Oslo: Universitetsforlaget.
Andreassen, Bengt-Ove. 2014. "Introduction: Theoretical Perspectives on Textbooks/Textbooks in Religious Studies Research." In *Textbook Gods: Genre, Text and Teaching Religious Studies*, eds. Bengt-Ove Andreassen and James R. Lewis, 1–15. Sheffield: Equinox Publishing.
Aronsen, Camilla Fines, Lene Bomann-Larsen and Henry Notaker 2008. *Eksistens*. Oslo: Gyldendal.
Bakken, Elisabeth, Per K. Bakken and Petter A. Haug. 1997. *Broene 5*. Oslo: Universitetsforlaget.
Behr, Harry Harun et al. 2008. *Saphir 5/6. Schuljahr—Religionsbuch*. München: Kösel.
Bondevik, John Harald, Ariane B. Schjelderup and Anne Borgersen. 2010: *Vivo 5-7*. Oslo: Gyldendal.
Bondevik, John Harald, Ariane B. Schjelderup and Anne Borgersen. 2010: *Vivo-Fortellingsbok*. Oslo: Gyldendal.

Borchgrevink, T. 2002. "Makten eller æren. Kristendom og felleskultur i det flerreligiøse Norge." *Sand i maskineriet. Makt and demokrati i det flerkulturelle Norge*, eds. Grete Brochmann, Tordis Borchgrevink and Jon Rogstad, 108–45. Oslo: Gyldendal Akademisk.

Bråten, Oddrun. 2014. "Bruk av lærebøker i RLE." In *RLE i klemme. Ein studie av det erfarte RLE-faget*, ed. Kåre Fuglseth. Bergen: Fagbokforlaget.

Børresen, Beate, Tove Larsen and Peder Nustad. 2006–2008. *Vi i verden*. Oslo: Cappelen Damm.

Douglass, Susan L., and Ross E. Dunn. 2003. "Interpreting Islam in American Schools." *American Academy of Political and Social Science* 588: 52–72.

Egeland, Elen, Anne Grete I. Husan, Kjerstin C. D. Jacobsen and Ariane Schjelderup. 2009. *Vivo 3-4*. Oslo: Gyldendal.

Eggen, Nora S., ed. 2008. *De rettvises hager. Al-Nawawis samling overleveringer om profeten Muhammad*. Oslo: Bokklubbene. (Verdens hellige skrifter.)

Eidhamar, Levi Geir. 1997. *Under samme himmel 5*. Oslo: Cappelen.

Engen, Dagrun Astrid Aarø et al. 2009–2011. *Inn i livet. Religion, livssyn og etikk*. Oslo: Samlaget.

Flaskerud, Ingvild. 2002. "Det kontroversielle bildet. Profeten Muhammed i islamsk bildekunst." *Din* 2-3: 56–63.

Flaskerud, Ingvild. 2010. "Bildebruk og bildestrid i islam." *Din* 3-4: 117–40.

Flood, Finbarr Barry. 2002. "Between Cult and Culture: Bamiyan, Islamic Iconoclasm, and the Museum." *The Art Bulletin* 84(4): 641–59.

Flood, Finbarr Barry. 2013. "Inciting Modernity? Images, Alterities, and the Contexts of 'Cartoon Wars'." In *Images that Move*, eds. Patricia Spyer and Mary Margaret Steedly, 41–72. Santa Fe: SAR Press.

Gruber, Christiane, and Avinoam Shalem. 2014. "Introduction: Images of the Prophet Muhammad in a Global Context." In *The Image of the Prophet between Ideal and Ideology*, eds. Christiane Gruber and Avinoam Shalem, 1–9. Berlin: Walter De Gruyter.

Gruber, Christiane. 2016. "Prophetic Products: Muhammad in Contemporary Iranian Visual Culture. *Material Religion*. 12 (3): 259–293.

Heiene, Gunnar, Bjørn Myhre, Jan Opsal, Harald Skottene and Arna Østnor. 2008. *Tro og tanke. Religion og etikk for den videregående skolen*. 1. utg. Oslo: Aschehoug.

Heiene, Gunnar, Bjørn Myhre, Jan Opsal, Harald Skottene and Arna Østnor. 2014. *Tro og tanke. Religion og etikk for den videregående skolen*. 2. utg. Oslo: Aschehoug.

Hodne, Hans, and Helje Kringlebotn Sødal. 2009–2011. *Du og Jeg. RLE*. Kristiansand: Høyskoleforlaget.

Holter, Knut. 2010. "Bildeforbudet i Det gamle testamentet." *Din* 3-4: 28–44.

Härenstam, Kjell. 1993. *Skolboks-islam: analys av bilden av islam i lärobøcker i religionskunskap*. Göteborg: Acta Universitatis Gothoburgensis.

Härenstam, Kjell. 2000. *Kan du höra vindhesten? Religionsdidaktik—om konsten att välje kunskap*. Lund: Studentlitteratur.

Jackson, Robert. 2014. *Signposts: Policy and Practice for Teaching about Religions and Non-Religious Worldviews in Intercultural Education*. Strasbourg: Council of Europe Publishing.

Janson, Torsten. 2012. "Imaging Islamic Identity: Negotiated Norms of Representation in British-Muslim Picture Books." *Comparative Studies of South Asia, Africa, and the Middle East* 32(2): 323–38.

Jensen, Tim. 2003. "Mange muslimer, mange islamer." In *Islam i bevægelse*, eds. Mona Sheikh, Fatih Alev, Babar Baig and Noman Malik, 23–64. København: Akademisk forlag.

Jonker, Gerdien, and Shiraz Thobani. 2009. "Introduction: Interpretations of the Muslim World in European Texts." *Narrating Islam. Interpretations of the Muslim World in European Texts*, 1–10. London: Tauris Academic Studies.

Karimi, Pamela, and Christiane Gruber. 2012. "Introduction. The Politics and Poetics of the Child Image in Muslim Contexts." *Comparative Studies of South Asia, Africa and the Middle East* 32(2): 273–93.

Kress, Gunther. 2010. *Multimodality. A Social Semiotic Approach to Contemporary Communication*. London: Routledge.

Kress, Gunther, and Theo van Leeuwen. 1996. *Reading Images. The Grammar of Visual Design*. London: Routledge.

Kress, Gunther, and Theo. van Leeuwen. 2001. *Multimodal Discourse. The Modes and Media of Contemporary Communication*. London, Arnold.

Kvamme, Ole Andreas, Eva Mila Lindhardt and Agnete Steineger. 2013. *I samme verden*. Oslo: Cappelen Damm.

L97 = Det kongelige kirke-, utdannings-, og forskningsdepartement. 1996. *Læreplanverket for den 10-årige grunnskolen*, Oslo, Det kongelige kirke-, utdannings-, og forskningsdepartement.

Leirvik, Oddbjørn. 2006. "Kva var karikatursaka eit bilete på?" *Kirke og kultur* 111(2): 147–59.

Løvland, Anne. 2007. *På mange måtar. Samansette tekstar i skolen*. Fagbokforlaget.

Leirvik, Oddbjørn. 2013. *Islam i Norge. Oversikt, med bibliografi* (14.1.2014). Hentet fra: http://folk.uio.no/leirvik/tekster/IslamiNorge.html

Lied, Sidsel. 2008. "KRL-faget i Strasbourg. Presentasjon av dom og dissens i EMD og skisse av en mulig vei videre." *Norsk Teologisk Tidsskrift* 01/2008: 55–70.

Løvland, Anne. 2011. *På jakt etter svar og forståing: samansette fagtekstar i skulen*. Bergen: Fagbokforlaget.

McCutcheon, Russell T., ed. 1999. *The Insider/Outsider Problem in the Study of Religion: A Reader*. London: Cassell.

Maagerø, Eva. 2010. "Hva skal vi med trollene?" In *Sammensatte tekster. Barns tekstpraksis*, ed. Elise Seip Tønnessen, 138–56. Oslo: Universitetsforlaget.

Midtbøen, Arnfinn, Julia Orupabo and Åse Røthing. 2014a. *Beskrivelser av etniske og religiøse minoriteter i læremidler*. Institutt for samfunnsforskning, Rapport 2014: 10.

Midtbøen, Arnfinn, Julia Orupabo and Åse Røthing. 2014b. *Etniske og religiøse minoriteter i læremidler. Lærer og elevperspektiver*, 11. Institutt for samfunnsforskning, Rapport 2014.

Natvig, Richard, ed. 2008. "Muslim Devotional Posters." Department of Archaeology, History, Cultural Studies and Religion (AHKR), University of Bergen. http://www.org.uib.no/popularikonografi/default_eng.html (accessed 26.06.2015).

Opsal, Jan. 2006. "Karikaturer og krenkelser." *Religion og livssyn* 18(1): 45–50.

Otterbeck, Jonas. 2005. "What is Reasonable to Demand? Islam in Swedish Textbooks." *Journal of Ethnic and Migration Studies* 31(4): 795–812: 806.

Otterbeck, Jonas. 2014. "What is Islamic Arts? And What Makes Art Islamic?: The Example of the Islamic Discourse on Music." *CILE Journal* 1(1): 7–29.

Rasmussen, Tarald, and Einar Thomassen. 1999. *Kildesamling: til kristendomskunnskap med religions- og livssynsorientering*. Nasjonalt læremiddelsenter.

RLE 2008 = Utdanningsdirektoratet. 2008. *Læreplan i religion, livssyn og etikk*. Oslo, Utdanningsdirektoratet. http://www.udir.no/kl06/RLE1-01/ (accessed 12.08.2014).

Rogne, Magne. 2009. "Læreboka—ein garantist for læreplannær undervisning?" *Acta Didactica Norge* 3.1.11: 1–21.

Rothstein, Mikael, and Rothstein Klaus. 2006. *Bomben i turbanen*. Århus: Tiderne Skrifter.
Skeie, Eivind mfl. 1997. *Reiser i tid og tro 5*. Oslo: Gyldendal.
Thobro, Suzanne Anett. 2014. "Cartographic Representations of Religion(s) in Norwegian Textbooks." In *Textbook Gods: Genre, Text and Teaching Religious Studies*, eds. Bengt-Ove Andreassen and James R. Lewis, 157–76. Sheffield: Equinox Publishing.
Undheim, Sissel. 2013. "RLE-religion. Religionsbegrepet i RLE-læreverkene for småskoletrinnet." *Prismet* 2013/4: 251–65.
Undheim, Sissel. 2015. "Bilder og bildeforbud i KRL og RLE." In *Det tredje språket. Multimodale studier av interkulturell kommunikasjon i kunst, skole og samfunnsliv*, ed. M. Engebretsen, 247–266. Kristiansand: Portal forlag.
Winje, Geir. 2003a. *Valg og vurdering av kunstbilder i KRL. Rapport 2(2003)*. Tønsberg: Høgskolen i Vestfold.
Winje, Geir. 2003b. "Hvordan brukes kunstbilder i KRL-undervisningen?" In *Fokus på pedagogiske tekster 7. Fire artikler om lærebøker i kristendoms-, religions- og livssynskunnskap. Notat 2/2003*, eds. Staffan Selander and Dagrun Skjelbred, 102–15. Høgskolen i Vestfold.
Winje, Geir. 2008. "Lærebøkene i KRL—hva har skjedd på ti år?" *Norsk Teologisk Tidsskrift* 2008/01: 72–87.
Winje, Geir. 2010. "Å lese kunstbilder som religiøse tekster." *Religion og livssyn* 22(3): 11–16.
Winje, Geir. 2012. *Guddommelig skjønnhet: kunst i religionene*. Oslo: Universitetsforlaget.
Wiseman, Alexander W. 2014. "Representations of Islam and Arab Societies in Western Secondary Textbooks". *Digest of Middle East Studies* 23(2): 132–344.
Yılmaz, Ferruh. 2011. "The Politics of the Danish Cartoon Affair: Hegemonic Intervention by the Extreme Right." *Communication Studies* 62(1): 5–22.

Endnotes
1. This chapter is a revised translation of an article published in Norwegian as "Bilder og bildeforbud i skolens religionsfag. En analyse av lærebøker for KRL og RLE," in *Det tredje språket: Multimodale studier av interkulturell kommunikasjon i kunst, skole og samfunnsliv*. Portal forlag, 2015: 247–66. The material has also been presented at a workshop at Leibniz Universität Hannover, organized by the EASR Working Group on Religion in Secular Education in March 2015, and at the XXI World Congress of the International Association for the History of Religions in Erfurt in August 2015. I wish to thank Richard Natvig for some very helpful conversations, and to everyone else who contributed with questions and comments at my presentations at various stages in the work process.
2. More about these changes below.
3. Bråten 2014, cf. Rogne 2009 for textbooks in general.
4. Løvland 2007. The concept of multimodality is presented and discussed in Kress and Van Leeuwen 1996, Kress and Van Leeuwen 2001 and Kress and Van Leeuwen 2010.
5. Andreassen 2014: 4–5.
6. Andreassen 2014; Härenstam 2000, Wiseman 2014: 315.
7. Studies of textbook representations of Islam include Härenstam 1993, Douglass and Dunn 2003, Otterbeck 2005, Jonker and Thobani 2009 and Wiesemann 2014.
8. The concept of integrative religious education is here taken to cover all variants of Norwegian RE-subject post 1997, based on the definition given by Wanda Alberts as "an analytical category referring to a particular form of school religious education in which the children of a

class are not separated — as opposed to separative confessional approaches — but learn together about different religions" (Alberts 2007: 1; cf. Andreassen 2012: 31).

9. Although not at all irrelevant, it has been beyond the scope of this particular study to include more thorough analyses of the actual publication process of these textbooks. It would for instance be interesting to look closer at the role of reference groups, consultants and editors in the selection of images for these books.

10. For an overview of the historical process leading up to KRL in 1997 and the subsequent controversies and revisions, see Alberts 2011.

11. To the extent that Norwegians by 2015 were facing the forth curriculum revision and name change since the introduction of the subject in 1997, i.e. *Knowledge of Christianity — Religion and Views of Life* (KRL) 2002, *Knowledge of Christianity — Religion and Views of Life* (KRL) 2005, *Religion, Philosophies of Life and Ethics* (RLE) 2008 and *Christianity, Religion, Philosophies of Life and Ethics* (KRLE) 2015. Borchgrevink 2002 gives an overview of the controversy and legal cases in the Norwegian court system. For the cases that eventually were brought to The Human Rights Committee (in Geneva) and The European Court of Human Rights (in Strasbourg), see Alberts 2011.

12. The RE subject for upper secondary has its own curriculum, which has been revised at different intervals and which has not nearly been as controversial as the one for primary school. Since, however, this subject builds on the one for primary and lower-secondary school, the most recent textbooks will occasionally be brought in to the analyses as comparative references.

13. Christianity, Judaism, Islam, Buddhism and Hinduism, plus Humanism, with Christianity in general taking up a few more pages than the rest, as indicated by the curriculum. In addition, there are chapters on philosophy and ethics, which occasionally overlap with the other sections. Cf. Undheim 2013.

14. The role in Ninian Smart in the Norwegian RE curriculum is discussed in Andreassen 2010.

15. L97: 90. My translation. Original: "Den estetiske dimensjon har til alle tider vært en sentral del av det religiøse uttrykk. Det er nærliggende å la dette slektskapet mellom religiøs og estetisk arv komme tydelig frem i opplæringen gjennom vekt på bildende kunst, arkitektur, musikk, drama og litterære tekster".

16. (L97: 89). My translation. Original: "de samme pedagogiske prinsippene skal legges til grunn for arbeidet med kristendommen og andre religioner og livssyn." (in RLE 2008: "The principles of equivalent education shall be the basis for teaching in the subject"). Cf. RLE 2008: "Adapted education is a commanding principle for this subject. Teaching in the subject shall use varied and absorbing working methods, which can contribute to understanding in all aspects of the subject. Care must be used when selecting working methods. The careful choice of working methods is especially important when considering parents, guardians and pupils so that they feel their own religion or philosophy of life is respected and that the subject be experienced without seeming to exercise another religion or forming an affiliation to another philosophy of life. Respect for the views of individuals and local communities should be paramount."

17. The Education Act §2-3a. "The school shall respect the religious and philosophical of pupils and parents and ensure their right to an equal education. Following written notification from the parents, pupils shall be exempted from attending those parts of the teaching at the individual school that they, on the basis of their own religion or own philosophy of life, per-

ceive as being the practice of another religion or adherence to another philosophy of life, or that they on the same basis find objectionable or offensive. It is not necessary to give grounds for notification of exemption pursuant to the first sentence." It is further stated that exemption is not given from the academic content of the curriculum, and that the school has to provide adapted teaching to meet the curriculum aims.

18. RLE 2008, Winje 2003, 2008, 2010.
19. For the insider/outsider question, see McCutcheon 1999.
20. RLE 2008, official translation. Original: "Religion, "livssyn og etikk er et ordinært skolefag som normalt skal samle alle elever. Opplæringsloven legger til grunn at undervisningen skal være objektiv, kritisk og pluralistisk. [...] Likeverdige pedagogiske prinsipper skal legges til grunn. Det innebærer at alle religioner og livssyn skal behandles på en faglig og sakssvarende måte ut fra sitt særpreg og mangfold."
21. cf. Douglass and Dunn 2003: 52-54.
22. E.g. Rothstein and Rothstein 2006, Yılmaz 2011, Flood 2013.
23. Gruber and Shalem 2014: 3.
24. Cf. Kolrud and Prusac 2014.
25. Thus, to complicate this even further, questions of Islamistic aniconism have in the wake of terror events such as the Danish Cartoon crisis and the Charlie Hebdo assassinations also been politicized, mobilizing the extreme right as well as left (cf. e.g. Rothstein and Rothstein 2006; Yılmaz 2011) adding yet more layers to the didactic discussions of how Islam ought to be represented visually in the classroom. Gruber 2016 describes similar diachronic changes in visual representations of the prophet Muhammad in Iran, which she connects to the cartoon controversy of 2005-6 (2016: 262 and 271).
26. Qur'an 21. 52-71; Flaskerud 2010.
27. E.g. Eggen 2008: 345-46, cf. Flood 2013.
28. Flood 2002; Gruber and Shalem 2014; cf. Jensen 2003. Otterbeck 2014 points out many of the same issues in his discussion of Islamic art and music.
29. Flaskerud 2002: 56, cf. Gruber and Shalem 2014: 4-7.
30. Geir Winje's report *Valg og vurdering av kunstbilder i KRL* ("Choices and Assessment of Art Images in KRL") from 2003 provide a thorough presentation of the textbooks for primary and secondary school. Winje 2008 gives a full analysis of all the KRL textbooks published between 1997 and 2006. It should be noted that *Vi i verden* (Capplen 2006-) is placed in the 2008-generation, despite being originally produced in response to the 2005 revision of the curriculum. The name of the subject was however changed to RLE on the latest printed editions, as well as on the interactive website.
31. Gyldendal, *Vivo* i 2010-2011, Samlaget: *Inni livet* (2009-2011) Høyskoleforlaget (now fused with Cappelen Damm): *Du og jeg* 2010-2011. In addition, Cappelen Damm had started publishing *Vi i verden* in 2006. See Undheim 2013.
32. *Under samme himmel 5*, 24 illustrations in total, of which 12 are photos (many "custom made" illustrations) *Reiser i tid og tro 5. klasse*, 20, of which nine are photos, *Fortell meg mer 5*, 28, of which 20 are photos, *Broene 5*, 26, of which 22 are photos. There is a significant degree of variation in sizes. This quantitative overview also counts maps, symbols on historical time lines etc.
33. According to Kress and van Leeuwen (1996: 159-60) photography and models, including maps, will in a Western cultural context convey a high degree of modality, cf. Løvland 2011: 63-74. Artistic aesthetic expressions, also abstract ones, may on the other hand better express

or convey other truth claims, not least religious, as the example referred to by Kress and van Leeuven demonstrates. For an analyses of the role of maps in textbooks, see Thobro 2013.

34. *Kildesamlingen* 1997: 235.

35. The miniature picture referred to here is available at https://commons.wikimedia.org/w/index.php?curid=4137203 (accessed 13 April 2016).

36. Rasmussen and Thomassen 1999: 234–35, my translation. Norwegian text: "Illustrasjon i et persisk håndskrift fra 1500-tallet laget for Shah Tahmasp. I persisk tradisjon har man ofte vært mindre tilbakeholdende med avbildninger enn i den islamske kulturen for øvrig. Profetens himmelferd har vært et yndet motiv. Tradisjonell sunni-islam forbyr denne type bilder."

37. A contemporary version of the same motif is reproduced in the upper secondary textbook *Tro og tanke* (2008 and 2014), 158, cf. n. 46 below.

38. Bakken et al. 1997: 111.

39. Aarflot et al. 1997: 131. My translation. Norwegian text: "Muslimene utviklet også egne kunstformer. Koranen forbyr avbildning. Noen tolket dette slik at en ikke kunne avbilde levende vesener i det hele tatt. Andre mente forbudet bare gjaldt gudebilder. I alle fall ble resultatet en kunst uten bilder av levende vesener i moskeene. De spesielle formene denne kunsten fikk, kaller vi kalligrafi (skjønnskrift) og ornamentikk, en kunstform som bruker farger og figurer." Cf. Winje 2003: 51, 53.

40. Eidhamar 1997: 100. My translation. Norwegian text: "Dette gamle maleriet viser astronomer som arbeider med instrumenter for å studere sol, måne og stjerner. På den måten kunne de blant annet finne den riktige retningen mot Mekka."

41. Bakken, Bakken and Haug 1997: 130. This picture by Ala ad-Din Mansur-Shirazi is in possesion of Istanbul University Library (F 1404, fol. 57a, Şehinşename, Book of the King of Kings). It is also available at https://commons.wikimedia.org/w/index.php?curid=4932717, cf. Eidhamar 1997: 100.

42. Flaskerud 2002, Natvig 2008.

43 The relevant pages are reproduced in Undheim 2015: 257.

44 Aarflot, Aarflot and Opsal 1997: 96–97.

45. However, the bird is indeed depicted, together with the spider in *Vivo* 5-7: 184. This book was published two years after *Vivo 3-4*.

46. Once again, the absence is probably most evident when contrasted to one of the few exceptions in Norwegian RE textbooks. The textbook *Tro og Tanke* (Heiene et al. 2008 and 2014) for students in upper secondary school (year 13) renders as many as four different figurative Islamic art works, covering different styles and historical periods (see pages 121, 126, 138 and 158). Of these, the latter is a contemporary interpretation of the Mi'raj which covers an entire page, and is the subject of an assignment in art analysis. The other two textbooks for upper secondary contain two (Kvamme, Lindhardt and Steineger 2013, pages 109 and 133, with a possible third being the rendering of a Turkish 11th century miniature of Socrates in the section on Philosophy, page 252) and one (Aronsen, Bomann-Larsen and Larsen 2008: 186) works of figurative art in the chapters concerning Islam.

47. Winje 2003: 17; Holter 2010.

48. Winje 2003: 60–61.

49. Bondevik et al. 2010: 78. My translation. Norwegian text: "På grunn av jødenes bildeforbud er det ikke vanlig med bilder av mennesker i synagogene. Derfor fikk figurene i Chagalls kunstverk tre, fire eller seks fingre, så han kunne si at det ikke var mennesker."

50. Andreassen 2012: 88–89, cf. Härenstam 2000.

51. Winje 2003: 22–23, my translation.

52. https://www.stortinget.no/no/Saker-og-publikasjoner/Vedtak/Beslutninger/Odelstinget/2008-2009/beso-200809-042/#a2

53. Flaskerud 2010: 133, cf. Borchgrevink 2002: 128.

54. Although cf. Borchgrevink 2002: 138, note 40 for issues raised concerning textbook images.

55. Jan Opsal 2006: 49. My translation. Norwegian text: "Det var tale om en pedagogisk vurdering ut fra KRL-fagets mål om å bekrefte muslimske elevers identitet. Følgelig må en framstille den enkelte religionen ut fra dens kontekstuelle form Norge. Da ville det ikke være riktig å presentere elevene for kunst som ville oppfattes som fremmed I forhold til deres egne religiøse tradisjoner. Hadde muslimene i Norge kommet fra tradisjoner hvor slike bilder var naturlig akseptert, ville vurderingen blitt en annen." It should however be noted that Opsal is the author of the section about Islam in the RE textbook for upper secondary school that reproduces the most varied selection of figurative images representing central protagonists in the history of Islam. See Heiene et al. 2013 and note 46 above. The primary school subject's role in confirming and supporting the pupils' religious identity is where the most notable changes have been made the last years, both in the curriculum and in classroom practice. Since the subject has moved significantly from the original dominant "learning from religion" ideology to an approach funded in "learning about religion," this argument may however be slightly more problematic now than in 2006. However, since the balance many had hoped was achievable with RLE in 2008 seems to be further from reach with the 2015 revision that quantitatively favors Christianity, there will probably be even less time to explore different Muslim identities post-2015 than before. Instead of a more nuanced perspective on plurality of Muslim communities, it is likely that the Islam the students encounter after the changes of 2015 will be even more essentialist and simplified.

56. With the exception of the small embroidery depicting Burak in *Du og Jeg* 4. Cf. p. 136 above.

57. Maagerø 2010; Undheim 2013.

58. Cf. Undheim 2013.

59. Janson 2012: 338.

60. In the conclusion to his review of the textbooks' use of images in representations of Islam, Winje also underlines that "examples of art [ought to] reflect the plurality within one of the world's largest and most important religions. Thirdly, the long history of Islam in Europe should be made visible in both text and images" (Winje 2003: 55, my translation).

61. Jonas Otterbeck indicated already in 2005 that certain strands or representatives of Islam have had more influence than others in the production of Swedish RE textbooks. It is particularly the ahistorical ideology of Islamists that he identifies as prominent. "Islamists try to delegitimize the historical development of Islam. Thus, the law schools, dynasties, philosophical trends and the development of Shia and Sufi understandings are criticized. Another strategy is to silence any discussion of them [...]" (Otterbeck 2005: 806).

62. Cf. the statistics from 2013 presented by Oddbjørn Leirviks, which show the increasing pluralism within Muslim: http://folk.uio.no/leirvik/tekster/IslamiNorge.html#statistikk (accessed 03.03.2017).
63. Andreassen 2014: 5.
64. Gruber and Shalem 2014: 4.

8. UNDERMINING AUTHORITY: THE REPRESENTATION OF BUDDHISM AND DISCOURSE ON MODERNITY IN RELIGION EDUCATION TEXTBOOKS

Kai Arne Nyborg

INTRODUCTION

Textbooks are an integral part of school education. In the school subject Religion Education (RE), textbooks represent knowledge about religion and culture. While some people are aware that the status of knowledge in textbooks are not ideologically neutral, but based on cultural beliefs, few contest the common sense view of textbooks as authorities of knowledge (Andreassen 2014). In this chapter I will attempt to provide reasons for being critical towards the authoritative status of textbook representations of Buddhism specifically. Textbooks do not simply reflect and transmit objective and true descriptions of Buddhism. Knowledge is constructed through selections, structure, adapting to curricula and so on, as much as constituted out of discourses influencing the representation of Buddhism.

By connecting Steven Berkwitz' study of misconceptions based upon orientalist practices (2004) and Craig Martin's study of interpretative strategies involved in maintaining authority in the reading and use of religious scripture (2009), in this study I will focus on how the representational strategies in the RE textbooks undermine Buddhist authority. From a science of religion perspective, textbook representations of religion and culture that reproduce common sense ideas and ideological propagations rather than communicate theoretical generalizations (Martin 2014), are problematic.

By focusing on the representation of Buddhism in terms of interpretative strategies, scholarly perspectives, and the effects these strategies might have on Buddhist authority, I will identify aspects of the discourse(s) that constitute knowledge about Buddhism in RE textbooks. If RE textbooks, as I will attempt to show, misrecognize Christian language as cross-cultural and comparative, and use national social values and practices to normatively evaluate Buddhist discourse and practice, then RE textbooks can be said to perform, with Bourdieu

(1977/2005), a type of *symbolic violence*. I will argue that symbolic violence is a consequence and expression of the discourse on religion and modernity.

EMPIRICAL MATERIAL, METHOD AND STRATEGY OF ANALYSIS

The empirical basis for this study is five RE textbooks applied in upper secondary school; two textbooks applied in the subject Victorian Certificate of Education (VCE)[1] Religion and Society in the state of Victoria in Australia, and three textbooks that are used in the subject Religion and Ethics in Norway. There are practical reasons as to why I have included textbooks from Australia such as language barrier, and accessibility. And, there are professional reasons such as the fact that Australia has adopted an explicit multicultural policy where religion is recognized as an important marker of identity, and it has also installed a private/public distinction that gives religion the opportunity to operate in the sphere of health, education, social services etc.

The two national contexts are similar. In both culture is heavily influenced by Western customs and traditions, and Christianity is the majority religion. The national contexts are different in geographical location, and in offering RE as part of its educational design. The subject VCE Religion and Society is currently elective, while Religion and Ethics in Norway is mandatory.

In the Australian and Norwegian study design for religious education the textbooks are structured according to curriculum organization and ideas, and facilitate comparison. In the subject *VCE Religion and Society* religion is understood "in a general way as meaning systems that have eight interrelated aspects" that can "guide students through their study of one or many religious traditions" (Victorian Certificate of Education Design [VCCED] 2014: 7). The Norwegian curricula state explicitly that "Education in the subject (Religion and Ethics) shall develop the theoretical and practical competence to analyze and compare religions, views on lives and philosophical disciplines" (The Norwegian Directorate for Education and Training 2006: 2). Both national curricula entertain a dimensional model or aspective approach, wherein the ethical aspect of religions are emphasized. I have strategically limited the aim and scope of this chapter to looking at the presentation of Buddhism and especially Buddhist ethics. One of the competence goals in the Norwegian curriculum is to describe central aspects and discuss a religion's ethics. Similarly, in the Australian context and curriculum one is to learn about the ethical perspectives of religious traditions as well as particular ethical positions on particular issues and themes (VCE Religion and Society 2014: 19).

Buddhism is chosen because it does not in all of its discourses and practices qualify as a religion (Faure 2003; Lincoln 2003), and because several misconceptions regarding representation of Buddhism prevail in the study of religion (Berkwitz 2004). Although Buddhism challenges the understanding of the category "religion" in RE, it is still recognized in the curricula as well as in the textbooks as a world religion. Accordingly, knowledge about the ethical dimension of Buddhism is to be expected in textbooks, as well as the opportunity to compare with other religions on the basis of ethics.

In the Norwegian as well as the Australian RE-subject, learning about religion is fundamentally a *comparative project*. This is stated in the Norwegian curriculum as a specific competence goal, and in the Australian curriculum as the basic approach to studying religion. Comparison is both a method and an approach to acquire knowledge about religion. For the analysis in this chapter it is crucial to investigate the premises for comparison.

Analyzing Questions
In analyzing the Australian and Norwegian RE textbooks I take a discursive approach (cf. Fairclough 1992, 2003; Laclau and Mouffe 1985/2001; Lincoln 2003). The textbook representation of Buddhism is investigated in light of the following questions:

1. How do the textbooks articulate and contextualize Buddhist discourse and practice?
2. How does the textbooks' articulation and contextualization of Buddhist discourse and practice relate to perspectives in the science of religion?
3. How do the textbooks facilitate and provide for comparison?
4. How do the different national contexts compare in the textbook representation of Buddhism?

All the textbooks make use of interpretative strategies. Some interpretative strategies are visible in all textbooks. Other strategies are specific to a particular textbook. All the emphasized interpretative strategies in the representation of Buddhism reflect a discourse on modernity.

In analyzing the textbooks I have chosen to present the textbooks in a particular order according to the difference between the various interpretative strategies, their relations, as well as the degree of complexity involved in their identification as expressions of a particular discourse.

MEDIATING STRATEGIES IN THE TEXTBOOK *EXISTENCE* (2008) — COMPARISON USING CHRISTIAN LANGUAGE

In the textbook *Existence* (Norwegian, *Eksistens*) (Fines Aronsen et al. 2008) readers immediately experience that Buddhism is represented using Christian language. This interpretative strategy is not particular to this textbook as this move can be found in the other textbooks as well. The textbook exemplifies the use of Christian concepts, theories and models to describe and explain Buddhist theory and practice. This has profound consequences to the students' development of a competence in analyzing and comparing religions and life views, as stated in the Norwegian curriculum.

The textbook *Existence* starts by outlining and explaining Buddhism in relation to Hinduism. Practices such as the caste system, offerings, and concern with gods, soul and reincarnation as well as karma become the background for the explanation of Buddhism (Fines Aronsen et al. 2008: 40–45); what the authors call "the common Indian platform" (Fines Aronsen et al. 2008: 52). However, monotheistic ideas quickly become implicated in conceptualizing Buddhist ideas and practices, and signal the default position of having a religion. The authors explain the cyclic view of history, universe and man in contrast to a monotheistic version:

> The circuit of rebirth applies to the world as much as humans. As we can understand, there is no creation, and Buddhism therefore has no creator god. Accordingly, the Buddhist avoids that which in Jewish and Christian tradition is called "the problem of evil": How could a loving and almighty God, allow for evil in the world (Fines Aronsen et al. 2008: 50, my translation).[2]

In this paragraph, the monotheistic conception of religion becomes a prototype to understand Buddhism.[3] However, when relating to Christianity it becomes evident that the concept of rebirth in Buddhism is different from a Christian concept of creation, and that the concurrent idea of evil establishes a difference between the two systems.

Two pages later, the author seek to explain karma and rebirth, and the same strategy of comparing and contrasting with monotheistic ideas is still operative. The paradox using Christian terms to describe and explain Buddhist theory, and at the same time distinguish Buddhism from Christianity, become inevitable, when the author disregards his previous conclusion:

> Therefore Buddhists do not discern between 'evil' and 'good' humans. Between 'righteous' and 'unrighteous.' They are only concerned with setting free humans from their sufferings. Salvation is therefore to be redeemed from the evil circle of rebirth (Fines Aronsen et al. 2008: 52, my translation).[4]

In the first paragraph, the author takes monotheism as a starting point, and draws up a distinction based on the concept of creation and its concurrent problem of evil, as invalid in describing and explaining Buddhism. In the second paragraph, evil is reintroduced as a comparative category central to the understanding of religion.

The problem is not that the textbook takes a singular monotheistic concept and uses it to misrepresent Buddhism in this one instance, but that Christianity becomes the model for understanding religion using a family of concepts belonging to a monotheistic, Christian understanding of religion. The problem is that the textbook uses Christian concepts, in plural, to demarcate Buddhism. The projection of the circle of rebirth as "evil" is a construction based upon the Christian ideas of salvation and redemption. To "set people free," is a project characteristic of the Christian messianic figure Jesus. Buddhists, Buddha's and bodhisattvas do not set people free they proclaim to help others attain liberation.

According to the Buddhist scholar Peter Harvey:

> The Buddhist perspective on the cycle of rebirths is that it is not a pleasant affair, but that all unenlightened people are reborn whether they like it or not, and whether they believe it or not. The process of life and rebirth is not seen to have any inherent purpose; for it was not designed and created by any being. Thus it is known as samsara, or 'wandering on' from life to life. Thus the only sensible aim, for one who understands samsara to some extent, is to strive, firstly, to avoid its more unpleasant realms, and ultimately to transcend it altogether, by attaining Nirvana (Skt; Pali Nibbana), and to help others to do so (Harvey 2000: 14).

Normative evaluations might be customary in some understandings of rebirth, both in and outside of texts and practices, warranting the characteristic of evil and resulting in a practice where fear of rebirth function as a motivation for action, however, it cannot, from a scholarly perspective be presented as the singular understanding of Buddhist rebirth.

Seen in light of the map/territory metaphor; the textbook *Existence* uses terms such as belief, salvation, evil, creation, redemption, that do not completely fit with the signified phenomenon of Buddhism; defined in its own terms through concepts such as samsara (rebirth), karma, dukkha (suffering), and nirvana (awakening). Christian concepts are used to compare and contrast with Buddhism, other times they are implicated. In all circumstances and uses the presuppositions are not explained, nor is there an attempt at signalling possible implications or negative consequences. The use of Christian terms is not innocent as one singular term draws on a whole complex of ideas and thoughts. A Christian perspective consists of particular assumptions, concepts and ways of thinking that is coherent on its own. Used as a mediating strategy the Christian perspective presupposes and builds on values that might be in conflict with the represented universe or world of the other. No steps are taken to make up for the incongruence.

These are just a selected few examples of local, Christian categories used to describe Buddhism in the textbook *Existence*. This textbook is rich in its use of Christian language and implicitly comparing Buddhism with Christianity, but it is not unique.

MEDIATING STRATEGIES IN THE TEXTBOOK *VCE RELIGION AND SOCIETY*, UNITS 1–4 (2012) — REDUCING COMPLEXITY AND GENERALIZATION

Another textbook operating on similar premises is the Australian textbook *VCE Religion and Society* (Green et al. 2012). In describing the ethics of different religions, this textbook provides a comparative chart. However, the problem is not only the use of concepts, categories and models that privilege monotheistic religions, but that the language use connected with shortcomings in explanation and misconceptions disfavors and constructs Buddhism negatively.

Buddhism is presented schematically using Christian and monotheistic terms/categories as headlines and supplementary explanation. The two main headlines: *Divine Authority for Ethical System* and *Worldly Authority and Religious Leadership* are based on a monotheist distinction and reflect several Christian ideas; among these Augustin's teaching of the two regiments. As this model is not representative for Buddhism several problems are created. The main category *Divine Authority of Ethical System* is structured according to three sub-headlines: *Ultimate Reality*, *Divine Reward and Punishment* and *Expression—Beliefs*.

Stating the concept of ultimate reality in Buddhism: "No concept of a personal or creator God" (Green et al. 2012: 225), signals that the category *Divine Authority* is construed on a Christian understanding, wherein divine authority is aligned with a "personal or creator God." As there is no distinction between a divine and a worldly authority in Buddhism, Buddhism represents a deviation from the prototype. In the second sub-headline: *Divine Reward and Punishment*, the Christian conceptual universe again is alluded to explicitly in the category, and implicitly by reference through comparison: "Ignorance rather than sin is the source of problems in the system of *Karma*" (Green et al. 2012: 225).

Defining religion in terms of Christianity and monotheist systems is an interpretative strategy already mentioned in association with the textbook *Existence*. The problem in *VCE Religion and Society* is related to the practice of generalization and reduction of complexity. As these are moves normally associated with scholarly practice, they are conceived as legitimate and therefore easily overlooked, even when they are compromising cultural phenomena. By explaining the concept of karma in relation to rebirth exclusively, and by uncritically reproducing a simplistic, popular understanding, complexity is reduced, but at the same time Buddhism is distorted: "good actions enable one to ascend through various life forms and levels of creation. Bad actions enable a descent to lower life forms" (Green et al. 2012: 225).

Simplifying the concept of karma is in one sense understandable given the nature of the chart and comparative scheme; by using bullet points the textbook signals that the content included is basic, essential and that the presentation as a whole intends to give a brief but coherent overview. It is however highly tendentious to make rebirth a cornerstone in Buddhist ethics and trivializing the karma/rebirth-complex. According to buddhologist Keown – karma is for Buddhists "a complex of interrelated ideas which embraces both ethics and belief in rebirth," and "For Buddhism, karma is thus neither random — like luck — nor a system of rewards and punishments meted out by God. Nor is it destiny or fate: instead it is best understood as a natural — if complex sequence of causes and effects" (Keown 2010: 437).

The consequence of the presentation strategy in *VCE Religion and Society* is that it misconstrues and gives untruthful information about Buddhism and Buddhists. According to the authors "one can escape the cycle of karma by reaching enlightenment and release *themselves* (my italicization) from the cycle extinguishing karma (Nirvana)" (Green et al. 2012: 225). In this statement samsara is mistakenly explained as karma. Buddhist terminology is trivialized, and this communicates how the author perceives Buddhism.

Under the third sub-headline: *Expression — Beliefs*, the so-called main doctrines and/or beliefs having ethical significance is formulated: "Buddhists believe that suffering is the nature of existence," "Disputes there being a God (akin to Epicurus and atheist thinkers)," and "Buddhists believe that escape from suffering comes from following the eightfold path and the ethics of Buddhism" (Green et al. 2012: 225). Could the use of the word belief in these sentences in some way be misleading? Do Buddhists really "believe that suffering is the nature of existence"?

Regarding the question of suffering, Harvey (2010) argues that the popular understanding of the four noble truths in the first sermon of the Buddha, wherein dukkha (suffering) is mentioned, needs to be corrected. As the sermon outlines the first of the truths with the intention to be understood, the second—suffering – to be abandoned, the third to be realized and the fourth to be developed or cultivated, suffering cannot be the nature of existence nor can it be escaped. Further, Harvey explains that these noble truths or ennobling realities "are not something that Buddhists should respond to with "belief." To "believe" them is to mishandle them, rather than treat them appropriately by respectively understanding, abandoning, realizing and developing them" (Harvey 2010: 320).

The sentence, "Buddhists believe that the escape from suffering comes from following the eightfold path and the ethics of Buddhism" is simply false. Karma cannot be escaped only managed. Could it be that this managing must be seen in a context of practice and a working process, and not predominantly in a context of beliefs and faith, as is done in this textbook? Thus, the textbook frames suffering and the management of suffering negatively by using the terms *believe* and *follow*, emphasizing aspects disqualifying action and the exercise implied in practice. Paradoxically, in the summary of *Ethical Ideas and Concepts* at the end of the chart this is acknowledged implicitly in the statement: "Desires generate karma (unethical actions form attachments) which must be dealt with either in this lifetime or others" (Green et al. 2012: 225). However, it has no consequence for the presentation that must be seen as an incoherent unorganized lapsing of ideas and concepts in a random design where meanings go in every direction.

Under the second major headline: *Worldly Authority and Religious Leadership*, the textbook presupposes an organization and authority structure determining standpoints on ethical issues. The sub-headline: *World Movements and Denominations who Formulate Stances on Ethical Issues and Advise Individual Religious Leaders as to Their Rulings on Ethics*, assumes a structure that is expected of organized religious traditions. However, when explaining this structure in Buddhism the author directs focus away from the fact that this structure cannot be identified and instead redirects it to schisms, and oppositional group rhetoric:

> Theravada (Orthodox), claims to have the original untainted teachings of the speeches of the Buddha compiled at a time closer to his life.
>
> Mahayana was compiled later and some elements clash with Theravada doctrine [...]. Some influence from locality led to different form of Buddhism, for example Zen Buddhism in Japan and Tibetan Buddhism (Green et al. 2012: 225).

Instead of addressing the different non-unitary organizational structure in Buddhism, the textbook focuses on distinctions between traditions and schools based on narrow group rhetoric. Naturally there are schisms and sectarianism in Buddhism as elsewhere in religions, but describing the Theravada tradition/Buddhists using the banal standpoint: "claims to have the original untainted teachings," because "the speeches of the Buddha" were "compiled at a time closer to his life," is projecting the standpoint of a narrow insider position. This rhetoric is also reminiscent of ideas defined as orientalist where the development of the Buddhist tradition is explained as going from an original untainted version to a diversity of inauthentic forms (King 2006).

The authors' concentration on conflict is problematic. By using strong wording such as "some elements (in Mahayana) clash with Theravada doctrine" without explaining the reason for diverging views between Theravada and Mahayana, signals an underlying motivation or deliberation. Current research, both in relation to theory and to practice having a bearing upon this distinction, denies the conflict or construed opposition between Theravada and Mahayana. The statement that "influence from locality led to different form of Buddhism," can against this background — the idea of a development from an original Buddhism to its many inauthentic forms, and in the context of opposition and conflict, seem to implicate a negative reduction and denigration of Tibetan Buddhism and Zen Buddhism.

In presenting *Worldly Authority and Religious Leadership in Christianity* it is merely stated that: "Each denomination has its own ethical authority structures through Church leadership," wherein Catholicism, Orthodox, Protestantism, Church of England and Pentecostal are described briefly with no antagonism, or sectarian language implied (Green et al. 2012: 219–20). Nor is there any mention of why these denominations are different — as in the case with Buddhism where it is implied that elements clash, that oppositions are based on insider rhetoric, and that different forms have developed influenced by locality.

The only organization mentioned in regards to Buddhism is "the Foundation for the Preservation of Mahayana Tradition," which is taken as representing the Mahayana internationally. Instead of adjusting the terms in the comparative chart, Buddhism is forced into a scheme, based on an understanding of Christian religion in particular. As a way of justifying the comparison the authors mention the Dalai Lama who "presides over a pontificate (*sic*) of his (Tibetan) sect of Vajrayana Buddhism only" (Green et al. 2012: 225). Paradoxically, the authors' rectifying views on the position of the Dalai Lama, fails to mention that organization and authority structures in Buddhism are different to e.g. Christian ones. The use of the term *sect* is hardly incidental having negative connotations signalling deviance.

In opposition, most scholars on Buddhism agree that authority structures and organization in Buddhism are primarily located to settings like the monastery or temples. However, the authority is restricted and does not have implications everywhere and for everyone. The second last sub-headline: *Ideas and Ethical Concepts—Revelation, Righteousness, Sin, Salvation, Free Will, Acts, Faith,* and *Grace* are telling of how Christian ideas and language are expressed as cross-cultural comparative terms (Green et al. 2012: 225). This fact is also affirmed as the concepts are identical to the ones displayed and used in the explanation of Christian ethics.

The problem with giving a presentation only delimited to a comparative chart is that the level of precision must be higher than normal, so that there is no opportunity for misunderstanding. This has not happened here.

MEDIATING STRATEGIES IN THE TEXTBOOK *FAITH AND THOUGHT* (2008) — CONTEXTUALIZING BUDDHISM IN NORWEGIAN AND WESTERN SOCIETY

In the textbook *Faith and Thought* (Norwegian, *Tro og tanke*) (Heiene et al. 2008) several problematic strategies can be identified. One strategy is that it relates to a Norwegian lifestyle and values rather than explaining the Buddhist practice, action or expression in the context where it is operative. Another strategy is the presentation of a narrow insider rhetoric constructed for the purpose of translation to a western context, as representative for a Buddhist tradition. A third strategy is to act as proficient enough to construct a religious expression and perform a Buddhist practice reserved for Buddhist masters or teachers on the highest level! A fourth strategy is to express doubt on the basis of historical research concerning the validity of a Buddhist practice, text or story.

While all textbooks take a dimensional approach, and give attention to ethics as a dimension of particular importance, *Faith and Thought* presents Buddhist ethics in one paragraph only, whilst presenting Christian ethics in an exclusive ten-page chapter! Taken into consideration that one of the competence goals is "to discuss central features of the ethics of the religions" (The Norwegian Directorate for Education and Training 2006: 2) and comparison is one of the major competences to be developed in the course, the presentation of Buddhism is limited in light of curriculum ambitions and aims. Nevertheless, as the description of social practices and institutions can explicitly or indirectly, refer to aspects of Buddhist ethics, I direct attention to an example in the textbook describing the relationship between monks and laypeople.

Buddhist Social Practice Contextualized and Explained in a Norwegian Context
Rather than explaining the relationship in terms of the Buddhist principle and practice of generosity (skr. dana), as normally done, the author reflects on the practice of giving alms seen from the perspective of a cultural outsider: "For the laypeople it is not experienced as a heavy duty, it is rather a privilege for them to give"[5] (Heiene et al. 2008: 83). Instead of taking the context wherein the practice is operative as a starting point to explanation, the author projects an immediate reaction to a social practice and arrangement that is unfamiliar to him. By contextualizing almsgiving as potentially experienced as a burden, the author implicitly, compares with a context and situation he defines as normal and installs his own would-be experience.

From a Buddhist perspective generosity located within the context of the relationship between monks and laypeople is emphasized as a virtue that is to be practiced and manifested in the provision of basic needs to the monks who in return provide for the highest gift that can be distributed, namely the teaching of dharma (Heim 2004: 196; Keown 2010: 341).

In a scholarly context on the other hand, this custom of giving and practice of generosity is explained as a mutually beneficial relationship that on a functional level upholds the sangha and maintains the distribution of dharma, as well as making available a situation where laypeople can establish karmic rewards. Further, this practice is operative predominantly in a so-called southern Buddhist context, rather than East Asian or Western, which makes it ungeneralizable. The textbook authors depict it as a universal Buddhist practice, and do not address this concern.

The problem with the textbook's implicit comparison is that it is in conflict with the scholarly principle of presenting the other on his/her own premises. Speaking on behalf of others in a cross-cultural, comparative study of religion, demands paying attention to the others first-order description. By taking into account ideas or structures in his own context — social values and norms, and projecting them onto the phenomenon as a way of explaining, the authors construct the other in their own image. The consequences of not being explained in its own terms is that the other instead is described as non-identical and therefore implicitly in a negative way, as one's own context and way of thinking is elevated simultaneously. In this way, the author presents local norms and values as universal.

From a single interpretative move, a whole series of problems are manifest. Implicitly the authors make a valuation of this arrangement that raises questions about its status and integrity, and further assess its validity and truth. In Norway, this social arrangement and institution of almsgiving/practice of generosity, expressed on the surface as begging, falls outside the social order, and is defined as a social problem. It is because the authors take the Norwegian culture/society as a point of departure, and make no reservations regarding the difference in context, that the operation is fallacious. Both the Buddhist and the scholarly perspective are compromised.

Zen Buddhism and the Koan—Reproducing Insider Rhetoric
A rather different strategy reflected in this textbook concerns the presentation of Zen Buddhism. In explaining Zen and the practice of Zen koan, the authors explain:

> Zen looks at religious rituals and dogmatic discussions as useless. The way to awakening is through sitting down and meditating. This happens in connection with education/learning where the zen master breaks down the students dispositions to think logically, for example by giving the students the task of meditating on a koan. A koan is a paradoxical expression that cannot be understood by help of logic, but demands insight on another level. [...] Logical thinking is understood as a barrier in relation to awakening and a koan is a means to destabilize logical thinking (Heiene et al. 2008: 100, my translation).[6]

According to scholars of religion studying Buddhist religion "the koan is not best understood as purely instrumental and without cognitive content, nor at a blank, non-cognitive state of mind" (McMahan 2010: 445-46). The incompleteness of presenting the koan "as a device to propel the mind out of calculating, rational thought, releasing it to the realm of the intuitive and trans-rational" is testified by the fact of a vast commentarial literature in the Zen tradition. The "Zen tradition values intellectual comprehension of koans" (McMahan 2010: 446), and the example of the "one hand clapping" reflects metaphorical and symbolic content in relating to the doctrine of non-duality.

From a scholarly, science of religions point of view, explaining Zen Buddhism as looking "at rituals and discussion as useless," is not explaining religion. That is confirming one insider account, and by extension a way of looking at religion through the lens of mysticism, or religionism. Reproducing insider rhetoric of Buddhism, or popular comprehensions, describing the Zen master's relationship and task vis-a- vis the student as consisting of breaking "down the dispositions to think logically," and that the koan "cannot be understood by help of logic," hardly provides for any cultural understanding. Conceived as beyond reason, and completely different from other practices of religious learning, Zen Buddhism and the koan practice is placed on the margins of what is defined as religion.

Explained as insider-rhetoric, expressions such as the one reproduced in the textbook can be thought of as instrumental to the reproduction of authority and of social formation. Seen from such an outsider-perspective this rhetorical practice and discourse, becomes the center of understanding Zen Buddhism and religion as a phenomenon in general (Sharf 1998). According to such a theory of religion, that also takes into consideration the empirical data, ritual and discussion in the Zen Buddhist tradition is presupposed and verified (Wright 1992). The textbook as such, could be claimed to reproduce insider terminology and rhetoric. But that is not all. The author reproduces one, particular insider rhetoric associated with the introduction of and recontextualizing Zen Buddhism into a Western context (Borup 2004).

The Author as Zen Master

In addition to mentioning the popular Zen Buddhist koan "What is the sound of one hand clapping?" the author incorporates in the presentation: "If you got ice-cream I will give you some. If you don't have ice-cream I will take it away from you,"[7] as another example. As this latter is not to be found within any known Buddhist texts nor any Buddhist discourse, cannot be related to any traditions, schools, and teacher or otherwise, it is an invention made by the author. Through this operation the author, in employing his creative freedom, claim to have a particular religious understanding and that it is hierarchically on the level of a Zen Buddhist master.

The author's assumption claiming insight on "another level," according to the above quotation, making him capable of constructing Zen koans on par with Zen Buddhist masters, transgresses the limits of professionalism. Since the constructed ice cream phrase is not related to Zen Buddhism, its status and use in the presentation of Zen Buddhism have the effect of misconstruing the Zen Buddhist practice and discourse, the Zen groups, and the Zen tradition. By employing his creative freedom, the author is trivializing and implicitly denigrating the phenomena he is representing.

The Representativity of the Dhammapada and Representation of the Buddha

In *Faith and Thought*, the analysis of religious texts are emphasized as an important skill to be learned and therefore accommodated for in the organization of the textbook. Texts are a major focus, and after introducing the concept of sacred texts in a separate chapter, the textbook makes an attempt at integrating one or several texts in the presentation of the individual religions. In the presentation of Buddhism, the Dhammapada is denoted as the most popular text, and the only textual source relied upon with the exception of three paragraphs quoted from a dialogue between the Buddha and a king about the fruits of a monkhood life. This becomes a paradox when the author, rather than take responsibility for his selection of the Dhammapada text, constructs a scholarly opposition undermining its validity: "Buddhists think that Buddha is the originator of the text, but that it was first written down after Buddha's death" (Heiene et al. 2008: 90, my translation).[8]

It seems clear from this formulation that the Buddha is not constituted as author, but influential to the thoughts and ideas communicated in the verses contained in the text. This understanding reflects in the presentation of the point of view of Buddhists. Who is saying that "the text was first written down after Buddha's death," is not clear, but it does seem to reflect the position of an outsider perspective. The juxtaposition of an insider perspective and an outsider observation in the same sentence can make the reader precarious about its meaning. The formulation becomes problematic because it is using an outsider position to modify an insider perspective.

From the standpoint of science of religion — the Dhammapada is taken as a text containing phrases and content not specific to Buddhism, but is constructed mostly out of the stories and sayings fluctuating in society at the time.

Rather than being unique, it is very general to life and society in India at the time. The problem here does not concern whether or not this text is representative of Buddhism, but the authors contextualization and use of it. After initially compromising the status of the text, the authors ascribe Dhammapada authority as a representative text in Buddhism because of their own use of it. The authors cannot use the text and take the standpoint of the Buddha without ascribing authority upon it. Strategic formulations such as: "Buddha underlined..." "Buddha formulated..." (Heiene et al. 2008: 89), "Buddha understood..." (Heiene et al. 2008: 91), "Buddha himself said..." (Heiene et al. 2008: 91), "Buddha described..." (Heiene et al. 2008: 91), are used to ascribe authority to the presentation and give it validity. No matter how problematic this presentation is, the authority of the authors would be impossible without the Dhammapada status as representative.

From an outsider perspective, staking a claim of truth on behalf of a being/person that lived some 2500 years ago, recounted in a text of a more dubious status, is rather problematic: "This is how Buddha resonated when he concluded that all the five processes (skandhas) are continually changing" (Heiene et al. 2008: 93). As if it is possible to insist upon knowing other people's thought processes, less how they reasoned and built their argumentation, based on a collection of aphorisms reported and written down some years after the so-called originator's death. While it is problematic that the Dhammapada is the primary text referred to explaining the Buddhist teaching, it is more problematic that the author takes upon himself the responsibility to give voice to the Buddha.

Using Religious Texts and Narratives, Applying Historical Critical Principles
Perhaps the most conspicuous of strategies in the presentation of Buddhism in the textbook *Faith and Thought*, is the artificially adopted outsider perspective giving the reader the impression of being based on a scholarly basis. This strategy, mentioned above, as constructing an opposition between an insider and an outsider account, is repeated in several other paragraphs such as these paragraphs outlining the life of the Buddha:

> Siddharta was son of Maya and Suddhodana Gautama, which in the Buddhist narrative is a royal couple in the kingdom of Shakya. Historians question this, as the kingdom was not a monarchy at this time. One figures that Siddharta was born around year 560 BC and lived until he was 80 years old. He could have been the son of a prominent man in the capital of Kapilavastu, but historians do not believe he lived in such an excessive luxury as some of the stories tell" (Heiene et al. 2008: 93, my translation).[9]

> Despite the remonstrations it is the stories in the Buddhist sources that depict the image of the Buddha most Buddhists relate to. These are also the basis of this presentation (Heiene et al. 2008: 94, my translation).[10]

As there are no sources mentioned in the authors' presentation, we are left bewildered as to which historians are referred to, and the purpose of mentioning them in the presentation. Why mention them at all if the presentation was going to be based on Buddhist sources exclusively? A similar compromising position is taken later when referring to a council after the death of Buddha where the author writes that: "It is said that the (whole) text was recited, written down and collected into the Tripitaka ("three baskets"), even though the historians think that the final assembling must have happened somewhat later (Heiene et al. 2008: 97).[11] Again, as the reference to historians is baseless, and serves no other purpose than taking credibility away from a Buddhist insider point of view, the authors' use the historical perspective as scholarly justification for compromising the authenticity of an event and/or a practice.

A professional historical perspective would demand self-reflexivity and consistency in its use of historistication, not allowing random comments emphasizing divergence between religious insiders and science of religion outsiders, based on historical facts without any references. A historical perspective is not compromising to the studied position by intent; it is so by nature (Lincoln 1996). It does not take anything away from the insider, but reframes the religious practice or discourse in focus, in terms of theory. In reference to the assembling of texts in the mentioned example, an outsider perspective would make a point of the authorization process involved in selecting and omitting texts. From a theoretical point of view the Buddhist canonization of texts is a concrete and specific example of a more general and universal phenomenon in the domain of religion (cf. Smith 1982: 43).

MEDIATING STRATEGIES IN THE TEXTBOOK IN THE SAME WORLD (2008) — COMPARING THEORY AND PRACTICE

In the presentation of the Buddhist view on nature, humans, gender and gender roles and other religions and life views, the textbook *In the Same World* (Norwegian, *I samme verden*) (Kvamme et al. 2008) constructs an opposition between theory and practice, the ideal and the real:

> Buddhism also teaches that we are all part of the same circuit of life. Nature and animals have a right to life on the same level as humans, and if we destroy nature, we injure/damage ourselves as all things are connected. That everything is interconnected has an ecological dimension. Nevertheless, there are still environmental destructions in Buddhist countries. In countries such as Burma and Thailand there are great environmental pollutions and forests are devastated (Kvamme et al. 2008: 255, my translation).[12]

> Buddha's point of departure was that all humans were equal independent of race, gender, and social status. But the actual reality in many Buddhist countries are characterised by an array of discriminating circumstances and continual human rights violations. One example is Sri Lanka, where the Buddhist majority for years have been in conflict with the Tamils, that mainly are Hindus and Catholics (Kvamme et al. 2008: 241, my translation).[13]
>
> Buddha's teaching expresses that both genders can achieve nirvana equally. Still we have seen that the spiritual equality is not always expressed in social life. Men have usually had a dominant position in Buddhist societies (Kvamme et al. 2008: 256, my translation).[14]
>
> Buddhism are in many ways an open and tolerant religion and have easily let itself be influenced by other cultures and religions met in its surroundings. [...] Today Buddhists must relate to Christianity and Islam when they transmit the teaching in the West. Buddhism here shows signs of adaption by taking up Christian and humanistic ideals (Kvamme et al. 2008: 257, my translation).[15]

The textbook constructs an opposition between Buddhist theory, where all of existence has the same value and humans are equal regardless of race, gender and social status, and social institutions and practices in many Buddhist countries and societies. By characterizing Buddhist countries and societies in terms of "environmental destruction," "pollution," "forest devastation," "human rights violations," "discriminating circumstances," gender and social inequality, paternalistic structures, and so on, in context of and opposition to Buddhist theory, Buddhist religion is held responsible for discrimination, human rights violations and environmental damages in Asian countries and Asian societies. Assuming Buddhism to have a causal role to social change and development in a modern world according to its system of beliefs, contradicts social theories emphasizing complex processes and the involvement of multiple factors (Benavides 1999), and is therefore not acceptable as a scientific explanation. Comparing Buddhist theory with practice (in an Asian country and society) is in conflict with scholarly principles (Jensen 1994: 8). Religious discourse and practice do not exist *sui generis*, as an independent and constant variable (Jensen 2003).

Christianity in Comparison — Creating Buddhism as a Problem
As the textbook *In the Same World* is predominantly oriented towards comparison, organizing the chapters on individual religions according to several competence goals, and by providing answers to the competence goals formulated as questions, for example, What is the religion's view on gender and gender-roles?, comparison between different religions and life-views are facilitated and encouraged. Applying the same questions to the presentation of Christianity one would find that Christianity is presented in alignment with democracy, human rights, and

manifesting humanist ideals and principles (Nyborg, forthcoming 2017). Against the background of such an understanding and theory of religion, Christianity is presented as a solution whilst Buddhism is a problem. The implicit functionalist model of religion and assumption that Christian religion contributes to social progress and welfare, whereas Buddhism does not, explains why social problems are connected to Buddhism and not to Christianity. Consequently, Buddhism, according to the textbook, must relate to Christianity (and Islam) in a Western society, and take up Christian and humanistic ideals. There is no explicit answer to the question why Buddhism must adapt to Western society by relating to Christianity and take up Christian and humanistic ideals, it is simply assumed.

MEDIATING STRATEGIES IN THE TEXTBOOK *RELIGION AND ETHICS IN A PLURALIST SOCIETY* (REPS) (2012)—INTERFAITH RELIGION

The textbook *Religion and Ethics in a Pluralist Society* (Tuohy et al. 2012) does not reflect one particular interpretative strategy, but an approach—interfaith, where Buddhism is presented as an ideal version. Buddhism is constructed in the image of a project aimed at defining the role and place of religion in a modern, secular and pluralist society. In representing Buddhism as identical to other religions, as a privileged perspective addressing ethics, social and political questions, this textbook provides a normative definition of what religion ought to be, rather than presenting Buddhism descriptively. The authority of Buddhism is undermined by representing it as a social project, affirmative of values defined as important in current society.

Interfaith Buddhism
In REPS religions are presented as oriented towards happiness, and the individual religions reflecting distinctive paths to this goal. This goal is realized, in all religions, through a focus on relationships towards self, others, society and the world. Religions are structurally similar in being paths to happiness and by focusing on relationships. This goal of happiness and focus on relationships are inscribed into the presentation of Buddhism through formulations such as:

> to reach perfect happiness and peace as exemplified by the Buddha (Tuohy et al. 2014: 241).

> One who is genuinely at peace with themselves will spontaneously want to help others and establish peace within their family, neighbourhood and society at large (Tuohy et al. 2014: 260).

> From the Buddhist point of view, cultivating harmony at a family level is extremely important and forms the basis for creating peace in the world (Tuohy et al. 2014: 261).

Buddhism is consolidated as a social perspective placing value on helping others, creating peace in the family, the neighborhood, the society at large, and the world as such. Further, in addressing themes and issues such as war, sexuality, environment, poverty, family and rights, Buddhism as well as other religions, are represented as professing a strong social commitment. Although the doctrines and theory (beliefs) in religions are different, they have relevance to current social and political issues. The consequence of this way of presenting religion in the textbook is that beliefs and doctrines become both trivial and central at the same time. As Buddhist doctrines and theory they are trivial. As addressing particular social issues and problems they become relevant. Thus, theory and doctrines become central constituents of religion. Buddhist doctrine and theory, as examples of religion are depicted as causal to ethical actions and discourses. This becomes clear when seeing how the textbook explains the relationship between religion and morality, and religion and ethics more broadly:

> Morality is not dependent upon religion. To be moral is part of learning how to exist in human community. We are social creatures who choose to live together in many ways, so learning how to do this for mutual and communal harmony and benefit is essential. Yet religion and morality are intertwined, intricately so. Attempts to separate religion and morality, placing religion into the 'interior, spiritual realm', while seeing morality as 'an exterior, social construct' does not acknowledge the complexity of either, or their very human-based relatedness (MacKay 2004: 43).

> The ethical position of a religion on an ethical issue of society is usually supported by the communication of values and beliefs through several aspects of the tradition. Such ethical positions, perhaps expressed through moral codes, flow from and are grounded in the stories, beliefs, rituals, religious experience and social structure of the traditions that express them (Tuohy et al. 2012: 228).

This ideal version constructs religion as a social perspective inherently ethical, antithetical to conflict and providing solutions to social, political and ethical issues primarily detected through beliefs, but also through the other aspects wherein religion is manifested. The aspective approach belongs to a family resemblance theory of religion (McCutcheon 2007: 92) and is instituted in the curriculum as educational (cf. Andreassen 2010). In REPS the aspective approach is employed as explanation of religion as predominantly ethical.

Both these issues in the presentation, the focus on beliefs (doctrines and theory) and concern with ethics, reflect a distinct Christian understanding of religion and a development related to modernity. Implicitly the interfaith project and pluralist theology of religions' position identifiable in the textbook reflects and addresses a general discussion in contemporary society; the issue of religion and its relationship to and place in a modern, secular society. More explicitly this is shown in the textbook presentation of Buddhism through its emphasis on *reason* as an integrated element and defining characteristic of religion. Under the headline *The Teachings and the Importance of Reason* it is stated that:

> In Buddhism it is extremely important to analyse, investigate and test the teachings against your experience. Through reason if we find that the teaching is logical, it is our personal responsibility to integrate what we have learned into our daily lives (Tuohy et al. 2012: 241).

Through the use of science-related terms such as analyze, investigate, test against experience, reason, logic, Buddhism is presented as fundamentally rational. The textbook signals that the presentation of the individual religions are ideal, but make no reservations concerning how the presentations ought to be understood, and reflect as such a view on religion. The ideal version of particular religions and more importantly religion as such, is a consequence of the interfaith project and pluralist position, and the attempt to define the situation of and negotiate the conditions for religion in current society. Presenting Buddhism as a social perspective and in alignment with reason is in conflict with perspectives arguing that Buddhism lacks a social ethic, and that a rational Buddhism is a modern, Western interpretation. More importantly, this approach diminishes differences between Buddhist positions, and between religious traditions. As the interfaith approach excludes any focus on conflicts in learning about religion, it is less a historical approach than a normative theological approach.

The interfaith approach operates with a positive understanding of religion. Not only does the interfaith approach have a formative function upon the different religions. Religions can be understood through its different aspects. Through the explanation of the ethical aspect the different religions are constructed as social perspectives, addressing social problems. As such, the textbook has recalibrated Buddhism as an ethical resource and a social and political force. In doing this the textbook has created/defined the conditions of possibility for the existence and maintenance of religion in the modern, secular world. According to Jensen and Rothstein (2002), addressing social and ethical problems and questions is necessary for religion's survival.

THE REPRESENTATION OF BUDDHISM AND THE DISCOURSE ON MODERNITY

In the analysis I set out to investigate the premises for comparison in textbooks from the school subjects *VCE Religion and Society* and *Religion and Ethics*. As demonstrated, comparisons in RE textbooks are based on concepts and categories that are not cross-cultural and comparative, and the readers are not informed of the presuppositions comparison is based on. This happens in the textbook *Existence*, as well as in other textbooks. Concepts such as "evil," "setting people free," "salvation" and "redemption" form part of a Christian discourse and practice. They are local, not universal terms, encapsulated in a particular cosmology where concepts have their meaning defined relationally in similarity and contrast to other terms to which they are interconnected and dependant on. As insider terminology, the monotheistic concepts cannot be applied to Buddhist discourses and practices without clarifying their basis, function and use. Reservations and precautions are necessary. The comparativists' interest must be clarified and made explicit. To clarify the interest of the comparativist and inform the readers of the presuppositions the comparison is based on, are professional criteria preventing scholarly transgressions.

Buddhism becomes a problem to the category "Religion," defined in Christian terms. Conceptualizing Buddhism also becomes a problem when there is a lack of knowledge, and when the presentation is schematic and knowledge condensed. As generalization and reduction of complexity are conceived as legitimate scholarly moves, uncritical readers may overlook compromising presentations. In the textbook *VCE Religion and Society* I have identified practices simplifying, distorting, trivializing, misconstruing, as well as disqualifying Buddhist discourse and practices. Because cultural representations have social consequences (Dyer 1993), neither in a scholarly nor in an educational context, indifference to how cultural phenomena are presented are allowed.

In the textbook *Faith and Thought* a scholarly perspective is used to express doubt concerning the validity of a practice, a text and a story. In another instance, the same textbook takes the perspective of an enlightened Zen Buddhist master creating a Zen koan of its own! Seen from a science of religion point of view, these examples cannot be judged successful honoring scholarly demands of presenting religion from an insider and an outsider perspective. By reproducing a narrow insider rhetoric created for the meeting with, and translation of Buddhism into Western society, without any notification, the textbook distances itself from scholarly research. The textbook authors reveal themselves as completely oblivious to the origin and context for the rhetorical discourse they have reproduced. Similarly, the textbook ignores the context explaining the social arrangement and practice of almsgiving by omitting accompanying principles and virtues. Instead the arrangement and practice is evaluated in terms of norms and values related to a Norwegian context. Reproducing information from out-dated scholarly sources cannot be justified by claims that RE in upper secondary school is not science of religion. To insist that describing phenomena in an RE-textbook cannot include all the available information only warrants more reflected and reasoned evaluations and choices, as well as demands of higher precision in writing.

The fact that Buddhism does not live up to the theory and ideals it communicates is hardly a distinctive trait describing Buddhism, as this incongruence is common to all religions (Smith 1993: 289–309). To claim Buddhism responsible for social and political problems in Asian countries and societies, as the textbook *In the Same World* seems to imply, is theoretically inconsistent. The idea of religion as a causal factor to the elimination of social problems; having a preventive effect on environmental destruction and human rights violations and operating as an ethical corrective, lacks a scholarly basis. There is no necessary relationship between holding a view, and acting out its ethical implications. This reasoning is both logically and empirically unfounded.

Seen in a context where Christianity is presented in alignment with democracy, human rights, and humanist ideals and principles, and where a functionalist model of religion implicitly ascribing Christianity as the cause of social progress and welfare is operative – making comparisons with Buddhism creates a problem for the category "Religion." When Buddhism provides no solution to social problems, as implied in the textbook *In the Same World*, social progress and welfare in Asian countries and societies are not seen as the result of Buddhism. Asian countries and societies are on the contrary depicted as constricted by Buddhism. This is most visibly expressed in the representation of the conflict in Sri Lanka as religious, rather than made up of social and economic differences.

In the textbook *REPS*, Buddhism is presented as an ideal version constructed in the image of a project defining the role of religion in secular pluralist society. In this interfaith project Buddhism is identical to other religions — a social perspective affirmative of values defined as important to current society. The difference — doctrines and theory, is trivial and vital at the same time; trivial as defining a particular religious tradition and vital as defining religion in general. It is vital to the explanation of religion as a social perspective, because it is through the beliefs (doctrines and theory) that the relevance and potential actuality of a religion can be identified. Social issues and concerns are related to beliefs and vice versa, and an ethical relationship is established. In this way, the interfaith approach emphasizes an understanding of diversity diminishing differences between religions, valuing religion as a particular dimension of life, and as a consequence excludes perspectives that focus on conflicts in religion and between religions.

In spite of these scholarly objections, the interpretative moves can be read as expressions of discourses present in the current communication about and discussion of religion. From a discursive point of view the textbooks' implicit use of Christianity as an example of the place and role of religion in a modern world, and thus, alignment of Christianity with modernity, construct a theory of modernity based on a Christian idea of religion of which Buddhism is compared and evaluated negatively.

The interpretative strategies in the textbooks are aspects of a larger discourse concerning the place and position of religion in modern society. In this larger discourse Christianity takes center stage, as both an example of a religion reframed as a social perspective and a model to be replicated. When a major part of the thinking about religion is based upon Christian ideas, small wonder then that the presentation of Buddhism uses Christian language. Coupled with a functional theory emphasizing the influence of religion on society, social practices and institutions are depicted as not only affected, but causally determined by religion. When the implicit comparison of Buddhism and Christianity become a comparison of Asian countries and societies with Western countries and societies, the shortcomings of the functional theory are obvious. The social development and growth in a Western context are communicated indirectly in the textbooks as a consequence of Christianity through their construction of Buddhism as a cause of various social, human rights and environmental problems in an Asian context.

Comparing the presentations in the Australian and the Norwegian textbooks there are both similarities and differences. All textbooks use Christian language describing Buddhism. The three Norwegian textbooks – *Existence, In the Same World, Faith and Thought* and the one Australian textbook *VCE Religion and Society* – use explicit Christian terminology. The other Australian textbook, *REPS*, employs a theological structure, describing Buddhism as a social perspective with an ethical basis in accordance with values in modern society. The major difference despite the structural reduction of differences in presenting religions as more or less the same is the inclusion of a Buddhist insider point of view in the same textbook. One could expect a more extensive treatment of Buddhism in the Australian textbooks because of the geographical location, where Australia and the East are nearby, whereas Buddhism is a stranger to the Norwegian context. However, this is not the case. In *VCE Religion and Society*, Buddhism is barely mentioned, and what is communicated is in large part misguided. From a Norwegian, Western point of view, Buddhism is depicted as different, as something strange. This is the reason Buddhism is depicted not in its own terms, but through translations of different kinds. In language, in context, in scholarly understanding, and in a context of a modern, secular, pluralist society. The difference in emphasis on society in the Australian textbooks consistently present doctrine and theory from the vantage point of ethics actualizing doctrine and theory, constructing the role of religion in modern society.

Orientalism – Representing the Other
The interpretative strategies identified in the textbooks can, more specifically, be said to reflect aspects of an orientalist discourse. Although, textbooks are obviously not involved in colonial projects, Said's characteristics of Orientalism (1978/1991) somehow justify the application (cf. Fairclough 1992, on the concept of intertextuality). The textbook authors profess knowledge of religion and culture (in Asia and elsewhere) and transmit this knowledge in textbooks. The textbook presentations of Buddhism reflect a way of thinking based on the distinction between orient and occident; in language use, in contextual frame, in lack of knowledge, in construction of the category religion, and in the theological interfaith projects' elimination of differences. Taking the interpretative strategies involved in the textbook representation of Buddhism into consideration, this distinction arguably is employed to demarcate Eastern and Western thinking and ways of living. According to Said, the phenomenon orientalism has an extensive meaning and also refers to the Western discourse and institution, conceived as "a Western style for dominating, restructuring, and having authority over the Orient" (Said 1991: 2–3).

Symbolic Violence in RE Textbooks
The representation of Buddhism in the textbooks is reminiscent of orientalism. Seen in a context of cultural encounter, the misrecognition of Christian language and the national context as universal and normative can be understood as an example of symbolic violence. Textbooks perform symbolic violence through their representation of Buddhism, by way of interpretative strategies taken as common sense and employed to communicate knowledge about differences in cultures and people. According to cultural theorist Pierre Bourdieu, symbolic violence, an intrinsic aspect of communication, is a result of unconsciously accepting common sense ideas and misrecognizing the social world they validate. By internalizing the structures, or more explicitly the categories of the dominant point of view, the dominated are prone to see the conditions as natural and therefore do not question them. The common sense ideas in the context of religious education correlate with the above-mentioned interpretative strategies, and manifest in religious education as a way of understanding and managing Buddhism.

Symbolic violence in school textbooks is a two-stage process that can inhibit learning about the comprehensiveness and complexity of religion. Explaining Buddhism in the language of Christianity is a direct expression of symbolic violence. Instilling a theory of religion wherein Buddhism is a subtype of the Christian prototype or model, legitimized through study of religion and cross cultural, comparative categories, is an implicit act of symbolic violence. Taking religion as transcending violence or antithetic to violence and conflict, is contradicting and denying science of religion, and establishing and maintaining an ideological project. This symbolic violence obviously can affect Buddhists, but also students adopting the taxonomic system, and by extension the society we live in where encounters between people are based on such cultural representations as the textbooks produce and reproduce.

ABOUT THE AUTHOR

Kai Arne Nyborg is Research Fellow and University lecturer at the Department of Education, UiT—The Arctic University of Norway. He is currently working on a project on textbook representations of religion and culture. This chapter forms part of his research project. Email: kai.arne.nyborg@uit.no

REFERENCES

Andreassen, Bengt-Ove. 2010. "Bruk eller misbruk? Ninian Smarts dimensjonsmodell i tilnærmingen til religion i norsk religionsdidaktikk." *Religionsvitenskabeligt Tidsskrift* 55: 55–73.
– 2014. "Introduction: Theoretical Perspectives on Textbooks/Textbooks in Religious Studies Research." In *Textbook Gods. Genre, Text and Teaching Religious Studies*, eds. B.-O. Andreassen and James R. Lewis, 1–15. Equinox Publishing: Sheffield.

Benavides, Gustavo. 1998. "Modernity." In *Critical Terms for Religious Studies*, ed. Mark Taylor, 186–204. Chicago: University of Chicago Press.

Berkwitz, Stephen C. 2004. "Conceptions and Misconceptions about 'Western Buddhism': Issues and Approaches for the Classroom." *Teaching Theology & Religion* 7(3): 141–52.

– 2015. "Textbook Buddhism: Introductory Books on the Buddhist Religion." *Religion* 14 (October): 1–26.

Borup, Jørn. 2004. "Zen and the Art of Inverting Orientalism: Religious Studies and Genealogical Networks." In *New Approaches to the Study of Religion*, eds. Peter Antes, Armin W. Geertz and Randi R. Warne, 451–87. Regional, Critical, and Historical Approaches, 1; Berlin: Verlag de Gruyter.

Bourdieu, Pierre. 1977/2005. *Outline of a Theory of Practice*. Cambridge Studies in Social and Cultural Anthropology, 16; Cambridge: Cambridge University Press.

Dyer, Richard 1993. *The Matter of Images: Essays on Representations*. New York: Routledge.

Fairclough, Norman. 1992. *Discourse and Social Change*. Cambridge: Polity Press.

Faure, Bernard. 2003. *Double Exposure: Cutting Across Buddhist and Western Discourses*. Stanford: Stanford University Press.

Fines Aronsen, Camilla, Lene Bomann-Larsen and Henry Notaker. 2008. *Eksistens*. Oslo: Gyldendal.

Green, Damien, Shayndel Samuel and Meaghan Paul. 2012. *VCE Religion and Society Units 1–4*. South Yarra, Victoria: Macmillan.

Harvey, Peter. 2010. "Ennobling Truths/Realities. In *Encyclopedia of Buddhism*, eds. Damien Keown and Charles S. Prebish, 318–37. London: Routledge.

Heiene, Gunnar, Bjørn Myhre, Jan Opsal, Harald Skottene and Lars Østnor. 2008. *Tro og tanke*. Oslo: Aschehoug.

Heim, Maria. 2004. "Dana." In *Encyclopedia of Buddhism*, Vol. 1, eds. Robert E. Buswell. A-L. Thomson Gale.

Jensen, Tim, ed. 1994. *Islam i skolen*. København: Danmarks lærerhøyskole.

Jensen, Tim, and Michael Rothstein. 2002. *Etikken & religionerne*. København: Aschehoug.

Jensen, Tim 2003. "Mange islamer, mange muslimer." *Islam i bevægelse*, ed. Mona Sheikh. København: Akademisk.

Keown, Damien. 2010. "Karma." In *Encyclopedia of Buddhism*, eds. Daimien Keown and Charles S. Prebish, 437–39. London: Routledge.

King, Richard. 2006. *Orientalism and Religion. Postcolonial Theory, India and 'The Mystic East'*. New York, Routledge.

Kvamme, Ole A., Eva M. Lindhardt and Agnethe Steineger. 2008. *I samme verden*. Oslo: Cappelen.

Laclau, Ernesto, and Mouffe Chantal. 1985. *Hegemony and Socialist Strategy: Towards a Radical Democratic Politics*. London: Verso.

Lincoln, Bruce. 1996. "Theses on Method." *Method & Theory in the Study of Religion* 8(3): 225–27.

– 2002. *Holy Terrors: Thinking about Religion after September 11*. Chicago, IL: The University of Chicago Press.

Martin, Craig. 2009. "How to Read an Interpretation: Interpretive Strategies and the Maintenance of Authority." *The Bible and Critical Theory* 5(1): 6.1–6.26.

Martin, Luther. 2014. *Deep History, Secular Theory. Historical and Scientific Studies of Religion*. Religion and Reason 54; Berlin: De Gruyter.

McCutcheon, Russell T. 2007. *Studying Religion: An Introduction*. London: Equinox Publishing.

McMahan, David L. 2010. "Koan." In *Encyclopedia of Buddhism*, eds. Daimien Keown and Charles S. Prebish, 445–46. London: Routledge.

Norwegian Directorate for Education and Training. 2006. *Religion and Ethics — Common Core Subjects in Programme for General Studies*.

Said, Edward. 1978 [1993]. *Orientalism: Western Conceptions of the Orient*. London: Penguin.

Smith, Jonathan Z. 1982. "Sacred Persistence: Towards a Redescription of Canon." *Imagining Religion: From Babylon to Jonestown*, 36–52. Chicago, IL: The University of Chicago Press.

Smith, Jonathan Z. 1993. "Map is Not Territory." *Map is Not Territory: Studies in the History of Religions*, 289–309. Chicago, IL: University of Chicago Press.

Sharf, Robert. 1998. "Experience." In *Critical Terms for Religious Studies*, ed. Mark C. Taylor, 94–116. Chicago, IL: University of Chicago Press, 1998.

Tuohy, Mary, Ray Elliott, Paul Rule and Shaun Harper. 2012. *Religion and Ethics in a Pluralist Society: VCE Religion and Society. Units 1 & 2*. South Melbourne: Nelson Cengage Learning.

Victorian Curriculum and Assessment Authority. 2014. *Religion and Society, Victorian Certificate of Education Educational Design*.

Wright, Dale S. 1992. "Rethinking Transcendence: The Role of Language in Zen Experience." *Philosophy East and West* 42/1 (January): 113–38.

Endnotes

1. The Victorian Certificate of Education is a credential awarded to secondary school students in the Australian state of Victoria Students must complete two or more years of study to attain the certificate, normally in years 11 and 12.

2. Gjenfødelsens kretsløp gjelder verden like mye som mennesket. Som vi forstår er det ingen skapelse, og buddhismen har ingen skapergud. Dermed unngår buddhisten det som i jødisk og kristen tradisjon blir kalt "det ondes problem": Hvordan kan en gud som er både kjærlig og allmektig, tillate ondskapen i verden? (Fines-Aronsen et al. 2008: 50).

3. This can easily be confirmed by looking into the textbook description and presentation of Christianity. When presenting Christian ideas, Buddhism or other religions are not mentioned.

4. "Derfor skiller ikke buddhistene mellom 'onde' og 'gode' mennesker, mellom 'rettferdige' og 'urettferdige'. De er bare opptatt av å befri menneskene fra lidelsene. *Frelsen* er derfor å bli forløst fra gjenfødelsens onde sirkel" (Fines-Aronsen et al. 2008: 52).

5. "For lekfolket oppleves ikke dette som en tung plikt, det er heller et privilegium for dem å få gi" (Heiene et al. 2008: 83).

6. "Zen ser på religiøse ritualer og dogmatiske drøftinger som nyttesløse. Veien til oppvåkning går gjennom å sitte ned og meditere. Dette skjer i tilknytning til en undervisning hvor en zen-mester bryter ned elevenes tilbøyelighet til å tenke logisk, for eksempel ved å gi elevene i oppdrag å meditere over et *koan*. Et koan er et paradoksalt uttrykk som ikke kan forstås ved hjelp av logikk, men som krever innsikt på et annet nivå. [...]. Logisk tankegang blir regnet som et hinder i forhold til oppvåkningen, og et koan er et hjelpemiddel til å sette den logiske tankegangen ut av spill" (Heiene et al. 2008: 100).

7. "Hvis du har iskrem, vil jeg gi deg litt. Hvis du ikke har iskrem, vil jeg ta den fra deg" (Heiene et al. 2008: 100).

8. "Buddhistene mener at Buddha er opphavsmann til teksten, men at den ble først skrevet ned etter Buddhas død" (Heiene et al. 2008: 90).

9. "Siddharta var sønnen til Maya og Suddhodana Gautama, som I den buddhistiske fortellingen er et kongepar I Shakyariket. Historikerne stiller spørsmål ved dette, da riket ikke var et monarki på den tiden. Man regner med at Siddharta ble født omkring år 560 f.Kr. og levde til han ble 80 år. Han kan ha vært sønnen til en stormann i hovedstaden Kapilavastu, men historikerne tror ikke at han har levd i en så overdådig luksus som enkelte av fortellingene kan tyde på" (Heiene et al. 2008: 93).

10. "Til tross for motforestillingene er det fortellingene i de buddhistiske kildene som tegner bildet av den Buddha som de fleste buddhister forholder seg til. Disse ligger også til grunn for denne framstillingen" (Heiene et al. 2012: 94).

11. "Det fortelles at alle tekstene som ble resitert, ble skrevet ned og samlet til *Tripitaka* ('De tre kurvene'), selv om historikerne mener at den endelige samlingen må ha skjedd noe senere" (Heiene et al. 2008: 97).

12. "Buddhismen lærer også at vi alle er en del av det samme kretsløpet. Natur og dyr har livets rett på lik linje med mennesker, og ødelegger vi naturen, skader vi også oss selv siden alt henger sammen. Det at alle ting er gjensidige avhengige av hverandre, får dermed en økologisk dimensjon. Likevel skjer det miljøødeleggelser også i buddhistiske land. I land som Burma og Thailand er det store miljøforurensninger, og skoger blir rasert" (Kvamme et al. 2008: 255).

13. "Buddhas utgangspunkt var at alle mennesker var likeverdige uavhengig av rase, kjønn og sosial status. Men den aktuelle virkeligheten i mange buddhistiske land er preget av en rekke diskriminerende forhold og stadige brudd på grunnleggende menneskerettigheter. Et eksempel er Sri Lanka, der det buddhistiske flertallet i årevis har vært i konflikt med tamilene, som i hovedsak er hinduer og katolikker" (Kvamme et al. 2008: 241).

14. "Buddhas lære uttrykker at begge kjønnene kan nå nirvana på lik linje. Likevel har vi sett at det åndelige likeverdet ikke alltid viser seg i det sosiale livet. Menn har stort sett hatt en dominerende posisjon i buddhistiske samfunn" (Kvamme et al. 2008: 256).

15. "Buddhismen er på mange måter en åpen og tolerant religion og har let latt seg påvirke av det den har møtt I omverdenen av andre kulturer og religioner. [...]. I dag må buddhister forholde seg til kristendom og islam når de formidler læren i Vesten. Buddhismen viser her tendenser til tilpasning, ved at den for eksempel tar opp i seg kristne og humanistiske idealer" (Kvamme et al. 2008: 257).

9. SIGNIFICANT OR INSIGNIFICANT ABSENCE? RELIGION AND VIOLENCE IN RE TEXTBOOKS FOR NORWEGIAN TEACHER EDUCATION

Bengt-Ove Andreassen

TEACHER EDUCATION IN NORWAY

There are different ways of becoming a teacher in Norway. In the general teacher education, which expanded from four to five years in 2017, student teachers have to choose to specialize in teaching primary (1–7 grade) or secondary school (5-10 grade).

At (some) universities students can apply for a one-year practical didactic education course after they have completed their Master's degree in e.g. social sciences or humanities. To attend this one-year teacher education, their degree must comprise of at least one subject with at least 60 European Credit Transfer and Accumulation System credits (ECTS)[1] that qualifies for teaching specific subjects in school. Academic subjects such as history and sociology qualify for teaching social science in school and the study of religions at university, for teaching RE in secondary or upper-secondary. This one-year practical didactic education "on top" of a Master's degree is a qualification for teaching in secondary and upper secondary schools.

A second possibility at the universities is the five-year integrated teacher education course. During a period of five years, students specialize in two subjects, pedagogy and subject didactics. The main difference from the one-year practical didactic education course is that pedagogy and subject didactics are integrated during the five years from the very beginning, while the one-year practical didactic education is an additional year with only pedagogy and subject didactics after five years of study (a total of six years). This also qualifies one to teach in secondary and upper-secondary schools.

To specialize in teaching RE is an option in all teacher education. The teacher education programmes that students can attend at the universities do not have national guidelines in the same way as general teacher education. The regulations (Norwegian, forskrift) for these education programmes only state that the subjects and courses must be relevant for teaching in school and that students should have 15 ECTS subject didactics related to each of the two subjects they study. To get an insight into what is considered relevant, one must go to the different institutions and look at the locally developed descriptions and course plans. Due to limited space, I will not give examples of such locally developed descriptions and course plans.

For the general teacher education programme, there are comprehensive national guidelines. Here the different subjects have aims for knowledge, skills and general competencies. The names of the subjects in the general teacher education are usually the same as in primary and secondary school. In 2015 the RE subject in primary and secondary school changed its name from Religion, Worldviews and Ethics (RLE) to Christianity, Religion, Worldviews and Ethics (KRLE). The name was not changed in teacher education until 2017 as new national guidelines were presented as a part of a reform in the general teacher education. In the national guidelines for general teacher education there is one description for KRLE1 (the first 30 ECTS) and one for KRLE2 (additional 30 ECTS). The course description for KRLE in the national guidelines is clearly adapted to the curriculum for primary and secondary school. It includes more or less the same teaching content: philosophy and ethics, secular world views, and the typical world religion approach (Judaism, Christianity, Islam, Hinduism and Buddhism), with a special emphasis on Christianity.

There is no mention of conflict or violence in the guidelines for KRLE in teacher education. If the institutions follow these guidelines, future teachers will not have met these kinds of topics in their training to become an RE teacher. Consequently, their education has not prepared them for dealing with questions from pupils concerning such issues. From a study of religions perspective, the national guidelines for general teacher education continue the theological and empathetic tradition from the earlier Christianity subject in teacher education (which applied until 1998). There is still a focus on existential perspectives that relate religion to a pupil's existential questions and moral development (cf. Andreassen 2014b).

There are of course rather big differences between KRLE at the university colleges and the study of religions at the universities. The latter provides students with familiarity with the academic study of religion, especially when it comes to theoretical and comparative perspectives. Although comparison of and reflection on insider and outsider perspectives are now integrated into the national guidelines for RE, theoretical perspectives on religion are more or less absent. The focus is dominated by a basic introduction to different religions, philosophy and ethics.

Traditionally, teachers in general teacher education have been recruited from theological seminars or theological university colleges. Thus, RE in general teacher education has been regarded as the "theologians' subject" (cf. Skeie 2003: 192–93; Andreassen 2009b).

TEXTBOOKS IN RE FOR NORWEGIAN TEACHER EDUCATION

Textbooks designed for RE in teacher education have the character of typical introductory books in religion, yet adapted to national guidelines for teacher education and RE in school. Nevertheless, since the last reform in teacher education in 2010 there have been no completely newly-written or revised books adapted to the guidelines implemented that year. Instead, the books analyzed for this volume are adapted to national guidelines from 1998 or 2003, and some are slightly revised to be in accordance with the adjusted national guidelines in RE dating from 2009. The general impression is that there is a need for newly-written and updated books in RE for teacher education. One could especially wish for books written by scholars in the study of religions.

Of all the books designed for RE in teacher education, there are only two comprehensive books that include introductions to "world religions" and secular worldviews. The book *Religioner og livssyn* (*Religions and (Secular) Worldviews*) was published in 2004 (Eidhamar 2004). There are five contributors to this edited volume that consists of 13 chapters (427 pages), covering secular worldviews, Judaism, Islam, Hinduism, Buddhism, Sikhism, Bahá'I, Mormons, Jehovah Witnesses and New Age. In addition there is an introductory chapter and chapters on "Faith and Revelations in the World Religions" and "The Religion's Narratives [Myths]".

The second comprehensive introductory book is entitled *Logos og Dharma. Religioner, livssyn og etikk* (*Logos and Dharma - Religions, Secular Worldviews and Ethics*) (Neegaard 2006). Published in 2006, this is also an edited volume with six contributors. The book consists of nine chapters covering Judaism, Islam, Hinduism, Buddhism, New Age, Secular worldviews and a chapter on "Ethics in World Religions - Differences and Community."

There is no chapter on Christianity in either of these books. Instead, there is a range of separate textbooks on Christianity, which I will return to below. This reflects the emphasis on Christianity in RE in the national guidelines for teacher education as well as in the RE subject in primary and secondary school.

The publisher, Høyskoleforlaget,[2] which published *Religioner og livssyn* (Eidhamar 2004), also publishes two separate books on Christianity: *Kristendommen I—Bibelen* (*Christianity I - The Bible*) (Sødal 2009a) and *Kristendommen II—Tro og tradisjon* (*Christianity II - Faith and Tradition*) (Sødal 2009b). The foreword in the second edition of the second volume states that the content is adapted to the RLE curriculum that was implemented in primary and secondary school in 2008 (Sødal 2009b: 11). This publisher also published a book entitled *Kristendommens historie. En innføring* (Meistad 2000) that also was adapted to the current RE curriculum at that time. The two later books on Christianity seem to have replaced this.

Høyskoleforlaget has also published separate books on different religions that were designed for RE in teacher education after the KRL subject replaced Christianity in primary and secondary school in 1997 and thus created a need for textbooks on other religions than Christianity. The two books, *Jødedommen. Islam*

(*Judaism – Islam*) (Rian and Eidhamar 2001) and *Hinduismen. Buddhismen* (*Hinduism – Buddhism*) (Jacobsen and Thelle 2000), were the only textbooks adapted to RE in teacher education that covered these religions in Norwegian in the late 1990s and early 2000s. First editions of both books were published in 1999.

Fagbokforlaget, which published *Logos og Dharma – Religioner, livssyn og etikk* (Neegaard 2006), has also focused on textbooks adapted to RE in teacher education. In 2004 this publisher launched the series labelled *KRL-biblioteket* (*The KRL-library/The RE-library*), which is a series of smaller introductory books to various themes and issues in RE. Nineteen books were published in the period from 2004 to 2007, 11 of which are on Christianity, four are on philosophy and ethics, and the last four are on Sami religion and the Laestadian movement (a Christian revival movement), religious narratives (myths), Old Norse religion and the Christening process in Norway, and on secular worldviews and New Age.[3] This series has no textbooks on other "world religions" than Christianity. The same publisher also published the book *Illustrert norsk kristendomshistorie* (*An Illustrated Church History of Norway*) (Elstad and Halse 2002).

All in all, Fagbokforlaget has published 21 books on religion adapted for RE in teacher education. A large part of these deal with Christianity, while the only book that deals with other religions[4] is the book, *Logos og Dharma* (Neegaard 2006). Høyskoleforlaget has published six books: three on Christianity and three on other religions, one of which is *Religion og livssyn* (Eidhamar 2004) that covers other "world religions."

The basis for this chapter is 23 books in RE designed for teacher education in Norway.

ANALYTICAL FOCUS – DEFINING TERMS

Analyzing textbooks to find out *if* and *how* they treat religious violence, calls for some clarifications concerning what can be identified as "religious violence," or "religious conflict." However, this is not an easy task (cf. Carlson 2011; Juergensmeyer et al. 2013). In his book on religious violence, William T. Cavanaugh (2009: 15–54), has found that a common feature in works on religious violence is an absence of conceptualization of these terms. The meaning of religion, violence and conflict varies and are generally unclear in most contributions, according to Cavanaugh. This calls for an extensive, almost exhaustive, task of clarification but nevertheless an important one.

To use "religion and violence," "religion and conflict" or "religious extremism" as analytical tools there must be an idea of what constitutes these terms. I have chosen to use all these terms simply to perform a wide analysis that will capture or include whatever examples are used in the textbooks or whatever the textbook authors have associated with such terms. More precisely, my analysis of textbooks draws on an understanding of violence and conflict from the works of Bruce Lincoln (1998, 2003) and Robert A. Segal (2008). A conflict is a situation in which disagreement, conflict or a clash between interests is encountered. Lincoln defines conflict as:

> the situation that arises when rival interests can no longer be denied, deflected, negotiated, or contained by the structures and processes ordinarily competent to do so. As a result, after an indeterminate period of confusion and crisis, normal competition moves into phases that are more open, bitter, confrontational, costly, and violent (Lincoln 1998: 65).

In religious conflicts enemy images are also created where people with other beliefs are stereotypically understood as "the others" and objectified as "the devil's messenger," "witches," "heathens" or "infidels" (the list could of course be longer). Based on this clarification this also implies that conflicts do not only mean violence, such as war or terrorism. Conflicts can be related to issues such as power and leadership, gender and economy.

Dealing with religious violence Robert A. Segal (2008: 13) uses a distinction between violence committed against religion and violence committed in the name of religion. It is the later form which usually describes religious violence and religious extremism as it is used in the public sphere. This understanding is an important distinction in my analysis. A further distinction is to capture an understanding of religious violence, as violence which is committed against fellow members of a religion and violence committed against outsiders, again according to Segal. Investigating religious violence through the works of scholars such as James Frazer, Renè Girard and Walter Burkert, Segal emphasizes that religious violence has always been present in religions in other forms than terror or random violence against innocents. Through ritual practices and social actions, violence has always been a part of religion, although disruptive, it is not a recent phenomenon. Segal concludes his investigation:

> Violence occurs regularly rather than *in extremis*, is controlled rather than uncontrolled, operates as part of the normal functioning of religion rather than only with the radicalization of religion, and can be beneficial rather than harmful. Seen from the standpoint of these theories, religious violence need be neither bemoaned nor excused. It is simply the way religion works (Segal 2008: 36).

However, the presence of religious violence as emphasized by Segal is perhaps not the one which is most difficult to deal with in public education. In spite of the perspective which sees violence as a natural ingredient of religion, it is religious terror and violence which appears as random and striking innocent victims, which is difficult to deal with in education. Although Segal's important and informative review of violence and religion is based on research and studies of classical religion in ancient times, it might communicate that violence in religion is something of a historical matter. The most challenging in today's RE subject in public education, whether we like it or not, is the religious violence which we usually understand as random and often associated with terror. This is religious violence which happens today and not purely a historical phenomenon.

Segal's article still provides an illustrative distinction when it comes to dealing with religious violence as a topic in public education. Religious violence as a part of a religion's ritual is internal and serves a distinct purpose (Segal 2008: 36). However, this is also the case with external religious violence. It is intended to serve a distinct purpose, and thus is often based on some sort of religious grounds which provide motivation. The problem of religious violence, especially the kind which strikes random victims, is that it is not arbitrary for those who are committing it. It is a planned action, and motivated by a higher power. Charles Kimball (2002: 6) argues that religious violence is likely to appear in the wake of absolute truth claims, blind obedience, the establishment of "ideal" time, the belief that the end justifies any means, and a declaration of holy war. With reference to such factors, religious violence, although committed on innocent victims, has an "inner logic" for the one who is executing it. Mark Juergensmeyer (2003) points to similar factors when he argues for a distinction between secular and religious violence. The religious violence is always, according to Juergensmeyer, symbolic. It refers to cosmic images which are larger than life, and includes references to battles in a legendary past, and to metaphysical conflicts between good and evil (Juergensmeyer 2003: 149).

In analyzing the textbooks I have tried to identify *if* and *how* textbooks present religions and relates them to the above mentioned issues or perspectives. As the work has proceeded, and worried about not finding "anything," I have also tried to identify if textbooks relate religion(s) to anything that is at all negative.

THE GENERAL TEXTBOOKS INTRODUCING "WORLD RELIGIONS"

The contents of the two textbooks offering a general introduction to "world religions," *Religioner og livssyn* (Eidhamar 2004) and *Logos og Dharma* (Neegaard 2006), are much the same. Both books leave out Christianity and are also structured in more or less the same way. *Religioner og livssyn* (Eidhamar 2004) also contains separate chapters on Sikhism, Bahá'I, Mormons and Jehovah Witnesses, making it about 60 pages longer than *Logos og Dharma* (Neegaard 2006). The chapters in both books introduce the religion's founder, a short history, texts, geographical spread, religious practice (from an insider perspective), diversity and the specific religious tradition in a Norwegian context.

The aim of *Logos og Dharma* is described through the following question: "In what way can this subject [RE in school] contribute to the pupil's growth and development? This question is the value guide[5] for this book" (Neegaard 2006: 10). The book quite clearly connects to a traditional understanding of RE as contributing to the pupil's moral and existential growth. However, it stands out as a little different because of the heading "Religion and Society" in each chapter. Under this heading, topics like religion and violence, or religion and conflict, religion and extremism are treated explicitly. Issues of conflict and violence are thus treated and related to all religions through cases from different regions and countries in the world. Buddhism is related to nationalistic Buddhism in Sri Lanka and seen as an inspiration for social reformation in India under Ambedkar in the 1900s. Hinduism is related to conflict in India and to religious nationalism in the Bharatiya Janata Party (BJP). In the chapter on Islam there are examples concerning sharia and *hudud* punishment, jihad and Islamism in addition to examples from different national contexts such as Turkey and Pakistan. Interestingly enough, 9/11 is not mentioned at all. In this way, the issue of religion and violence is treated through a range of specific examples from different national contexts. Religion is thus presented as a contextual phenomenon and must be understood as such, and not only in reference to a broader religious tradition. However, there are no sections of the book, in the chapters on specific religions, which deal with religion and violence more principally.

With the Norwegian context as a vantage point, all the mentioned examples of religious violence and extremism are far away, in other parts of the world, thus signalling that this has little or nothing to do with the Norwegian or European reality. This can be related to the term "othering" which primarily is a term used in social anthropology and indigenous studies to characterize a process through which people or groups of people (cultures) are being categorized as not being "one of us" (Moreton-Robinson 2000: 179). In reference to the analyzed textbooks, "other religions" than Christianity and other continents than Europe, can be related to violence, conflict or extremism in some way or another. Europe and Christianity are not related to such issues at all.

In *Religioner og livssyn*, there are no headings that relate religion(s) to conflict, violence or extremism. However, there are some topics that can be related to conflict. In a chapter on myths in *Religioner og livssyn*, the authors also discuss what they describe as "Parallel and rivalling myths"[6] (Eidhamar 2004: 382–84, my translation). "Parallel myths" are explained as myths that tell about the same person but in slightly different ways. Sometimes these myths can be contradictory and the person whom the myth is about can be presented in a completely opposite manner within two religious traditions. These are described as "rivalling myths." Jesus and Buddha are used as examples of both parallel and rivalling myths.

The authors mention three ways of dealing with parallel and rivalling myths in teaching: (1) to harmonize the myths, (2) to present one version as more "true" and correct than the other, and (3) to let the myths stand side by side (Eidhamar 2004: 383, my translation). They conclude that the third way is the only alternative if RE is supposed to have the aim of strengthening the identity of pupils in a school characterized by diversity. The authors also mention gender issues related to myths, which also can be related to religion and violence. However, the myths are primarily presented as stories in mythical times. There is no discussion on how religious groups present and interpret their myths, which could display conflict and legitimation of religious extremism and violence. Rather, the authors seem to take for granted that teachers present myths in their teaching from different religious traditions without using the opportunity to say anything about different traditions of interpretation and how myths are used to legitimize extremism and violence. One reason why they do not discuss this could be that they have focused their work principally on teaching in primary school. To relate myths to religious violence is therefore not something they find appropriate. However, this is not something that is explicitly stated in the text, and therefore it is difficult to know exactly why the myths are presented in this particular way.

TEXTBOOKS ON CHRISTIANITY, ISLAM, JUDAISM, BUDDHISM AND HINDUISM

The many textbooks developed about Christianity and reviewed in this chapter are all written by theologians and church historians. It is the insider perspective that dominates these books, especially those concerning the Bible (e.g. Lybæk 2007; Sødal 2009a; Tobiassen 2004) and Christian teachings (e.g. Schanke 2006; Sødal 2009b). These textbooks are in general primarily oriented to introducing Christian teachings as a "source and inspiration for the pupil's interpretation of life" (Sødal 2009b: 165–66, my translation). This is a perspective that is also formulated in the RE curriculum for primary and secondary school, as well as in national guidelines for teacher education from 2003/2009. Compared to textbooks on "world religions," the textbooks on Christian teachings have an even more explicit existential perspective and thus aim to be an inspiration for interpretation of life. Here, there is seemingly no place for topics like violence, conflict or extremism. Conflict is only mentioned in respect of internal theological conflicts concerning differences in understanding and interpreting Christian teachings and the Bible. This confirms the dominating so-called "resource perspective" on religion as pointed out in earlier works (cf. Andreassen 2014b). The teaching about religions should be related to existential perspectives and the pupil's interpretation of life. This means that religion is rather seen as having a predominantly reconciling effect and function when it comes to matters of conflict.

There are several books on church history. Some of them also provide an overview of Christian denominations in Norway (cf. Meistad 2000; Sødal 2009b). One of the books in the KRL-library aims only at presenting an overview of Christian denominations and ecumenical organizations (Schanke 2005). This book does not focus on historical background but uses Ninan Smart's dimension model as an approach in presenting the different denominations. In his book, *Dimensions of the Sacred* (1997), Smart added an eighth dimension: the political dimension. One could think that religion and violence, conflict or extremism could be related to this dimension. However, the political dimension is not included in Schanke's (2005) presentation and use of Smart's model.

The books on church history aim to present an overview of important historical events. They are structured chronologically, with special emphasis on Reformation and Lutheran Protestantism in Norway (e.g. Elstad and Halse 2002; Elstad 2005; Furre 2006). It is interesting to note that the "cultural heritage" perspective on RE is more or less absent in these books. This perspective has been seen as an important part of the teaching of RE in primary and secondary school. In the debate on the recent changes in the RE curriculum in primary and secondary education, the "cultural heritage" perspective was used as an argument for stating that at least half of the teaching in the new KRLE subject should be on Christianity. In the national guidelines from 2010 and 2017, the general description for RE in teacher education states that "Christian faith and tradition in particular have influenced Norwegian culture and history" (National guidelines 2010, RLE 5-10: 70; and National guidelines 2017, KRLE 5-10: 29, my translation).[7] Ever since the introduction of the KRL subject in primary and secondary school in 1997, and in teacher education in 1998, Christianity has been described as a "deep current in Norwegian culture and history" (Kunnskapsdepartementet 2003: 23, my translation, cf. Andreassen 2013). The special emphasis on Christianity as a "deep current in Norwegian culture and history" is not something that is discussed in the books on church history.

The textbook on Old Norse religion and the Christianization of Norway (Straum 2004) has a section in which the mission strategy of the "Mission Kings" is outlined. Their use of violence is also discussed as one of three mission strategies. The "Sword mission" implied use of force and is commented by the author as "necessary to complete the Christianization," but "was hardly the most important reason" (Straum 2004: 53). Compared to the book on Sami religion and the Laestadian movement (Kristiansen 2005), in which the Christianization of the Sami is treated in a section of the book, the more violent sides of the mission is not discussed as in the book on the Christianization of Norway. Although it lies implicit in the text that the mission among the Sami also implied the use of violence. In one small section of the text it states that: "Missionaries and priests had orders to destroy places of sacrifice when they came upon them, and it happened in several places" (Kristiansen 2005: 42-43). If one compares these two textbooks (Straum 2004; Kristiansen 2005), the one on Old Norse religion to a much larger extent offers a reflection on the use of violence as a mission strategy.

In the textbook on Judaism and Islam (Rian and Eidhamar 2001), only the section on Islam mentions conflict, violence and extremism. There are no such examples in the section on Judaism. However, the Holocaust is of course referred to in several places. There are also brief references to conflict that the state of Israel has been involved in. In the part on Islam, it is emphasized that "today's Muslims"[8] understand jihad as "the inner jihad" – the struggle with oneself (Rian and Eidhamar 2001: 172). Jihad is also related to the legitimation of violence and extremism in a paragraph on Islamism (Rian and Eidhamar 2001: 204-205). Islamism is explained as a diverse term but with a common aim to "establish an Islamic government/state that is based on sharia laws"[9] (Rian and Eidhamar 2001: 204).

It is also explained that the diversity of Islamists contains terrorists. Hassan al-Banna, as the founder of the Muslim Brotherhood, serves as an example on Islamism along with a brief mention of Islamist groups in Algeria and the Taliban in Afghanistan. The *hudud* punishment is put forward in an illustration that shows how different kinds of crime are punished (Rian and Eidhamar 2001: 175). One example is that theft is punished by "the amputation of the hand." Although this illustration provides several examples on religiously motivated violence, such as the death penalty, amputation of body parts, whipping, the *hudud* punishments are not discussed or explained as a kind of violence. Instead, it is stated that "only a limited number of Muslim states enforce the sharia" (Rian and Eidhamar 2001: 176, my translation). Thus, there are no principle discussions on religion and violence. Jihad and *hudud* punishments serve as examples of sides or dimensions of Islam.

In the textbook on Buddhism and Hinduism (Jacobsen and Thelle 2000: 165-67), there are three pages on Hindu nationalism that relate to religion and violence. There are no examples linked to violence or extremism in the part on Buddhism. In the section on Hinduism, Bal Gangadhar Tilak (1856-1920) is mentioned as a leading character, who, in reference to the *Bhagavad Gita*, argued that violent acts could be accepted in the fight for what is right (*dharma*) against what is unjust (*adharma*). A more updated example is given in reference to the political party BJP, which was established in 1980 and formed a government after the elections of 1996 and 1998. These are the only brief mentions of religion and violence, and there are no more principal discussions on religion and violence in Hinduism.

SIGNIFICANT OR INSIGNIFICANT ABSENCE?

The reading of the 27 books for this chapter has illustrated that religion and violence, conflict or extremism is something that is hardly touched on in RE textbooks for teacher education. Only one textbook addresses such issues more systematically, although under the heading "Religion and Society" (Neegaard 2006). There are also some references to related issues in the section on Islam in the textbook on Judaism and Islam (Rian and Eidhamar 2001) and in the section featuring Hinduism in the textbook on Buddhism and Hinduism (Jacobsen and Thelle 2000). The book, *Logos og Dharma*, thus stands out as different from the others, as it relates religions to national contexts and, in these sections, also discusses issues of conflict, violence and extremism. In the books on Christianity, such issues are not mentioned at all. The general finding is that issues that connect religion to conflict, violence and extremism are hardly mentioned explicitly as religious violence, nor is this topic treated more principally.

In reference to the attention such topics get in various media, one could argue that it is a paradox that textbooks in RE for teacher education fail to discuss religion and violence. The dominating absence of such themes is therefore something to ponder on: especially, whether this is a significant or an insignificant absence. Norman Fairclough has used the expression "significant absence" to describe relations between what is present and what might have been present in a text (Fairclough 2003: 37). Dealing with textbooks that are adapted to specific national guidelines for RE in teacher education, it is a relevant question whether the absence of issues of violence, conflict and extremism could be described as a 'significant absence,' or if it simply is an insignificant one.

Issues that relate religion to conflict, violence or extremism are not explicitly included in the curriculum or in the national guidelines for teacher education. If using the framework for RE in school and teacher education as a point of reference, the absence of such themes in textbooks for RE in teacher education is thus not a "significant absence". Publishers and authors strive to publish books that are adapted to the current framework and that are updated and relevant. This means that themes and topics that are not explicitly included in the curriculum and in the national guidelines are seldom, if ever, included in the textbooks.

The simple fact that hardly any textbook explicitly deals with religious violence, conflict and/or extremism might also be used as an argument for such issues being considered insignificant within the dominating discourse on RE – not just in the politically sanctioned framework such as curricula and national guidelines. The fact that the scholars writing textbooks do not consider it significant enough to include might also be a sign that confirms the dominating view in the RE discourse that this is not something that is relevant. The framework, curricula, national guidelines and textbooks in this sense substantiate a signal that religion and violence, conflict and extremism is insignificant in RE. Instead, the way religion(s) are approached in curricula, national guidelines and textbooks reinforces the impression of the discursive construction of religion(s) as something good, as something that provides ethical ideals, cultural and personal identity and a way to relate to all "big questions in life" (cf. Andreassen 2014b), what Katharina Frank (2008: 217–21) has characterized as "life world-related RE." If the overarching aim for RE in public school is to stimulate the pupil's personal and moral growth by relating to their life world, religion and violence will simply be a disruptive force in this line of thinking. The absence of religion and violence, conflict and extremism might therefore be understood as an active discourse production. Such issues have never been regarded as relevant and consequently are not mentioned in curricula, national guidelines or most textbooks. Within the isolated Norwegian scholarly discourse of RE, it is seemingly regarded as insignificant. In opposition to the dominating discourse, I will argue that it is a significant absence.

RELIGIOUS VIOLENCE, CONFLICT AND EXTREMISM AS CONTEXT FOR RELIGION EDUCATION IN SCHOOL

Religion is constantly mentioned in the media and popular culture, and very often this is as a part of conflict and related to violence (cf. Shaheen 2008; Marsden and Savigny 2009) or to extremism in some way (cf. Bangstad 2014; Østberg 2013). Bruce Lincoln (2003) has referred to the paradox of religion that there is religion and religious motivation behind figures like Gandhi and Mother Theresa, and they might serve as ethical ideals. Nevertheless, there is also religion behind Bin Laden, the Christian extremist, Joseph Kony, in Uganda and the terrorists that attacked Charlie Hebdo in Paris in January 2015 and carried out the coordinated attacks in Paris in November 2015.[10] Extremists like these are a part of the context for teaching RE and something that pupils regularly hear about in the news or read about on the Internet (cf. Moore et al. 2008).

Pupils bring their observations and questions to school and will often have a need to discuss or to ask questions about these. Norwegian scholar, Marie von der Lippe (2011), has shown that pupils' talk about religion is influenced by "overarching macro structures" and the dominating discourse in public debate and the media. In another Norwegian study (Anker and von der Lippe 2015), on pupils' thoughts about the terror in Oslo and Utøya in July 2011, the pupils clearly expressed a wish to talk about this and mentioned RE as a possible arena for that in school. Some also stated that they experienced teachers seeming to avoid the topic.

The English scholar, Joyce Miller (2013: 127), refers to English research in which pupils think that the classroom is the best arena to discuss religious extremism and violence. In a more recent UK study, Angela Quartermaine (2016) has researched pupils' perceptions of terrorism and found that, concurring with Miller (2013), many RE teachers feel badly equipped to deal with the issues that might arise from terrorism discussions. The research by Anker and von der Lippe, Miller and Quartermaine displays an urgent need to deal with such issues in teacher education.

If we expect teachers to teach in a way that is relevant to the pupils, referring to society and life outside the classroom, there is no way to escape the challenge of religious violence, conflict and extremism. Teacher education should try to prepare for that, regardless of how difficult that is. The important question is thus, rather, how they should be prepared. It is obvious that as long as the topic is avoided in textbooks for teacher education, it is also easy for teachers in teacher education not to make these issues explicit in their teaching. Thus, student teachers might go through their entire teacher training in RE without dealing with such topics.

EXPLAINING ITS ABSENCE: UNDERMINING THE LEGITIMACY OF TEACHING RELIGION IN PUBLIC EDUCATION?

I have already addressed some possible explanations for why the issue of religion and violence is absent in RE in teacher education. How religion in public education is understood is closely connected to how teaching religion is legitimized in public education. Internationally there is no consensus on the comprehensive meaning of what an RE subject in public education should imply. Nevertheless, meanings and intentions are many (cf. Jackson 2004; Jensen 2008; Schreiner 2007; Webb 2002).[11] However, some recommendations have been presented by the Council of Europe in the report *Religious Diversity and Intercultural Education: A Reference Book for Schools* (Council of Europe 2007), by OSCE in *Toledo Guiding Principles on Teaching about Religions and Beliefs in Public Schools* (OSCE/ODIHR 2007), and by the Council of Europe in *Signposts: Policy and Practice for Teaching about Religions and Non-Religious World Views in Intercultural Education* (Jackson 2014). These recommendations and guiding principles primarily promote a view that religion is a positive factor providing identity and meaning and fostering tolerance and peace. Therefore, it is implied, teaching about religion should reflect this. These recommendations do not say anything about how teaching, in compulsory public schooling or teacher education, should face or treat issues regarding religious violence, conflict or extremism. Instead, it seems, it is taken for granted that any RE subject will provide pupils with attitudes that in the long run will help prevent such things. These recommendations also confirm the dominating Norwegian discourse on RE: that these are insignificant issues and there is no need to deal with them explicitly. However, the first paragraph in the section, "The Religious Dimension in Intercultural Education," written by Canadian scholar Michelin Milot in the Council of Europe report, points to the more challenging sides of religion in public education:

> Globalisation requires that education must rise to the challenges inherent in the growth of cultural and religious diversity in order to form citizens who are able to live together peacefully. Due attention paid to the religious dimension of intercultural education can make a significant contribution to peace, openness to other cultures, tolerance and respect for human rights in Europe. Religious differences continue all too often to be a source of tension, conflict and discrimination (Council of Europe 2007: 19).

It is worth noting that religion is given attention as a source of tension, conflict and discrimination. This will continue to be a challenge for religion in public education, as it is in teacher education and in the academic study of religions as well. Dealing with such issues requires strategies that are thought through and not only limited to a presentation of the dialectically opposite perspective: religious ethical ideals. However, in the different international guidelines, there lies a consensus to primarily present religion and religions as a positive source for human beings and societies. To deal with conflict, violence and extremism is therefore a disruptive force that potentially could undermine this understanding.

It is not only the public school system that has found these issues challenging. American scholar, Hector Avalos (2005: 24), has remarked in his book, *Fighting Words*, that the academic study of religion was not intended to focus on the possible negative sides of religion. Instead, intentions were rather to be sympathetic to religion. Avalos also points to the fact that most academic institutions in America were funded by taxpayers. Religions should therefore be understood as resources for ethical ideals and tolerance and not criticized. Avalos' comment implies that there could be a risk of losing funding (or even their jobs) if academic scholars of religious studies perform a critique of religion instead of pointing to its intended positive sides.

This becomes even more crucial when it comes to pointing at religion's disruptive force in teaching religion in public education. It raises the question: What is the purpose of teaching religion in public education? In the Norwegian and European context, religion as a school subject has been, and still is, considered as a means or tool for integration and is believed to foster tolerance, respect and identity. Teaching about religion, as in the Norwegian context, is globally intended to be about fostering peace, tolerance, integration, understanding and personal growth and identity (cf. Jackson 2004; Schreiner 2007).

Many teachers will argue that the best strategies to deal with the topics of religious violence and conflict is to present the ethical ideals or religious strategies for dealing with such topics, which are found in ecumenism and interreligious dialogue. It seems as if an expected, and quite usual, strategy is to manage the difficult topics by minimizing them and then, and as a next step, to nurture mutual understanding and tolerance through religious dialogue. This is a rather typical way of facing such issues (cf. O'Keefe 2009; Streib 2001).

Embedded in a discourse that promotes all the good intentions in teaching RE, arguments about including violence, conflicts and extremism might be considered arguments for including something that is not only insignificant but possibly a disruptive force that might undermine the aims of RE. The question at stake is: if an RE subject cannot foster peace and tolerance, then what is its rationale and legitimacy in public education? Should peace and tolerance be the main aims of RE even if one cannot guarantee that that is the result? If the students or their parents should not expect to be stimulated in their personal belief and get confirmation of their religious identity, then what is the rationale of teaching religion in public education? These are intricate questions and involve different levels. There is a big difference between the role of religions in international conflicts and wars, and how national states can deal with these issues in a national curriculum. A study of religion based RE will point to analytical critical competencies and knowledge about religion as crucial for understanding "religion," and, in the words of Tim Jensen (2008: 130), "the various ways religion and religions interact with and influence other human, social and cultural formations and discourses." A study of religions based RE will rather stress the potential in providing pupils with analytical critical competencies and knowledge about religion, also about how religions can be used and misused to legitimize violent acts, because that is important in educating pupils to be enlightened, critical and, hopefully, tolerant people. A "life world-related RE" on the other hand, aims at using religion as a potential for spiritual growth for the individual. This approach in RE will not foster critical analytical skills, and potentially undermine pupil getting insight in that religion is something dynamic and appears in different forms and shapes in different cultural and historical contexts.

RELIGIOUS VIOLENCE – A POTENTIAL FOR LEARNING ABOUT RELIGIONS?

Many of the works cited in this chapter (cf. Kimball 2002; Lincoln 1998; Juergensmeyer 2003; Segal 2008) all seem to agree that religious violence is not as arbitrary and random as one might (like to) think. On the contrary, religious violence is disturbingly planned and is based on a sort of "inner logic" which is difficult for the outsider to see and understand. This "inner logic" contains a use, or abuse, of religious symbols, which is dependent on human interpretation. In analyzing how religious violence and extremists are pointing to cosmic images, a legendary past, and to metaphysical conflicts between good and evil, there lies a possibility for learning something about religion(s). From a terrorist's insider perspective, religious violence could be considered necessary and might be about managing the truth, thus appearing symbolic and organized (Juergensmeyer 2003). To another insider, who belongs to the same tradition, religious violence might be understood as wrong and as nothing to do with religion at all. Both views are interpretations of the same religion (its texts, doctrines and tradition and so on) and illustrate that religions are cultural phenomena that do not give answers that everybody can agree the meaning of. It is important to learn something about how followers of the same religion can have diametrically opposite understandings of their religion.

It appears to be controversial to claim that religious violence is a part of religion when teaching religion in public education. Why? Because it might undermine what is understood as the reason and legitimacy for having religion as a subject in public education. An RE subject that investigates the violent or negative sides of religion (as well as more positive sides of religion), no matter how unpleasant it might be for teachers and students will ensure a broad and secular investigation of religion.[12] As in history or social sciences, we, as teachers, sooner or later will have to deal with unpleasant topics such as religiously motivated violence, extremism, oppression of indigenous peoples (Indians in America and/or Sami in Norway), gender or other issues. From my vantage point, which is a study of religions based RE, it is important to investigate all sides of religion to get as much knowledge about religion as possible.

There is no doubt that including religion and violence in textbooks and teaching challenges teachers as well as pupils. The danger of a superficial understanding of religious violence and extremism is of course evident. To learn something from such issues, student teachers and pupils need to develop their knowledge and competence in the use of critical thinking, textual analysis and historical reasoning and relate this to different historical and social contexts. Religious violence and extremism can thus provide a model for interdisciplinary, humanistic inquiry, as outlined by Brian K. Pennington (2012). Nevertheless, Pennington has also pointed to the ever-present difficulty of overcoming the cumulative effect of pulsating images and sound-bite new coverage to stimulate critical analysis among students reared in that media climate (Pennington 2012: 3). The challenge for the teacher is thus to facilitate a learning process, in which student teachers are stimulated to see through the dramatic happenings in pictures and on TV and to focus on the intentions and legitimations of the actions. In teacher education this can create an example of how to integrate such perspectives in teaching. However, this seems to me to be an area of RE which needs to be developed.

CONCLUSION

Textbooks in RE for Norwegian teacher education hardly deal with issues like religious conflict, violence and extremism. This absence might, in reference to Norman Fairclough's terms, be considered an "insignificant absence" because such issues are mentioned neither in the curriculum for RE in primary or secondary school nor in the national guidelines for teacher education. However, as a part of the public discourse on religion, it is an important part of the context for RE. Research also shows that pupils want to learn more and discuss such issues.

To make religious conflict and violence topics in teaching religion, however politically incorrect, is to present a complementary picture of the phenomenon of religion that allows for the distinctiveness of religions, the constantly changing nature of religion, and the notion that religions are believed to be in possession of the truth. To integrate such topics in teaching religion indeed displays a study of religions based RE and thus secular teaching of RE in public education, which is the opposite of the dominating discourse on RE. A study of religions based RE approach aims to develop the pupil's analytical skills and enable him/her to deal with complex phenomena. That also means teaching about religion as a social and historical fact including all its variables. Religiously motivated violence and conflict is also among those variables, whether we like it or not. In teaching religion in public education we simply have to deal with this issue, no matter how disruptive it is. And, most importantly, it provides knowledge of religion and religions.

ABOUT THE AUTHOR

Bengt-Ove Andreassen is Professor in the Study of Religions at the Department of Education, University of Tromsø – The Arctic University of Norway. Andreassen's doctoral thesis was an analysis of textbooks on religion used in teacher education. He has written a number of articles and books for RE, and especially addressed the lack of literature on conflict and violence in RE. He was also one of the editors (with James R. Lewis) of *Textbook Gods* (Equinox, 2014). Additionally, he has written several articles in various journals about the Study of Religions based Religion Education.

REFERENCES

Alberts, Wanda. 2008. "Didactics of the Study of Religions." *Numen* 55(2-3): 300-34.
Andreassen, Bengt-Ove. 2008. "Konfliktperspektiver i religionsundervisning og religionsdidaktikk – en bredere og bedre tilnærming til religion?" *Acta Didactica Norge* 2(1). Available at: http://www.adno.no/index.php/adno/article/view/71/96.
Andreassen, Bengt-Ove. 2009a. "Om fraværet av konfliktperspektiver i den religionsdidaktiske faglitteraturen." *Norsk Teologisk Tidsskrift* 110(3): 167-86.
Andreassen, Bengt-Ove 2009b. "Seige strukturer – perspektiver på endring og diskursivt arbeid i norsk religionsdidaktikk." *Din* 1: 5-29.
Andreassen, Bengt-Ove. 2012. *Religionsdidaktikk – En innføring*. Oslo: Universitetsforlaget.
Andreassen, Bengt-Ove. 2013. "Religion Education in Norway: Tension or Harmony between Human Rights and Christian Cultural Heritage?" *Temenos* 49(2): 137-64.
Andreassen, Bengt-Ove. 2014a. "Theoretical Perspectives on Textbooks/Textbooks in Religious Studies Research." In *Textbook Gods – Genre, Text and Teaching Religious Studies*, eds. Bengt-Ove Andreassen and James R. Lewis, 1-15. Sheffield: Equinox Publishing.
Andreassen, Bengt-Ove. 2014b. "A Reservoir of Symbols: On the Conceptualization of 'Religion' in Introductory Books for RE in Teacher Education in Norway." In *Textbook Gods – Genre, Text and Teaching Religious Studies*, eds. Bengt-Ove Andreassen and James R. Lewis, 177-97. Sheffield: Equinox Publishing.
Anker, Trine, and Marie von der Lippe. 2015. "Når terror ties i hjel: en diskusjon om 22. juli og demokratisk medborgerskap i skolen." *Norsk pedagogisk tidsskrift* 99(2): 85-96.
Avalos, Hector. 2005. *Fighting Words – The Origins of Religious Violence*. New York: Prometheus Books.
Bangstad, Sindre. 2014. *Anders Breivik and the Rise of Islamophobia*. London: Zed Books.
Breidlid, Halldis, and Tove Nicolaisen. 2007. *På skattejakt i fortellingsuniverset*. Bergen: Fagbokforlaget.
Carlson, John D. 2011. "Religion and Violence: Coming to Terms with Terms." In *The Blackwell Companion to Religion and Violence*, ed. Andrew R. Murphy, 7-22. Oxford: Blackwell.
Cavanaugh, William T. 2009. *The Myth of Religious Violence: Secular Ideology and the Roots of Modern Conflict*. Oxford: Oxford University Press.
Council of Europe. 2007. *Religious Diversity and Intercultural Education: A Reference Book for Schools*. Strasbourg: Council of Europe.
Eidhamar, Levi Geir ed. 2004. *Religioner og livssyn*. Kristiansand: Høyskoleforlaget.
Elstad, Hallgeir. 2005. *Nyere norsk kristendomshistorie*. Bergen: Fagbokforlaget.
Elstad, Hallgeir, and Per Halse. 2002. *Illustrert norsk kristendomshistorie*. Bergen: Fagbokforlaget.
Fairclough, Norman. 2003. *Analysing Discourse – Textual Analysis for Social Research*. London: Routledge.
Frank, Katharina. 2008. *Schulischer Religionsunterricht – Eine religionswissenschaftligch—soziologische Untersuchung*. Stuttgart: Kolhammer.
Furre, Berge. 2006. *Røter, tistlar og blomar – Kristendom i eit historisk riss*. Bergen: Fagbokforlaget.
Gearon, Liam. 2006. "Human Rights and Religious Education: Some Postcolonial Perspectives." In *International Handbook of the Religious, Moral and Spiritual Dimensions in Education. Part One*, eds. Marian de Souza et al., 375-85. Dordrecht: Springer.
Jacobsen, Knut A., and Notto R. Thelle. 2000. *Hinduismen – Buddhismen*. Kristiansand: Høyskoleforlaget.

Jackson, Robert. 2004. *Rethinking Religious Education and Plurality – Issues in Diversity and Pedagogy.* New York: Routledge Falmer.

Jackson, Robert, ed. 2014. *Signposts – Policy and Practice for Teaching about Religions and Non-Religious World Views in Intercultural Education.* Strasbourg: Council of Europe Publishing.

Jensen, Tim. 2008. "RS based RE in Public Schools: A Must for a Secular State." *Numen* 55(2–3): 123–50.

Juergensmeyer, Mark. 2003. *Terror in the Mind of God – The Global Rise of Religious Violence* (3rd edn). Berkeley, CA: University of California Press.

Juergensmeyer, Mark. 2008. *Global Rebellion – Religious Challenges to the Secular State, from Christian Militias to al Qaeda.* Berkeley, CA: University of California Press.

Juergensmeyer, Mark, Margo Kitts and Michael Jerryson. 2013. "Introduction: The Enduring Relationship of Religion and Violence." In *The Oxford Handbook of Religion and Violence*, eds. Mark Juergensmeyer, Margo Kitts and Michael Jerryson, 1–12. Oxford: Oxford University Press.

Kimball, Charles. 2002. *When Religion Becomes Evil.* San Francisco, CA: Harper Publishing.

Kristiansen, Roald E. 2005. *Samisk religion og læstadianisme.* Bergen: Fagbokforlaget.

Kunnskapsdepartementet [Ministry of Education and Research]. 2003. Rammeplan for allmennlærerutdanningen [Framework Plan for General Teacher Education]. Oslo: Kunnskapsdepartementet.

Kunnskapsdepartementet [Ministry of Education and Research]. 2010. Nasjonale retningslinjer for grunnskolelærerutdanningen 5–10. trinn [National Guidelines 2010 5–10]. Available at: https://www.regjeringen.no/globalassets/upload/KD/Rundskriv/2010/Retningslinjer_grunnskolelaererutdanningen_5_10_trinn.pdf

Lincoln, Bruce. 1998. "Conflict." In *Critical Terms for Religious Studies*, ed. Mark C. Taylor, 55–69. Chicago, IL: The Chicago University Press.

Lincoln, Bruce. 2003. *Holy Terrors – Thinking about Religion after September 11.* Chicago, IL: University of Chicago Press.

Lybæk, Lena. 2007. *Evangeliene – den historiske Jesus: evangelienes tilblivelse, kulturelle kontekst og religiøse ideinnhold.* Bergen: Fagbokforlaget.

Marsden, Lee, and Heather Savigny, eds. 2009. *Media, Religion and Conflict.* Farnham: Ashgate.

Meistad, Tore. 2000. *Kristendommens historie – En innføring.* Kristiansand: Høyskoleforlaget.

Miller, Joyce. 2013. "Religious Extremism, Religious Education and the Interpretive Approach." In *Religion in Education – Innovation in International Research*, eds. Joyce Miller, Kevin O'Grady and Ursula McKenna, 121–33. London: Routledge.

Moore, Kerry, Paul Mason, and Jason Lewis. 2008. *Images of Islam in the UK – The Representation of British Muslims in the National Print News Media 2000–2008.* Cardiff School of Journalism, Media and Cultural Studies. Available at: http://www.irr.org.uk/pdf/media_muslims.pdf

Moreton-Robinson, Aileen. 2000. *Talkin' Up to the White Woman: Indigenous Women and Feminism.* Queensland: University of Queensland Press.

Neegaard, Gunnar, ed. 2006. *Logos og Dharma – Religioner, livssyn og etikk.* Bergen: Fagbokforlaget.

O'Keefe, Theresa. 2009. "Learning to Talk: Conversation Across Religious Difference." *Religious Education* 104(2): 197–213.

OSCE/ODIHR. 2007. *The Toledo Guiding Principles on Teaching about Religion or Belief in Public Schools.* Warsaw: Organization for Security and Co-operation in Europe, Office for Democratic Institutions and Human Rights. Available at: http://www.osce.org/odihr/29154?download=true

Østberg, Sissel. 2013. "Diversity and Citizenship in a Context of Islamophobia." In *Religion in Education: Innovation in International Research*, eds. Joyce Miller, Kevin O'Grady and Ursula McKenna, 58–71. London: Routledge.

Pennington, Brian K. 2012. "Introduction." In *Teaching Religion and Violence*, ed. Brian K. Pennington, 3–15. New York: Oxford University Press.

Quartermaine, Angela. 2016. "Discussing Terrorism: a Pupil-Inspired Guide to UK Counter-Terrorism Policy Implementation in Religious Education Classrooms in England." *British Journal of Religious Education* 38(1): 13–29.

Rennie, Bryan, and Philip L. Tite, eds. 2008. *Religion, Terror and Violence: Religious Studies Perspectives*. New York and London: Routledge.

Rian, Dagfinn, and Levi Geir Eidhamar. 2001. *Jødedommen. Islam*. Kristiansand: Høyskoleforlaget.

Schanke, Åge J. 2006. *Kristen tro - En innføring*. Bergen: Fagbokforlaget.

Schanke, Ragnhild. 2005. *Kristendommens kirker og trossamfunn*. Bergen: Fagbokforlaget.

Schreiner, Peter. 2007. "Religious Education in the European Context." In *Religious Education in Europe - Situations and Current Trends in Schools*, eds. Elza Kuyk et al., 9–16. Oslo: IKO Publishing House.

Segal, Robert A. 2008. "Violence Internal and External." In *Religion, Terror and Violence - Religious Studies Perspectives*, eds. Bryan Rennie and Philip L. Tite, 13–38. New York and London: Routledge.

Shaheen, Jack G. 2008. *Guilty: Hollywood's Verdict on Arabs After 9/11*. New York: Olive Branch Press.

Skeie, Geir. 2003. "KRL — et fag på frammarsj?" In *Norsk lærerutdanning - Søkelys på allmennlærerutdanningen i et reformperspektiv*, eds. G. E. Karlsen and I. A. Kvalbein, 189–206. Oslo: Universitetsforlaget.

Smart, Ninian. 1997. *Dimensions of the Sacred: An Anatomy of the World's Beliefs*. London: Fontana Press.

Straum, Olav-Kansgar. 2004. *Norrøn tro og kristningen av Norge*. Bergen: Fagbokforlaget.

Streib, Heinz. 2001. "Fundamentalism as a Challenge for Religious Education." *Religious Education* 96(2): 227–44.

Sødal, Helje Kringlebotn, ed. 2009a. *Kristendommen I: Bibelen*. Kristiansand: Høyskoleforlaget.

Sødal, Helje Kringlebotn, ed. 2009b. *Kristendommen II: Tro og tradisjon*. Kristiansand: Høyskoleforlaget.

Tobiassen, Tormod. 2004. *Bibelens første del - Det gamle testamente eller Tanak?* Bergen: Fagbokforlaget.

von der Lippe, Marie. 2011. "Young People's Talk about Religion and Diversity: a Qualitative Study of Norwegian Students Aged 13–15." *British Journal of Religious Education* 33(2): 127–42.

Webb, Stephen H. 2002. "The Supreme Court and the Pedagogy of Religious Studies: Constitutional Parameters for the Teaching of Religion in Public Schools." *Journal of the American Academy of Religion* 70(1): 135–57.

Endnotes

1. European Credit Transfer and Accumulation System (ECTS) is a standard for comparing the study attainment and performance of students in higher education across the European Union and other collaborating European countries. One academic year corresponds to 60 ECTS-credits that are equivalent to 1500-1800 hours of study.

2. Høyskoleforlaget is now a part of the Norwegian publishing house Cappelen Damm.

3. I have not included the books on philosophy and ethics in this chapter. The book on religious narratives [myth] is written by the same authors (Breidlid and Nicolaisen 2007) who have written the part on religious narratives in Neegaard 2006.

4. In the book *Bibelens første del. Det gamle testamente eller Tanak?* (*The First Part of the Bible: The Old Testament or Tanak?*) there are several references to Judaism. In some sections of the book (e.g. Tobiassen 2004: 18–20) the author briefly discusses Jewish and Muslim views on the Old Testament.

5. In Norwegian: "Denne problemstillingen er den verdimessige rettesnor for denne boken" (Neegaard 2006: 10). The Norwegian formulation "den verdimessige rettesnor" is difficult to translate. Hence, the translation "value guide," which to a certain degree corresponds with the Norwegian text.

6. The chapter is written by Halldis Breidlid and Tove Nicolaisen. Their ideas about myths is elaborated in several books and articles, mainly in Norwegian. The book on religious narratives/stores [myths] in the KRL-library is written by Breidlid and Nicolaisen (2007).

7. In Norwegian: "Kristen tru og tradisjon har i særlig grad prega norsk kultur og historie" (National Guidelines 2010, RLE 5–10: 70).

8. In Norwegian, "Vår tids muslimer" (Rian og Eidhamar 2001: 172)

9. In Norwegian, "Deres felles mål er å opprette et islamsk styre grunnet på sharia" (Rian og Eidhamar 2001: 204).

10. One could also mention the Norwegian terrorist, who, in July 2011, planted a bomb in Oslo killing eight people and then drove to Utøya outside Oslo where The Labour Party's youth organization had their summer camp. There he shot and killed 69 people. In the manifesto he distributed via email to several thousand recipients before the terrorist action, he made several references to Christianity and that he was a "Crusader" defending Europe. How to understand these references is discussed by scholars (cf. Bangstad 2014; Anker and von der Lippe 2015).

11. See also baseline studies by Tim Jensen and Karna Kjeldsen (2014) published online and available at: http://iers.unive.it/about/research/ (accessed 4 March 2016).

12. One challenge is regarding which classes and age groups could be presented with religion in relation to conflict and violence. I have no clear answers, but in a Norwegian context I have argued that pupils in upper secondary (age 17–19) should be able to deal with such topics and probably secondary pupils (age 14–16) as well (cf. Andreassen 2008).

10. TOWARD AN APPRECIATION OF NON-NORMATIVITY: A QUASI-AUTOBIOGRAPHY

Aaron W. Hughes

Textbooks produce "good" religion. This makes sense given the fact that the ostensible goal behind the genre is to introduce students to a religious tradition with which they are largely unfamiliar. Why, it is assumed, would such textbooks want curious yet largely uninformed students to begin their journey in and through a particular religion on the "wrong foot"? In so doing, however, such textbooks end up reifying their subject matter since they often define religion as if it exists independently of culture, politics, and ideology. There is some eternal core, it is often further assumed, that is perceived to link up disparate cultural — not to mention spatial or geographic — expressions. Since they are interested in establishing normativity, textbooks rarely entertain non-normative voices because such voices threaten, or at the very least undermine, the basic narrative supplied by the former. In order to introduce students to the presumed "beauty" of expression found in a specific religion as opposed to showing its messiness and complexity, textbooks necessarily silence or at best marginalize non-normative voices. The result is a preference to claim that, for example, groups like al-Qaeda, Boko Haram or the so-called Islamic State are not representative of an authentic Muslim expression. Rather than situate the violent rhetoric and actions of these groups within the framework of larger Islamic discourses, the expressions of such groups are instead often portrayed as hijacking an essentially peaceful Islam. Many are afraid, and here they certainly have a point, that bringing such violent voices into the larger Islamic narrative might confuse students into mistaking the non-normative for the normative and vice versa.

Textbooks streamline and essentialize religions. For all intents and purposes, they take a set of diverse and often contradictory voices, and then thinly paper over such differences by transforming them into a monolith. Rather than speak, for example, of rival Judaisms that have radical views concerning authority, tradition, and what constitutes proper interpretation, textbooks frequently speak of Judaism in the singular. This produces a set of cognitive difficulties in students. It also means that textbooks set students up to think that there is a "Jewish," to stay with this example, take on a given topic. The result is that textbooks actually have the potential to confuse as much as they do to clarify. If students think, for example, that there is a normative "Jewish" take on abortion, what happens to those voices or denominations that diverge from it? This necessarily means silencing all those voices that somehow detract or depart from the mainstream.

Textbooks are inherently conservative, reproducing the status quo. Textbooks, we must not forget, are meant to make money for their publishers and their authors because they are designed to appeal to the large and potentially lucrative undergraduate market. No publisher wants to invest the resources and publish a book for which there is no market. This means that textbooks are inherently conservative and operate within the well-defined parameters of the field as opposed to challenging them. A textbook on Islam, for example, that begins with the violence of the so-called Islamic State would rarely, if ever, be used in a classroom setting, since so many "Introduction to Islam" courses are, especially in the post-9/11 world, meant to correct popular stereotypes that want to claim that Islam is inherently violent. Those who might peer-review such a potential textbook — and here it is worth noting that most textbook manuscripts are often sent to eight to ten reviewers as opposed to the more customary two for non-trade academic titles — would either not recommend it for publication or demand that the author remove such egregious material. The result is that pretty much all of our introductory textbooks, regardless of the religion, tend to replicate the same old categories, terminology, and rhetoric as all the others already in existence.

If textbooks are inherently benevolent and conservative in their intentions and capitalistic in their teleology, we have to ask ourselves are they worth it? Can a critical study of religion — something that we are, ideally if not practically, all engaged in — make use of the introductory textbook, which seems to go against the very grain of what it is we want to do? This is especially the case when it comes to dealing with violence. Since religiously sanctioned and motivated violence is all around us, what are we to do with textbooks that want to argue that such violence is a bastardization or represents a "hijacking" of a true faith?

In order to address such questions, what follows uses this basic critique of textbooks to examine the question of religious violence. It argues that the type of textbooks we need to address such all important issues in the contemporary period do not yet exist and perhaps cannot even exist since they are unfortunately out of sync with so much of our regnant discourses. These discourses problematically constitute the field and work on the assumption that religion is a source of good in the world and that those who commit violence do not properly understand their religion, and thereby somehow exist outside of it. Such an argument, however, deprives actors of their agency and represents, what I have called elsewhere a "neo-Orientalist" approach to religion — even among those who are, paradoxically, critical of the Orientalist project (see Hughes 2015).

As in this introductory section, my concern is both with Judaism and Islam. My focus will be more on the latter, however, because I myself have written a textbook, *Muslim Identities: An Introduction to Islam* (2013), which seeks to counter the portrayals found in other textbooks meant to introduce this tradition to undergraduates. Yet, as I have already remarked, in order to get such a book published it nevertheless had to reproduce the time-honored categories of the field. Despite this, the goal of my textbook is to bring non-normative voices, especially those that emphasize violence, into the larger discourse about what constitutes Islam.

INTRODUCTORY TEXTBOOKS ON JUDAISM

In his *Introducing Judaism*, Eliezer Segal writes:

> It must be remembered that for Jews…the ultimate expression of divine revelation is in the form of laws. This is certainly true for traditional Jews who believe that the momentous event in history was when God revealed the Torah to the children of Israel at Mount Sinai. The Torah consists primarily of laws and commandments, and it has always been assumed that the intensive study of religious law is a fundamental act of religious devotion. Jewish religious law encompasses not only matters of belief, liturgy, and ritual, but also covers the full range of civil and criminal laws. For Jews, all these laws have their origin in a divine revelation, and their observance forms the basis of the eternal covenant between God and the people of Israel (2009: 7).

What do we do with all those Jews who might disagree with this statement? Perhaps it comes as no surprise to learn that Segal, an Orthodox Jew, makes the observance of the commandments into the essence of Judaism. These commandments are, according to him, a divine revelation that presumably all Jews (he makes no mention of what Jews in particular) believe is the central focus of the covenant between God and Israel. What are we to do with all those Jews — indeed, the overwhelming majority of Jews — who do not believe this?[1]

This becomes especially relevant when it comes to those voices within the tradition that emphasize violence. Textbooks on Judaism, for example, rarely mention Baruch Goldstein, the Orthodox Jew who shot 29 Muslim worshippers in the tomb of Abraham in Hebron, nor the larger contextual framework supplied by the late Meir Kahane and his now outlawed political party Kach (see Ravitzky 1993: 181–90) that made his murderous act possible. This larger context reveals Baruch Goldstein to be anything but a "lone wolf," and instead as a social actor who was motivated by religious zeal. David Shatz, providing a "Jewish Perspective" to *The Oxford Handbook of Religious Diversity*, states that "I do not explore here discomfiting teachings of those Jewish authors who see innate differences between Jews and non-Jews with respect to spiritual capacities and holiness or that denigrate non-Jews and diminish their dignity" (2011: 366). The immediate question we have to ask, however, is, why not? Does the author not mention such teachings because he considers them to be anathema to Judaism? But even if anathema, some Jews hold them and, therefore, they are surely worthy of further study so that we are able to contextualize them and thus better understand them. The alternative, to say that such actions do not represent some self-constructed "authentic" Judaism is no less helpful. Or, perhaps the author thinks that by including such voices, he will reinforce traditional stereotypes that Jews see non-Jews as less than human? Regardless, by not including the full diversity of Jewish voices in an introductory treatment of Judaism and religious diversity should strike us as odd and potentially misleading. I disagree with Shatz in that I maintain that these "discomfiting teachings" are important to examine. Even though they may not be "mainstream," they nonetheless provide important discursive sites wherein we can glimpse at both Judaism's multivocality and its ambiguity.[2]

Another example comes by way of a controversial book entitled *Torat haMelech* (Torah of the King) that was published in 2009 by Yitzhack Shapira and Yosef Elitzur, two rabbis associated with a seminary entitled Yeshiva Od Yosef Chai located in the West Bank. The authors, among other things, sought to advise Israeli soldiers how to conduct themselves in times of war. Basing their arguments on a highly particularist reading of the traditional canons of Jewish law (*halakhah*), they argued that under certain circumstances "non-involved" gentiles, including innocent women and children, may be preemptively killed. They reason that such force is permissible because these innocents may, at some indeterminate point in the future, take up arms against Jews. Although Arabs are nowhere mentioned by name in the book, it is not difficult to see that such a work both legitimates and justifies the murder of innocent Palestinians (including children) for the sake of some self-perceived religious struggle between Jew and non-Jew.[3] As problematic as the book's contents are, equally troubling is the fact that many notable and well-respected rabbis wrote legal endorsements of it, including Yaakov Yosef, the son of the late Chief Sephardic Rabbi, Ovadia Yosef.

The authors of *Torat haMelech*, as well as many of those who proffered endorsements for it, were subsequently investigated by the State of Israel's Attorney General's office on suspicion of incitement to racism and violence (though no charges have ever been laid). Some of the most prominent rabbis who had endorsed the book, most notably Kiryat Arba's chief rabbi Dov Lior, dismissed police summons by arguing that the secular and human law that currently governed the State of Israel could not infringe upon God's law, which alone was eternally binding on the Jewish people. When, a year later, the Israeli police finally arrested Lior, riots broke out with scores of religious Zionists burning tires in the streets and attempting to storm the Israeli Supreme Court. It is probably worth pointing out that, paradoxically, Lior and the other rabbis who endorsed *Torat haMelekh* are all state employees.

Despite, or perhaps because of, this work and its troubling repercussions, *Torat haMelekh* will not find its way into introductory textbooks on Judaism. I would certainly not want to argue that this work somehow represents "mainstream" Jewish opinion on the topic of religious diversity, but to show that Judaism — like any other religious tradition — constructs and legitimates itself through a complex process of self- and other-making. In order to create a discourse of the self, framed somewhat differently, it is necessary to do the same for the not-self. This means that self and other become dialectic opposites that require one another for mutual definition and ultimate exclusion. What Jewish sources say about non-Jews, not surprisingly, tell us more about Jewish concerns than they do about either the contents or validity of other religious traditions and beliefs. It is precisely these "non-religious" factors that are so missing in introductory textbooks because so many of them seek to convey the spiritual or religious side of religion as opposed to the historical, the social, or the political. Unfortunately, however, very few introductory textbooks are willing to undertake even this most basic of sociological explanations for group formation.

The worldview that informs *Torat haMelekh* shows this clearly. Non-Jews, unnamed and anonymous, become the marker whereby Judaism and its values can be both imagined and articulated. Jews are holy, chosen, and possess some intrinsic divine right to the land of Israel; non-Jews are less than human, threaten Jewish existence, and represent a potential pollutant in the land, a pollutant that can and must be removed. The killing of non-Jews, on this reading, is not immoral, but in fact now becomes a moral imperative. This could even be extended to Jews who support aiding non-Jews. Witness, for example, the religious justification and right-wing rhetoric of the murderer who assassinated Yitzhack Rabin, the Prime Minister of Israel in 1995. Read in this manner, something that we are accustomed to imagine as "the Jewish tradition" can certainly be used to nourish a highly racist and atavistic nationalism. And there certainly exist many Jews, especially among religious Zionists in the modern State of Israel, who would endorse such a reading. Is it normative? Certainly not. However, who gets to decide what represents so-called normative Judaism? Textbooks, I would argue. Textbooks, whether their authors would admit it or not, are in the habit of contributing to the discourse of "good" religion. Rather than attempt to push our understanding of the cultural, political, social, and ideological components that create group formation, the majority of textbooks simply repeat the stories that religions tell of themselves. The result is little more than color commentary.

INTRODUCTION TO ISLAM TEXTBOOKS

In Islamic studies the situation is not any better. In fact, one could say that it is actually much worse. As I have shown in several publications (Hughes 2007, 2012a, 2012b, 2015), the study of Islam as carried out in the field of religious studies is notoriously uncritical, apologetic, and unwilling to engage in pressing issues such as Islam's relationship — both in the past and in the present — to religiously sanctioned violence. This has only been exacerbated in recent years as many seek to downplay, even at the risk of excising completely, the fact that there are Muslims that commit violence in the name of Islam. Rather than try to contextualize such violence, for many the default position is either that such Muslims do not properly understand their religion or that they have hijacked it for "political" ends as opposed to upholding the religion's "spiritual" truths. This neat separation between "political" and "spiritual" is, of course, a politically motivated distinction. Consider, for example, the case of Karen Armstrong.[4] She is someone who, despite the fact that she has no training in Islamic studies, has nevertheless written several best-selling textbooks. In her *Muhammad: A Prophet for Our Time* (2007), she writes that "Muhammad literally sweated with the effort to bring peace to war-torn Arabia, and we need people who are prepared to do this today" (2007: 7). Bringing peace to "war-torn" places is our modern term that reflects recent headlines about places like Iraq and Afghanistan, but certainly not one that is relevant to 6th century Arabia, about which we know next to nothing since all our sources come from much later periods. Armstrong subsequently writes that Muhammad "had profound genius and founded a religion and cultural tradition that was not based on the sword but whose name — "Islam" — signified peace and reconciliation" (2007: 202). Implicit in such a statement, according to Armstrong and so many others like her, is that those who commit violence in the name of Islam, which we are frequently told comes from the same root as *salām* or "peace," are not really Muslims. Instead they have, to use another well-worn trope, "hijacked" the tradition for their own "political" purposes.

In her more recent *Fields of Blood* (2014), Armstrong takes her apologetic argument and seeks to provide a grandiose and highly problematic theory of religious violence — again for use in the classroom. She argues, among other things, that religion, rather than be intrinsically violent, instead absorbs the violence associated with the post-industrial world and, especially, the rise of the modern nation state. In particular, she claims that:

> If we can define the sacred as something for which one is prepared to die, the nation had certainly become an embodiment of the divine, a supreme value. Hence national mythology would encourage cohesion, solidarity, and loyalty within the confines of the nation. But it had yet to develop the 'concern for everybody' that had been such an important ideal in many of the spiritual traditions associated with religion. The national mythos would not encourage citizens to extend their sympathy to the ends of the earth, to love the stranger in their midst, be loyal even to their enemies, to wish happiness on all beings, and to become aware of the world's pain… Secular nationalism seemed to regard the foreigner as fair game for exploitation and mass slaughter, especially if he belonged to a different ethnic group (2014: 294).

Once again, in her desire to free the "spiritual" core of religion from the violence committed in its name, she puts the blame squarely on secularism. The political world of secularism, in other words, is diametrically opposed to the spiritual world of religion.

Returning to Islam, many textbooks are interested in showing the diversity of Islam by not confining the tradition to its Middle Eastern expression. This is certainly a good thing. However, while they increasingly refuse to make Middle Eastern Islam normative, they nevertheless still reproduce another normativity that refuses to acknowledge, let alone contextualize, the violent actions committed by groups that clearly describe themselves as Muslim. While this is certainly a noble initiative, it nevertheless often further reifies the same assumptions as those more traditional textbooks that make the Islam of the Arabian Peninsula and the Middle East normative. Also implicit in this is that there is an essential Islam that exists somewhere in the ether like a Platonic form and that manifests itself in different cultures. A more appropriate narrative, of course, would be one that ignores the form and simply looks at various cultural expressions. This is hard to do, however, because so few scholars are either savvy enough in religious studies method and theory *or* familiar with all of the cultural modalities that produce different, even competing, Islams around the globe. There is, then, no ideal textbook for Islam just as there can be no ideal textbook for any religion. The question we have to ask ourselves, and I will address this more fully in the concluding section, is why do we persist in the task? In the space that remains I wish to try to answer this from the perspective of what I have called in the subtitle to this chapter "quasi-autobiographical."

When I was an undergraduate student at the University of Alberta I first encountered Islam as an academic subject through Frederick Denny's highly popular *An Introduction to Islam* (1985; it is currently in its 4th edition, and I quote from the 2nd edition of 1994). I was really bothered by one particular sentence in the textbook that referred to the Qur'an. Therein Denny writes, "It is painful for Muslims to witness certain types of historico-critical, philological, and otherwise 'Orientalist' scholarly treatment of their sacred book" (1994: 148). Was Denny really telling me as an undergraduate student that I should not engage in certain types of questions — what he himself labels as "critical" and "scholarly" — because they might offend the sensibilities of Muslims? Was I not in a university setting where such critical and scholarly questions were the norm.

Just imagine, I realized, if we confuse history with salvation history, fact and fiction, and simply assume that what later Islamic sources tell us about the Qur'an's origin — namely that it was revealed by God to Muhammad via the archangel Gabriel — is what really happened. It would be akin to assuming that what the Bible had to say about the origins of the ancient Israelites was factual even though independent sources or the archeological record cannot corroborate it. All that Denny went on to elaborate worked on the assumption that the Qur'an fell from heaven and that any investigation into its historical origins was either "painful for Muslims" or "Orientalist." It should come as no surprise that this latter term, especially post-9/11, often functions as code for "Islamophobe" (see Ernst and Martin 2010). Another example of this hermeneutic may be found in the writings of Tariq Ramadan, another scholar whose works are used as textbooks to introduce undergraduates to Islam. In his *In the Footsteps of the Prophet* (2007), he writes,

> Our aim is more to get to know the Prophet himself than to learn about his personality or the events in his life. What is sought is immersion, sympathy, and essentially love...this is indeed the primary ambition of this work: making of the Messenger's life a mirror through which readers facing the challenges of our time can explore their hearts and minds and achieve an understanding of questions of being and meaning as well as broader ethical and social concerns (Ramadan 2007: x).

As this passage makes abundantly clear, Ramadan is neither interested in history nor the historical record. His goal is to present his own interpretation of Islam and its prophet as if it were based on a set of facts that anyone can access. The truth of the matter, however, is that they are not based on facts, but opinion. These opinions are then presented to undergraduates and other readers who know very little about the traditions as if they were quite literally true. As I have written elsewhere, just imagine if students at a secular university were introduced to Christian origins with a textbook that claimed that all they needed to understand Jesus and the early Jesus movement was love (Hughes 2012a: 27).

If the likes of Denny and Ramadan — and here I might add pretty much every other textbook — refuses to discuss the thorny issue of Islamic origins because it offends Muslim sensibilities, then what are they going to do when it comes to the topic of Islam and violence or Islamic violence? The answer should come as no surprise: they either ignore it or claim it is not really Islam. The easiest way to do this, and this seems to be the default position, is to do what John Esposito does and say, with a straight face, that those who commit violence in the name of Islam are not Muslims. In so doing, he sets himself up as the arbiter of who is and who is not a "true" Muslim. Our goal as scholars, it is worth underscoring here, is not to engage in the type of act, but to explain why and how some Muslims might legitimately engage in such actions. In his *The Islamic Threat: Myth or Reality* (1999 [1992]), however, Esposito writes,

> The demonization of a great religious tradition due to the *perverted actions* of a minority of *dissident and distorted voices* remains the real threat, a threat that not only impacts on relations between the Muslim world and the West, but also upon growing Muslim populations in the West (Esposito 1999: xiii, my italics).

Esposito's post-9/11 textbooks are certainly no better. In the 2005 edition of his *Islam; The Straight Path*, another very popular textbook, he tells his audience about Osama bin Laden,

> Terrorists like Osama bin Laden and others *have gone beyond* classical Islam's criteria for a just war. They recognize no limits but their own, employing any weapons or means... At the same time, many prominent Islamic scholars and religious leaders across the Muslim world have denounced this

hijacking of Islam by terrorists. The Islamic Research Council at al-Azhar University, one of the oldest universities in the world and a leading center of Islamic learning regarded by many as the highest moral authority in Islam, issued strong authoritative declarations against bin Laden's initiatives (2005 [1988]: 263).

This passage is problematic on so many levels. For one thing, it sets up a number of binaries. Bin Laden is described as a "terrorist," though of course he himself would never have used such a term to describe himself. He is then juxtaposed with "prominent Islamic scholars," who presumably represent the "authentic" Islamic teaching. Esposito then contrasts the "moral authority" granted to these Islamic scholars by virtue of their institutional affiliation with the "initiatives" of solitary individuals or rogue groups who "hijack" Islam's true and peaceful message.

When reading the likes of Denny, Armstrong, and Esposito, an undergraduate reaches the inevitable conclusion that such authors want them to reach: that those who perpetrate violence in the name of Islam are not real Muslims. Rather, their violent actions represent inauthentic religious expressions. Undergirding such claims, of course, is the old-fashioned Protestant notion that "authentic" religious sentiment is internal and spiritual, never political or external. Framed in the language of another Karen Armstrong textbook,

> The spiritual quest is an interior journey; it is psychic rather than a political drama. It is preoccupied with liturgy, doctrine, contemplative disciplines and an exploration of the heart, not with the clash of current events... power struggles are not what religion is really about, but an unworthy distraction from the life of the spirit, which is conducted far from the maddening crowd, unseen, silent, and unobtrusive (Armstrong 2000: ix).

This is the larger context that I faced when I decided to write my own textbook. Since the majority of other such books were primarily interested in either presenting a sanitized version of the tradition, I decided that I would not. This means that rather than worry about Muslim sensibilities in discussing early Islam, I had to address some of the real and historical problems associated with reconstructing this period. Unlike competing texts, I decided to offer readers a choice so that they could make their conclusions based on the facts or lack thereof. I thus have two sections: one on "later Muslim accounts of Islamic origins," which essentially retells the story of Islamic origins that Muslims tell themselves; and then juxtapose this with a section entitled "outsider and skeptical approaches to Islamic origins" (Hughes 2013: 32–37). In terms of introducing the later, I write,

> A skeptical approach to these sources regards them as historically very problematic as the attempts by later generations of Muslims to justify and legitimate their vision of what Islam should be. Such an approach ques-

tions all the 'facts' recounted in this chapter. The result is a very different account of the emergence of Islam. This section provides an overview of some of these theories as a way to show the diversity of opinions and research on these sources (Hughes 2013: 34).

This comment and the section that follows it offers what I consider to be a direct response to the likes of Denny and Ramadan that want to bypass the historical problems associated with using much later sources as if they were eyewitness accounts. (For those unfamiliar, our earliest sources documenting the rise of Islam date anywhere from 150-250 years after the fact. And there is absolutely no way to get around the fact that the sources we do possess reflect later political debates over legitimacy to rule).

In terms of dealing with religious violence I again make the point that it is a reality within contemporary Islam. No matter how much we want to deny this fact, we cannot. So rather than excise it from the tradition, I seek to account for it. I certainly have no desire to say that Islam is a violent religion — or at least any more inherently violent than any other tradition — or that all Muslims engage in violence. However, it is important for the beginning student of religion to understand both the nature and mentality of those who commit violence in the name of the tradition. As I claim in my textbook, it is necessary to use a larger frame of reference to try and understand the many types of Muslim responses to the perceived secularism of the modern world. In order to do this I find Bruce Lincoln's distinction between religious "minimalism" and "maximalism" to be useful (Lincoln 2003: 57–59). This distinction is also useful because it can be usefully applied to all religions. Minimalists, according to him, desire to curtail religion from the public sphere, whereas maximalists seek a greater role for religion in all spheres of society. Within this context, I make the point in my textbook that, based on Lincoln's distinction,

> suggests a convenient way to establish a taxonomy of Muslim encounters with modernity. Such a taxonomy, although by no means accurately mirroring the complexity of Islamic voices on the ground, should provide a convenient context to begin the process of sorting through at least some of these competing voices heard from Islam. Most important, it should also avoid the common assumption that all Muslims, whether synchronically or diachronically, speak with one voice or that they all react in the same manner to external and internal stimuli (2013: 233).

I then try to let these various voices speak for themselves by giving a series of case studies that I analyze. I have an entire subsequent chapter where I try to discuss what I call "Islam post-9/11." Therein my goal is to analyze the events of September 11, 2001, in addition to taking groups like al-Qaeda seriously as Islamic voices, while at the same time being quick to point out that they should not be seen as normative. It is only when commentators — either to the left or right

— desire to hold up one voice to the exclusion of others that, I argue, problems emerge:

> Because of these myriad voices, it is important not to take one and hold it up as normative, thereby mistaking a part for the whole. Unfortunately, however, various commentators, politicians, and even scholars try to make liberal Islam or militant Islam somehow representative of Islam. It is necessary to be aware that contemporary Islam is a polyphony of voices that are rarely, if ever, in harmony with one another (2013: 275).

My textbook, then, tries to address what I consider to be major lacunae in other introductory treatments of Islam. Was I successful? Time will tell. Although I do confess that even though I strayed from the basic narrative in addressing some of these issues, I still had to adopt the existing chronological framework so that my book would fit within the existing structure of the "Introduction to Islam" course. The next question, though, is because I strayed from this basic narrative does this mean that instructors will adopt the book? Although I have had some very favorable reviews (e.g. Hoffman 2014; Hershkovits 2014), others have criticized the book because much of my other work in Islamic Studies (especially 2012a, 2012b) has been so critical of others in the field whom I believe perpetuate what I called "disciplinary lying."

The following review of my book on the website Amazon.com by one "Kemal Kaygili" is indicative. Note that I do not think that this counts as a valid review because on such websites one can say anything about anything without proving one's credentials or even prove that s/he has read the book in question. At any rate, he writes,

> This book is extremely biased against Islam. The author writes in the beginning that he will follow a 'middle path between theological introductions to Islam and works that seeks to undermine the religion.' However, the book itself turns out to be a book that undermines Islam. The author did his best to find any single polemic [sic] that is around non-academic and anti-Islam settings [sic] and integrated them [sic] into his 'introduction to Islam.' Throughout the book, he tries to discredit very well established scholars of Islam such as Karen Armstrong, Tariq Ramadan, etc.... This is funny because the author himself is not a scholar on Islam. His major scholarship is on Judaism. He is the Philip S. Bernstein Professor of Jewish Studies at University of Rochester. I was really surprised how a prestigious press such as Columbia published this book as a textbook. It cannot serve as a textbook for Islam classes. This book doesn't introduce Islam. It introduces non-intellectual and polemical arguments against Islam.

I mention this comment solely as a discursive site, since it shows just what is at stake for those who want to try to do something new. This person seems to object that I hold an endowed chair in Jewish studies even though I specialize in Islam and Islamic-Jewish relations. He is bothered that I "discredit," even as I do here, the apologetic work of more traditional type textbooks produced by the likes of Armstrong and Ramadan — the former has no training in Islamic studies (I am not even sure if she can read a line of Arabic) and the latter has no training in the academic study of religion. Finally, this review objects — as I am sure many will who are contemplating using my book in their classes — that I introduce the skeptical approach to Islamic origins, something that is often referred to pejoratively as "revisionist" or "Orientalist." This does not amount to an "argument against Islam" as it is an attempt to provide an honest assessment about what we know and what we do not, what we can know and what we cannot.

CONCLUSION

As mentioned above, I decided to write my own textbook on account of what I, and others, consider to be the real paucity of good textbooks on Islam. In the post-9/11 world — where we read regularly about groups such as the Taliban, Hamas, al-Qaeda, Boko Haram, and ISIS — students, in addition to interested non-academics, want to know what these groups think and how they interpret their tradition. If we simply tell our students that such groups have nothing to do with Islam then either they will not believe us — in which case they may even accuse us of being "liars" — or gravitate to more sensationalist accounts that will try to make the case that Islam is inherently violent. Too many existing textbooks, for various political reasons, seek to present Islam in the best possible light. While this is certainly understandable given the woeful ignorance of most Americans and Europeans when it comes to this religion, it unfortunately does not make for the best analysis when it comes to understanding and contextualizing religious violence.

Violence is a part of religion. If we ignore this fact, we lie to ourselves. We do not have to be trained sociologists to acknowledge that social groups form and define themselves through an intricate process of privilege and denial. This means that the basic instinct of all social groups is to create others. Throw into this mix the perceived threat of secularism and we have the perfect mix for *some* groups to engage in violence. Yet, our textbooks rarely engage in this kind of analysis. This is because, as I mentioned in my opening paragraphs, textbooks procure good religion, try to silence non-normative voices, and endeavor to make money.

Textbooks, in conclusion, actually have the potential to exacerbate problems. In reading them we are told that Islam is synonymous with peace. Yet we see every day in the media violence committed by individuals who not only appear to be devout, but also use the language of those who are devout. In ignoring such voices in our introductory classes, we become the ones who do violence. This means that our textbooks, which we use in our classes, make a mockery of the headlines and what our students perceive all around them. It is perhaps for this reason that experts in religion are not qualified, according to the FBI, to be expert witnesses (see Weitzman 2013).

Ultimately we must conclude that in their refusal to take seriously religious violence, many of our textbooks do real violence to our ability to understand the range of human practices that we too neatly subsume under the category "religion."

ABOUT THE AUTHOR

Aaron W. Hughes holds the Philip S. Bernstein Chair of Jewish Studies in the Department of Religion and Classics at the University of Rochester. Hughes is a highly published scholar in the field of studies on Islam and Judaism. Among his published books are *Abrahamic Religions: On the Uses and Abuses of History* (Oxford University Press, 2012), *The Study of Judaism: Identity, Authenticity, Scholarship* (State University of New York Press, 2013), *Muslim Identities: An Introduction* (Columbia University Press, 2013), *Rethinking Jewish Philosophy: Beyond Particularism and Universalism* (Oxford University Press, 2014), *Islam and the Tyranny of Authenticity: An Inquiry into Disciplinary Apologetics and Self-Deception* (Equinox, 2015), and *Jacob Neusner: An American Jewish Iconoclast* (New York University Press, 2016). Email: aaron.hughes@rochester.edu

REFERENCES

Armstrong, Karen. 2000. *Islam: A Short History*. New York: The Modern Library.
Armstrong, Karen. 2007. *Muhammad: A Prophet of Our Time*. New York: HarperOne.
Armstrong, Karen. 2014. *Fields of Blood: Religion and the History of Violence*. New York: Knopf.
Denny, Frederick Mathewson. 1994. *An Introduction to Islam*. 2nd edn. New York: Macmillan.
Ernst, Carl W., and Richard C. Martin, eds. 2010. *Rethinking Islamic Studies: From Orientalism to Cosmopolitanism*. Columbia, SC: University of South Carolina Press.
Esposito, John L. 1999 [1992]. *The Islamic Threat: Myth or Reality*, 3rd edn. New York: Oxford University Press.
Esposito, John L. 2005 [1988]. *Islam: The Straight Path*. Revised 3rd edn. New York: Oxford University Press.
Hershkovits, Keren Abbou. 2014. "A Different Approach to an Introduction to Islam." H-Mideast-Medieval, H-Net Reviews. November, 2014. Available at: http://www.h-net.org/reviews/showrev.php?id=40468
Hoffman, Murad Wilfried. 2014. "Review of *Muslim Identities: An Introduction to Islam*." *Journal of Islamic Studies*. Available at: http://jis.oxfordjournals.org/content/early/2014/06/19/jis.etu049.extract
Hughes, Aaron W. 2007. *Situating Islam: The Past and Future of an Academic Discipline*. London: Equinox Publishing.
Hughes, Aaron W. 2012a. *Theorizing Islam: Disciplinary Deconstruction and Reconstruction*. London and New York: Routledge.

Hughes, Aaron W. 2012b. "The Study of Islam Before and After September 11: A Provocation." *Method and Theory in the Study of Religion* 24(4-5): 314–36.
Hughes, Aaron W. 2013. *Muslim Identities: An Introduction to Islam*. New York: Columbia University Press.
Hughes, Aaron W. 2015. *Islam and the Tyranny of Authenticity: An Inquiry into Disciplinary Apologetics and Self-Deception*. Sheffield: Equinox Publishing.
Hughes, Aaron W. 2016. "Theology: The Articulation of Orthodoxy." In *Routledge Handbook of Muslim-Jewish Relations*, ed. Yosef Meri, 77–94. New York and London: Routledge.
Lincoln, Bruce. 2003. *Holy Terrors: Thinking About Religion After September 11*. Chicago, IL: University of Chicago Press.
Ramadan, Tariq. 2007. *In the Footsteps of the Prophet: Lessons from the Life of Muhammad*. New York: Oxford University Press.
Ravitzky, Aviezer. 1993. *Messianism, Zionism, and Jewish Religious Radicalism*, trans. Michael Swirsky and Jonathan Chipman. Chicago, IL: University of Chicago Press.
Segal, Eliezer. 2009. *Introducing Judaism*. London and New York: Routledge.
Shatz, David. 2011. "A Jewish Perspective." In *The Oxford Handbook of Religious Diversity*, ed. Chad Meister, 365–80. New York: Oxford University Press.
Weitzman, Steven. 2013. "Religious Studies and the FBI: Adventures in Academic Interventionism." *Journal of the American Academy of Religion* 81(4): 959–95.

Endnotes

1. This paragraph reworks Hughes 2013: 24.
2. This and the following paragraph rework Hughes 2016.
3. Instead of mentioning Arabs, the authors use "children of Noah." In their synopsis of Chapter 1, for example, they write:

> In this chapter we deal with the notion that the prohibition of 'do not murder' [*lo tirtzach*] does not apply to non-Jews. And, the prohibition of Jews killing non-Jews is learned from the prohibition given to the offspring of Noah against killing others. In the appendixes of the chapter we deal with another principle that the Jews are obligated in the commandments given to Noah (Shapira and Elitzur: 17).

4. In my own opinion, Armstrong should not even be considered a "scholar of religion" because she lacks the minimum credentials (i.e., the PhD) to be considered as such. Nevertheless, since she regularly offers keynote addresses at the Annual Meetings of the American Academy of Religion, the largest professional organization of professional religionists, I include her here. She is also convenient to use because she, in my opinion, offers the most egregious example of downplaying or completely severing the connection between religion and violence.

11. SELF-CONTRADICTIONS AND PROJECTED OTHERNESS: IMAGES OF SIKH MILITANCY IN THE WRITINGS OF ORIENTALIST SCHOLARS AND CONTEMPORARY TEXTBOOK AUTHORS

James R. Lewis

Over the course of the past few decades, academics have invested increasing amounts of energy into analyzing the scholarly discourse of previous eras, particularly the scholarship that was carried out by colonialist nations with respect to subject peoples. The focus of most of this relatively recent work has been to point out how the images of non-European peoples presented in such discourse were shaped by the (often unconscious) presuppositions of European scholars, as well as how this scholarship ultimately fed back into, and helped to legitimize imperialistic attitudes. Within Sikh studies, a fair amount of analysis along these lines has been carried out with respect to the semi-scholarly works produced by British officials during the period of time leading up to the annexation of the Punjab.

As someone professionally involved in teaching of general courses on world religions, I became interested in examining how non-Western people were presented in contemporary survey treatments of world religions, especially the representations found in world religion textbooks. What follows is a short report of my findings in this area with respect to the Sikh community. The focus of the discussion will be on the representations of the Sikh martial tradition as well as an analysis of the factors that might be responsible for such misrepresentations.

SIKHISM AND MORAL CENSURE

H. H. Wilson, one of the major Orientalists of the 19th century, published an article on Sikhism during the time of the Anglo-Sikh wars. Predictably, considering the time period in which he wrote, his analysis was sharply critical:

> The great distinction between the Sikhs and the other Hindus is the abolition of the distinction of caste, and consequent extinction of many of the restraints, which, in the more orthodox system, supply, however imperfectly, the want of a purer code of faith and practice. The experiment has not been very successful, and the worship of the Book and of the Sword, and the moral declamations of the contributors to the sacred Granth, have led to as great, if not a greater, laxity of conduct, and as utter a disregard of both religious and moral obligations, as the superstitious belief and multiplied ceremonial of the Brahmans (Wilson 1958 [1848]: 68-69).

The more peculiarly Orientalist "contribution" of Wilson's critique is evident in his exaggerated deployment of the "early pure vs. later degenerate" contrast. The original elements of Nanak's Sikhism were, in his analysis, "deism of a mystical character, contemplative worship, peace and good-will" (Wilson 1958 [1848]: 64). Guru Gobind Singh, however, according to Wilson,

> changed the whole character of the community, and converted the Sikhs of Nanak, the disciples of a religion of spirituality and benevolence, and professors of a faith of peace and good will, into an armed confederacy, a military republic. The worship of 'steel' was combined with that of the 'book,' and instead of attempting to unite Muhammadans and Hindus into one family fraternity, he made his disciples vow implacable hatred to the followers of Mohammed (Wilson 1958 [1848]: 58).

This is, of course, a grossly unfair and inaccurate characterization of the contrast between Nanak and Gobind Singh. It is, however, easy to explain why Wilson adopted this condemnatory tone. From certain other passages in the text, it is clear that Wilson wrote this piece between the first and second Anglo-Sikh War, and wished to castigate the English's recent enemy, as well as to encourage the government to "finish off" the remains of Ranjit Singh's kingdom:

> [T]he Khalsa has been left in a state of utter imbecility which will ensure its spontaneous extinction at no distant period, if not kept alive by the undeserved protection of the Government (Wilson 1958 [1848]: 64).

In the example of Wilson, we are able to perceive one of the ways in which "knowledge" about other peoples is employed to legitimize imperialism. In this particular case, Sikhism's early period (a kind of idealized, Sikh "golden age" structurally similar to the Orientalists' Hindu classical age) is used to call into judgment contemporaneous Sikhs. Wilson argued that the Sikhs were degenerate, and implied that this state of affairs legitimized British conquest. The structure of this argument is not fully explicit in Wilson, but one can find clear, overt expressions of this line of reasoning in other 19th century sources — e.g., "Works like these [the abolition of widow-burning] are the credentials by which the Western civilization makes good its right to conquer and humanize barbarous races and to replace ancient civilizations" (Helms 1882, cited in Geertz 1980: 102).

The contrast between early and later Sikhism is, however, somewhat different from the contrast between early and later Hinduism. The fact that the theme seemed to obsess observers of the Sikhs, long after Europeans had ceased to condemn contemporaneous Hindus on the basis of an idealized Hindu past, indicates that the contrast within Sikhism set off certain resonances within the Western psyche that Hinduism's contrast did not. In the Orientalist picture of Hinduism, the contrast had been between a past that was seen as a pure monotheism and a present that was seen as superstitious and idolatrous. The Orientalist portrayal of the contrast within Sikhism was structured along different lines. Though Sikhism was also portrayed as having been (or as still being) a pure monotheism, Europeans focused on the supposed pacifism of Nanak and sharply contrasted it with the militancy of the Tenth Guru. This type of obsession indicates that the British were probably projecting one of their own repressed, internal conflicts onto the Sikhs.

In order to understand this fixation, it is important to be aware that it is not only biological drives which can be the subject of repression. Guilt about the gap between one's ideals and one's behavior, or uneasiness about the contradictions among one's own values, can also be pushed out of the circle of full consciousness only to re-emerge as a projection. A good example of this inner split is discernable in the tension between the teachings of Jesus and the martial self-image — not to mention the martial activity — of the British in India. An apparent, though false, parallel to this disjunction is evident in the contrast between Guru Nanak and Guru Gobind Singh, and as a consequence British writers almost never failed to call attention to it.[1] The tone of condemnation as well as the parallel to Britain's "forgetfulness" of Jesus's "tenets of peace" is evident in such statements as W. L. McGregor's observation that, "Nanak, as the founder of the Sikhs, is greatly venerated by that nation, though they appear to have entirely forgotten his tenets of peace" (W. L. McGregor 1970 [1846]: 41).

It is transparent (though it was not, of course, obvious to McGregor and his contemporaries) that this condemnation applied at least as well — and, considering that Nanak was not a pacifist,[2] probably a good deal better — to the British conquerors of India. We are thus probably justified in inferring that at some level the British were aware of the self-contradiction in which they were involved, but disliked the self-image that a full awareness of this state of affairs would have produced and thus repressed it out of consciousness — only to project their anxieties about themselves onto the Sikhs. My line of argument here may seem a little strained, but, if we were to examine a broad cross-section of British condemnation of Sikh militancy, we would find many other passages that apply equally well to the British themselves. For another instance of this phenomenon, we could go back to Wilson's article where he asserted that Ranjit Singh, confidently prosecuted his system of aggression, and trampled with impunity upon the rights of his neighbors, whether Muhammadans or Hindus The transactions that have taken place [have shown] the rottenness of his system; the instability of a dominion based upon military violence and individual ambition; the certain consequences of relying upon an army as the main instrument and stay of a government (Wilson 1958 [1848]: 64).

At the period when Wilson was writing the British were pursuing a policy of aggressive conquest, and furthermore based their dominion upon naked power — though they did not fully admit this state of affairs to themselves. Considering the close parallel between this portrayal of Ranjit Singh and the actual situation of the British it is not far-fetched to read autobiographical (using "autobiographical" to refer to British imperialists as a group rather than as individuals) overtones in Wilson's moral judgment. Yet other passages could be cited to demonstrate this pattern, but the point should be sufficiently clear.

After 1857, the constellation of factors shaping British perceptions of India changed. In addition to a new political situation, the intellectual climate was considerably different. The idea of unilinear progress had, for example, largely supplanted older models of cyclic growth and decay, at least as far as they applied to the West. However, the Orientalist theme of the "degenerate East" remained useful as part of the legitimating ideology of imperialism, and hence was retained.

On the whole, the Sikhs fared rather better than most other Indian groups. In the latter half of the 19th century, the British generally tended to perceive the Sikhs in a positive light. Nonetheless, because of the resonances that the Nanak/Gobind Singh contrast elicited from the inner tensions of European Christians, a trace of the degenerationist paradigm was retained in discussions, particularly academic discussions, of the development of the Sikh religion. In fact, the theme of the supposed contradiction between early and later Sikhism, often carrying with it the same undertone of moral censure that it originally carried, is repeated in Western discourse about Sikhism to this very day.

SIKHISM – A SYNCRETISM OF HINDUISM AND ISLAM

Next to the portrayal of Sikhism as a syncretism of Hinduism and Islam, the most frequent misinterpretation of the Sikh religion to appear in world religion textbooks is this same contrast between the supposed "pacifism" of Guru Nanak and the "militancy" of Guru Gobind Singh. Although a few authors of general surveys have recognized that the difference between the First Master and the Tenth Master on this point lay more in the circumstances of the time during which they lived rather than in their basic orientations, more often than not such authors have seen it fit to exaggerate the contrast until it appears that there is an actual contradiction between early and later Sikhism. To cite a few such misrepresentations:

> The Sikhs found themselves forced to abandon the non-violent teachings of the early masters... (Smart 1976: 152).
>
> One of the paradoxes of the Sikh religion is its pacifism in theory and militarism in practice (Hardon 1963: 231).
>
> Sikhism's transformation from a passive sect to a fighting theocracy is a well nigh complete reversal of basic values (Hutchison 1969: 201).

These statements clearly echo the negative judgment first leveled against the Sikhs by scholar-administrators such as Wilson. Though we might be inclined to be forgiving toward these 19th century figures — who were, after all, writing around the period of the Anglo-Sikh wars as well as engaged in the difficult task of legitimatizing British imperialism — we have to wonder what issue is at stake behind the very similar statements of contemporary scholars.

This brings us back to the hypothesis that perhaps the relevant scholars are uncomfortable with the contradiction between theory and practice in their own religious tradition, but have repressed the problem and have projected the contradiction onto Sikhism, a tradition that apparently (but not actually) contains the same contradiction. This point becomes clearer if one substitutes "Christians," "Christian," and "Christianity's" for "Sikhs," "Sikh," and "Sikhism's" in the above quotations. Such substitutions would render the above statements at least as accurate — if not more accurate — than the originals. Let us even push this a little further, and quote a series of longer passages from three different textbooks:

> *Another element in the religion of Nanak was his pacifism. This man, in all his travels and with all the rejection that he received, maintained the stance of a pacifist. He never struck out at his enemies, and apparently he taught his disciples to follow this pattern. In contrast to the teachings of Nanak, Sikhs, in their later history, became known as the most militant of warriors* (Hopfe 1987: 183).
>
> *Although the teachings of Nanak himself set forth a quietistic religion that laid stress upon the individual and his relationship to God, the religion, which developed after Nanak, became highly political, leading to a religious state in the Punjab. Also, the original emphasis on individual virtues and piety became in time a faith that emphasized strength, combativeness, and even militarism* (Stroup 1974: 104).
>
> *Guru Gobind Singh built up Sikh fighting strength, and what had begun as a group of believers in brotherly love turned into a formidable military brotherhood which waged war against Muslims, and which believed, as Muslims did, that death in battle was a passport to paradise* (Cavendish 1980: 49).

As a way of making this issue stand out more starkly, let us actually go ahead and substitute "Jesus" and "Christians" for "Nanak" and "Sikhs" in the extended quotation from Lewis M. Hopfe's *Religions of the World*, and "Jesus" and "Europe" for "Nanak" and "Punjab" in the above quote from Herbert Stroup's *Founders of Living Religions*:

> Another element in the religion of Jesus was his pacifism. This man, in all his travels and with all the rejection that he received, maintained the stance of a pacifist. He never struck out at his enemies, and apparently he taught his disciples to follow this pattern. In contrast to the teachings of Jesus, Christians, in their later history, became known as the most militant of warriors.

> Although the teachings of Jesus himself set forth a quietistic religion that laid stress upon the individual and his relationship to God, the religion, which developed after Jesus, became highly political, leading to a religious state in Europe. Also, the original emphasis on individual virtues and piety became in time a faith that emphasized strength, combativeness, and even militarism.

The point here is not to criticize Christianity, but rather to call attention to the differential treatment the Sikh religion has received at the hands of Western scholars. These kinds of evaluative statements would have been less objectionable had similar criticisms been leveled against traditions like Christianity. However, these textbook authors appear blind to the obvious.

All of the examples quoted in this section were drawn from world religions textbooks published more than two decades ago. Current surveys of world religions that address this same issue are typically less judgmental, but still represent later Sikhism as having turned away from the First Master's imputed pacifism.[3] To take one comparatively mild example[4] from the second (2005) edition of William Young's *The World's Religions*:

> The pacifism taught by Guru Nanak had fallen victim to the growing hostility between Sikhs and Muslims (Young 2005: 242).

I did, however, come across one highly judgmental treatment of Sikhism in the "Sikh History" entry of Johannes Schade's relatively recent *Encyclopedia of World Religions*:

> By rejecting nonviolence, they lost scruples against killing and eating animals. The history of the patriarchal period of Sikhism reflects a gradual shift, under the increasing hostility of the Muslims, from the pacifism of Nanak toward the political and militaristic character the movement acquired under Gobind Singh (Schade 2006).

As one might (unfortunately) anticipate, Schade does not subject the Christian tradition's rejection of nonviolence to a comparable evaluation.

SIKHISM – OBJECTIONABLE CHARACTERIZATIONS

A different theme one often finds in textbook discussions of the Sikh tradition is the question of Sikh syncretism. While it should be self-evident that every emergent religion necessarily relies upon prior religious traditions as points of reference for a new vision of spiritual reality, the relationship between early Sikhism and its religious environment appears to have captured the attention of observers of the Sikh religion more so than other religions. In particular, the question of the relative impact of Hinduism and Islam, and more especially the notion of a "syncretism" of these two traditions, has constituted almost an obsession in Western treatments of the Sikh religion.

Given the many critiques that have been leveled at the notion of Sikh syncretism since the 1970s, one might have expected that this idea would have been exorcised from academic discourse many years ago. This has not, however, been the case. Scholarly specialists have, with few exceptions (e.g. Cohn 1996: 107), dropped the term "syncretism," but certain textbook authors whose specialty is not Sikhism have not. This is especially the case with textbooks that are republished in multiple new editions.

A publisher's purpose in issuing successive editions of a textbook is to compel students to purchase the most recent edition because publishers gain no profit from sales of used texts. Except as updating influences sales, publishers are not particularly interested in bringing contents up to date. On the other hand, academicians write general textbooks as a way of supplementing their incomes. After the first edition appears, authors are typically not motivated to undertake revisions beyond the minimal revisions required by publishers.

The result, for Sikhism, is that the same objectionable characterizations are usually repeated edition after edition. Thus, for example, in the ninth (2005) edition of Lewis Hopfe's and Mark R. Woodward's *Religions of the World*, we find the following passage about Sikh syncretism:

> Sikhs believe their faith to be a new and independent religion based on the insights of their first teacher, Nanak. Scholars have long held that Sikhism developed in the context of a religious conversation between devotional Hinduism and Islamic mysticism. Like Buddhism and Jainism, Sikhism takes much of its worldview from and seeks to reform certain elements of Hinduism. Unlike other reform movements in Hinduism, however, Sikhism endeavors to incorporate elements from another major world religion, Islam. The blending of elements from two such diverse religions is a fascinating chapter in the history of religion in southern Asia (Hopfe and Woodward 2005).

In this passage, the authors state what Sikhs believe, and then proceed to assert that scholars have proven them to be mistaken (though not in so many words). Their real message becomes clearer if we insert "Although" at the beginning of the passage, insert a comma after Nanak, and substitute "syncretism" for their equivalent term, "blending":

> [Although] Sikhs believe their faith to be a new and independent religion based on the insights of their first teacher, Nanak[,] scholars have long held that Sikhism developed in the context of a religious conversation between devotional Hinduism and Islamic mysticism. Like Buddhism and Jainism, Sikhism takes much of its worldview from and seeks to reform certain elements of Hinduism. Unlike other reform movements in Hinduism, however, Sikhism endeavors to incorporate elements from another major world religion, Islam. The [syncretism] of elements from two such diverse religions is a fascinating chapter in the history of religion in southern Asia.

Though I have not thoroughly read *Religions of the World* cover to cover, I have not found — nor, frankly, would I expect to find — comparable discourse about other religions that disparages what adherents believe in contrast to what scholars "know is true."

Contemporary world religions textbooks that were not originally written three or four decades ago either ignore the syncretism characterization completely, or else approach it cautiously. Thus, for example, in the second (2005) edition of *The World's Religions: Worldviews and Contemporary Issues,* William Young portrays Sikhism as a syncretism, but, simultaneously, he is also careful to point out Sikhism's uniqueness:

> As we examine Sikhism we will point out Hindu and Muslim elements. However, its "syncretistic" context (combining and synthesizing beliefs) should not be allowed to obscure the uniqueness of Sikhism. It stands alone as a distinct and important religion (Young 2005: 240).

Though this is certainly a vast improvement over Hopfe and Woodward, it still begs the question of why only Sikhism's relationship with prior religions is characterized as a syncretism and not Christianity, Islam, *et cetera*.[5]

One can also find the same items of discourse cropping up in a wide diversity of places. Thus, for example, in the fifth (2003) edition — and probably in other editions as well — of *Cultural Anthropology: A Global Perspective*, Raymond Scupin states that: "The Sikh religion developed in the 15th century as a syncretic blend of Hindu and Islamic belief" (Scupin 2003: 383). One ameliorating aspect of Scupin's book is that, in sharp contrast with world religion texts, he at least characterizes other religions beyond Sikhism as syncretisms (e.g. Scupin 2003: 338–42).

The same characterization of Sikhism as a syncretism can be found in numerous studies that are not textbooks. Thus, for example, in an interdisciplinary study of terrorism, *Terrorism in Context*, the author of the chapter on Indian terrorism refers to the "pietistic syncretism" of Guru Nanak (Wallace 1995: 361).

These examples could be multiplied, but enough has been said to demonstrate that the notion of Sikh syncretism is alive and well, despite near universal rejection of the idea by scholars of the Sikh tradition.

ABOUT THE AUTHOR

James R. Lewis is a highly published scholar in the field of New Religious Movements and Professor of Religious Studies at the University of Tromsø (Norway). He currently co-edits three book series and is the general editor for the *Alternative Spirituality and Religion Review* and for the *Journal of Religion and Violence*. Recent publications include *Violence and New Religious Movements* (2011), (co-edited with Olav Hammer) *Religion and the Authority of Science* (2011), *Cults: A Reference and Guide* (2012), (co-authored with Diana Tumminia) *The Movement of Inner Awareness* (2013) and *Sects & Stats* (2014).

REFERENCES

Cavendish, Richard. 1980. *The Great Religions.* New York: Arco.
Deol, Harnik. 2000. *Religion and Nationalism in India.* London: Routledge.
Hardon, John A. 1963. *Religions of the World.* Westminster, MD: Newman.
Hopfe, Lewis M. 1987. *Religions of the World*, 4th edn. New York: Macmillan.
Hopfe, Lewis M., and Mark R. Woodward. 2005. *Religions of the World*, 9th edn. Upper Saddle River, NJ: Pearson/Prentice-Hall.
Hutchison, John A. 1969. *Paths of Faith.* New York: McGraw-Hill.
Juergensmeyer, Mark. 1979. "The Forgotten Tradition: Sikhism in the Study of World Religions." In *Sikh Studies*, eds. Mark Juergensmeyer and N. Gerald Barrier. Berkeley, CA: Graduate Theological Union.
Juergensmeyer, Mark. 1993. "Sikhism and Religious Studies." In *Studying the Sikhs: Issues for North America*, eds. John Stratton Hawley, and Gurinder Singh Mann. Albany, NY: State University of New York Press.
Lewis, James R. 1985. "Some Unexamined Assumptions in Western Studies of Sikhism." *Journal of Sikh Studies* 12(2).
Lewis, James R. 1989. "Misrepresentations of the Sikh Tradition in World Religion Textbooks." In *Advanced Studies in Sikhism*, eds. Jasbir Singh Mann and Harbans Singh Saraon. Irvine, CA: Sikh Community of North America.
Macauliffe, Max Arthur. 1909. *The Sikh Religion Its Gurus, Sacred Writings and Authors.* Oxford: Clarendon Press.
MacMunn, George. 1933. *The Martial Races of India.* London: Sampson Low, Marston & Co., Ltd.
Malcolm, John. 1986 [1812]. *Sketch of the Sikhs.* New Delhi: Asian Educational Services.
McGregor, W. L. 1970 [1846]. *The History of the Sikhs.* Patiala: Languages Department, Punjab University.
Noss, John B., and David S. Noss. 1984. *Man's Religions*, 7th edn. New York: Macmillan.
Philips, C. H. 1961. *Historians of India, Pakistan and Ceylon.* London: Oxford University Press.
Pincott, Frederic. 1984 [1885]. "Sikhism." In *Dictionary of Islam.* Lahore: Premier Book House.

Schade, Johannes P., ed. 2006. *Encyclopedia of World Religions.* Leeuwarden, Netherlands: Foreign Media Books.
Schoeps, Hans-Joachim. 1968. *The Religions of Mankind.* Garden City, NY: Anchor.
Scupin, Raymond. 2003. *Cultural Anthropology: A Global Perspective,* 5th edn. Upper Saddle River, NJ: Pearson/Prentice-Hall.
Singh, Daljeet. 1994. *Essentials of Sikhism.* Amritsar: Singh Brothers.
Singh, Darshan. 2004 [1991]. *Western Perspectives on the Sikh Religion.* Amritsar: Singh Brothers.
Singh, Khushwant. 1963. *A History of the Sikhs,* Vol. 1. Princeton, NJ: Princeton University Press.
Smart, Ninian. 1976. *The Religious Experience of Mankind.* New York: Charles Scribner's Sons.
Stokes, E. T. 1961. "The Administrators and Historical Writing on India." In *Historians of India, Pakistan and Ceylon,* ed. C. H. Philips. London: Oxford University Press.
Stroup, Herbert. 1974. *Founders of Living Religions.* Philadelphia, PA: Westminster.
Wallace, Paul. 1995. "Political Violence and Terrorism in India: The Crisis of Identity." In *Terrorism in Context,* ed. Martha Crenshaw. University Park, PA: Pennsylvania State University Press.
Wilkins, Charles. 2004 [1781]. "The Sicks and their College at Patna." In *"Sicques, Tigers, or Thieves": Eyewitness Accounts of the Sikhs (1606-1809),* eds. Amandeep Singh Madra and Parmjit Singh. New York: Palgrave Macmillan.
Williams, Bernard, ed. 2001. *One World Many Issues.* Cheltenham: Nelson Thornes.
Wilson, H. H. 1958 [1848]. "Civil and Religious Institutions of the Sikhs." In *The Sikh Religion: A Symposium,* eds. M. Macauliffe, H. H. Wilson, Frederic Pincott, John Malcolm and Sardar Kahan Singh. Calcutta: Susil Gupta.
Young, William. 2005. *The World's Religions: Worldviews and Contemporary Issues,* 2nd edn. Upper Saddle River, NJ: Prentice-Hall.

Endnotes

1. I say false because, though superficially similar, the difference between the First Nanak and the Tenth Nanak is not of the magnitude of a "contradiction," whereas the contrast between Jesus and Western imperialism is. Guru Nanak's attitude was no more "passive" than Guru Gobind Singh's was "violent."

2. This passage has been reproduced verbatim in the ninth edition (Hopfe and Woodward 2005: 159).

3. Though my critical focus is on the differential treatment of Sikhism and Christianity, I feel compelled to note that anyone familiar with the traditional stories of his often confrontational style of iconoclasm would have a difficult time characterizing Guru Nanak as a "pacifist" (unless one *defines* pacifism as restraint from *physical* assault).

4. Other comparably mild remarks can be found in, to use a couple of other contemporary examples: (1) Harnik Deol's *Religion and Nationalism in India*: "To recapitulate thus far: we have attempted to situate the metamorphosis of the pacifist followers of Guru Nanak to the militant brotherhood of the Khalsa within the context of the historical and social development of Sikh religion" (Deol 2000: 63). (2) Bernard Williams' *One World Many Issues*: "The first Sikh community founded by Guru Nanak followed a simple disciplined way of life, committed to strict pacifism. As Sikh fortunes fluctuated, later Gurus taught their followers that they should be prepared to defend themselves" (Williams 2001: 187).

5. Mark Juergensmeyer has also discussed the issue of the syncretism theme in world religions textbooks in a number of places (e.g. Juergensmeyer 1993: 19-20).

Index

Key Events
2011 Norway attacks 187
9/11 See September 11 attacks

A
Abrahamic 129, 137, 139
Abu Ghraib 18-19
Adharma 185
Allah 60, 63-64, 94, 130
Al-Qaeda 16, 27, 35-36, 39-41, 49, 196, 205, 207
Anathema 142, 198-99
Angel 132, 135, 138, 202
Anglo-Sikh wars 210-11, 214
Aniconism 5, 129-30, 136, 141
Anti-Semitism 5, 98-107, 109-16
Apologetic 200-201, 207
Arab-Israeli conflict 8, 11-13, 17, 19, 104, 199
Armstrong, Karen 201, 204, 206-207
Aum Shinrikyo 27-28, 41-44, 48-49

B
Bhagavad Gita 185
Bible 12, 47-48, 74, 80, 137, 178, 183, 202
Blasphemous 128-29, 139
Boko Haram 196, 207
Bourdieu, Pierre 5, 54-55, 57, 151-52, 172
Buddha 29, 155, 157-58, 162-66
Buddhism 5, 28-29, 38, 48, 87, 99, 151-59, 161-72
Burqa 39

C
Catholicism 4, 56, 63, 87, 93, 158, 165
Charlie Hebdo 90, 129, 187
Christian 4, 17, 18, 29, 35, 44, 60-61, 63, 66, 71, 74-81, 93, 116, 129, 135, 137-38, 151, 153-56, 158-59, 165-72, 179, 183-84, 187, 203, 213-15
Christian Extremism 187
Christianity 5, 18, 37-38, 44, 76, 78-80, 93, 99, 101, 127-28, 137-39, 152, 154-56, 158, 165-66, 170-72, 177-79, 181-85, 214-15, 217

Christianization 4, 71, 75-79, 184
Church of England 158
Cold War 31
Colonization 4, 12, 71, 73-79, 84
Concentration Camps 102, 105, 107-109, 113-14
Confucianism 38
Conservatives 17-18, 34-35, 45, 49, 81, 85, 197
Crusade 1
Cult 34, 41-43, 49

D
Denny, Fredrick 202-205
Dhammapada 162-63
Dharma 160, 178-79, 181, 185
Dialogue 12, 16, 29, 56, 67, 82, 88, 92-93, 95-96, 162, 189
Divine 90, 92-93, 156, 198, 200-201
Dukkha 155, 157

E
Elitzur, Yosef 199
Esposito, John 203-204
Extremism 5, 12, 28, 179-80, 182-91

F
Fiqh 130
Freedom of religion See religious freedom
Fundamentalism 12, 40-41, 85

G
Gabriel 132, 202
Gautama Buddha, See Buddha
Gaza Strip 13, 17, 19
Geneva conventions 19
God 32, 37, 40, 48, 62, 66, 78, 93-94, 103, 154, 156-57, 198-99, 202, 214-15
Goldstein, Baruch 198
Greek-Orthodox 136
Guru Gobind Singh 211-15
Guru Nanak 211-17

H

Hadith 130
Halakhah 199
Halal 35, 38, 90
Hamas 207
Hanukah 60
Haugianism 81-82
Heretics 113
Hijab 93
Hinduism 29, 87, 99, 154, 165, 177-79, 182-83, 185, 211-13, 216-17
Holocaust 5, 98-112, 114-16, 184
Holy Land 37
Holy War 40, 181
Hopfe, Lewis M. 214-17
Hudud 182, 185
Human Rights 37, 63-65, 116, 165-66, 169-71, 188

I

Iconoclasm 129, 142
Iconography 5, 99-101, 106-116, 135
Idolatry 94
Indigenization 72, 78, 83-84
Indigenous 4, 71-79, 81-85, 182, 190
Interfaith 166-68, 170-71
Internment of Japanese Americans 8, 10-11, 19
Invasion of Afghanistan 14-15
ISIS, See Islamic State
Islam 4, 5-6, 27, 28-29, 31-33, 35-37, 39, 40-41, 54, 56, 59-67, 92-94, 99, 115, 126-27, 129-42, 165-66, 177-79, 182-85, 196-98, 200-208, 213, 216-17
Islamic extremist 28
Islamic fundamentalism 40
Islamic mysticism 216-17
Islamic revival 27, 33, 40
Islamic State 35, 49, 90, 129, 196-97, 207
Islamism 38, 182, 184-85
Islamophobia 29, 36, 202
Israel 11-13, 17, 32, 40, 96, 103-104, 184, 198-200

J

Jainisim 216-17
Jesus Christ 29, 139, 155, 182, 203, 212, 214-15
Jews 11-12, 17, 56, 60-61, 63, 66, 90, 93-96, 98, 100-115, 136-37, 154, 196-200
Jewish extremist 12

Jibril 132
Jihad 17, 37, 182, 184-85
Juergensmeyer, Mark 1, 179, 181, 190
Judaism 5, 94, 98-108, 111, 113-16, 126-27, 129, 131, 136-39, 177-79, 183-85, 196-200, 206, 208
Judgement day 62
Jylland-Posten Muhammad cartoons controversy 129-30, 140

K

Ka'ba 130
Kach and Kahane Chai 198
Karma 154-57
Kautokeino Rebellion 4, 71, 80-82
Kippah 93-94
Kosher 90

L

Laestadianism 6, 80-82, 179, 184
Laestadius, Lars Levi 80
Lincoln, Bruce 152-53, 164, 179-80, 187, 190, 205

M

Mahayana Buddhism 158-59
Mass suicide 28
Middle East 14, 17, 202
Militarism 214-15
Missionaries 71, 78-79, 184
Monotheism 154, 156, 169, 212
Mosque 14, 60, 63, 65, 90, 92-93, 132-33
Muhammad 35, 37, 62, 94, 129-35, 139-40, 142, 201-202, 211
Muhammadans 211-13
Muslim Brotherhood 185
Muslim Veil 90, 92-94
Mysticism 161

N

Nanking Massacre 45
Nationalism 12, 31, 38, 46, 102-103, 182, 185, 200-201
Neo-Orientalist 197
New Religious Movements 28, 29, 41, 76
Nirvana 155, 157, 165
Norwegianization 74-75

O

Occult 42
Old Testament 12, 129, 137-38

Orientalism 6, 31, 151, 158, 171–72, 197, 202, 207, 210–13
Osama Bin Laden 15. 39, 187, 203–204
Ottoman Empire 62–63, 67

P
Pacifism 6, 212–15
Paganism 77
Palestine 11–13, 17, 114
Palestinian extremist 12
Patriotism 12, 14–15, 84
Pentecostal 158
People's Liberation Army 13
Pilgrimage 62
Prophet 54, 61, 129–33, 135, 139–42, 201–203
Protestantism 17–18, 158, 184, 204

Q
Qur'an 64–65, 130, 133, 202

R
Rabbi 199
Racism 98, 100, 102, 199
Radical movements 17–18
Ramadan 64
Redemption 59, 155, 168
Reformation 1, 76, 184
Refugees 13, 17, 53, 104
Religious education 5, 28, 47–48, 53–54, 56, 59–60, 64–67, 75, 82, 92, 102, 116, 126, 152, 172
Religious freedom 46–48, 88, 138

S
Sabbath 60, 93
Sacred 128, 130, 162, 183, 201–202, 211
Saddam Hussein 15–16
Salām 201, 202
Salvation 154–55, 159, 168, 202
Sámi 4, 71, 74–82, 84–85, 179, 184, 190
Samsara 155, 157
Sect 36, 38, 41, 43, 159, 214
Secular Humanism 127
Secular Zionism 104
Secularism 5, 33, 35, 49, 61, 64–66, 87–88, 92, 94, 116, 133, 139, 167–68, 170–71, 177–79, 181, 199, 201, 205, 207
Šehid 65

Separation of religion and state 28, 34, 36, 46–49, 201
September 11 attacks 1, 3, 8, 14, 27, 32, 35–37, 39–40, 182, 197, 202–203, 205, 207
Serbia-Orthodox 4, 56, 63
Shapira, Yitzhack 199
Sharia 65, 130, 182, 184–85
Shia 133
Shintō 28, 38, 45–49
Sikhism 6, 178, 181, 210–18
Social Injustice 58–59
Spiritual 41, 165, 189, 198, 200–201, 204, 216
Spirituality 96, 211
Suicide bombing 40
Sunnah 64, 130
Sunni 132–133, 140
Surah 60–61, 64
Symbolic violence 5, 151–52, 172

T
Taliban 15–16, 129, 185, 207
Tamagushi 46
Tanakh 137
Terrorism 3, 5–6, 14–15, 27–29, 31–32, 34–37, 39–43, 49, 90, 129, 180–81, 185, 187, 190, 203–204, 217
Theology 89–90, 167
Theravada 158
Tibetan Buddhism 158
Tilak, Bal Gangadhar 185
Torah 12, 198
Torat haMelech 199–200
Torture 18–19, 113
Tripitaka 164

U
Ultra-nationalism 38, 45–46
Ummah 60–61, 65–67
UN convention on children's rights 64
UN and the Eurpean Declaration on Human Rights 64
Utøya, See 2011 Norway attacks

W
War crimes 15, 45
War on Terror 3, 8, 14–16, 32, 39, 40–41
Weapons of mass destruction 15–16, 18
West Bank 13, 17, 199

Woodward, Mark R. 216–17
World War II 8, 10–11, 31, 37, 45–47, 74, 77, 99, 101–105, 107–15

X
Xenophobia 29

Y
Yasukuni Shrine 28, 45–49

Z
Zen Buddhism 158, 161–62, 169
Zen Koan 161–62, 169
Zionism 11–12, 103, 199, 200